Good des[ign]

for effective revision

Worked examples show you the answers the examiners expect

[ful]l coverage of the [sub]jects included in [the] examinations

[and] methods, [tec]hniques and [con]cepts you need to [kn]ow, and examples [illu]strating them

[r]eal exam [q]uestions of [d]ifferent types: [to] give you [the] practice on the [the] real thing [that] can be set as [class] tests or self-tests

[a]nswers at the [e]nd of the book [to h]elp you check [yo]ur progress

Glossary helps you with difficult terms

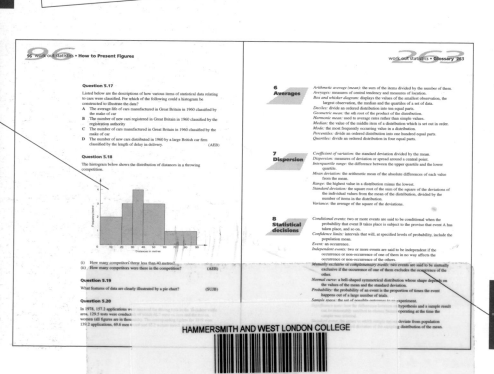

Good design

for effective revision

2

Collecting Information: Surveys

Objectives	By the end of this chapter the following terms and methods should be understood:			
		Date attempted	Date completed	Self-assessment
Survey design				
Survey methods				
Observation				
Interviewing				
Questionnaires				
Sampling				
Sampling methods				
Random sampling				
Quota sampling				
Panels				

Summary	This chapter describes survey methods used for collecting statistical information. It explains statistical sampling techniques used in surveys.

12

Start and completion column Keeps tabs on your progress – see at a glance which areas still need to be worked through

Self-assessment For you to note how well you've done or areas which need to be revised again

Chapter breakdown Shows you in detail what is covered in the chapters

Introduction

How to use this book

The aim of this book is to provide a full, thorough and concise coverage of the subjects included in the GCSE Statistics examinations, and the statistics in a range of business, professional and management courses, diploma and degree examinations.

All statistics examinations are different in their requirements, one concentrating on one area of techniques and methods, and another on other areas. This book covers all those examinations and courses that do not require advanced mathematical knowledge but are concerned with basic mathematical and statistical methods and their applications.

Each chapter is structured so that a description of techniques is followed by examples, questions and assignments with solutions and worked examples plus large numbers of recent examination questions. In order to make the best use of this book, you should study the techniques carefully, work through the examples and then attempt the questions and exercises so that you have plenty of practice in each section and gain experience in formulating answers.

There is a balance in each chapter between those questions for which solutions have been provided in the text and those for which the numerical answers are at the end of the book. In Chapter 6, for example, 48 questions have solutions provided in the text while 26 have answers at the end of the book. All the questions are examination questions or are based very closely on them, whether they are classified as worked examples, questions or exercises. Questions with answers at the end of the book can be set as tests or self-tests and the answers can be computed by following the methods set out in the chapter.

Examination papers have been analysed so that the book includes a wide spread of statistical methods, techniques and concepts to provide a solid foundation for success in understanding statistics for a broad range of people some of whom may have very limited mathematical knowledge. The book includes a section on basic mathematics as a reminder of simple numerical techniques.

This book should be read in conjunction with *Mastering Statistics* (Tim Hannagan, Macmillan) which is complementary in its scope with a more detailed description and analysis of statistical techniques and concepts.

Statistics in practice

Statistics is a practical subject concerned with obtaining and processing data in order to extract numerical information and to make inferences which will help in making decisions. GCSE syllabuses and vocational courses encourage the use of statistics in practice in order to facilitate learning. Practical work in statistics can develop the understanding of the subject and the application of statistical methods.

Practical work can develop skills in:

- identifying the statistical aspects of a problem;
- collecting data;
- selecting appropriate statistical methods;
- interpreting statistical evidence;
- communicating statistical results.

Practical work in statistics can include:

Measuring – (length, weight, volume/capacity, time, temperature);
Counting – (heads/tails, dice, vehicles, people);
Surveying – (opinions, results).

Course work on statistical techniques can be based on this practical work. Statistical comparisons can be made on samples of products and relative prices, weight or numbers; correlation can be based on age and weight, height and weight, price and sales; time series can be based on wealth, prices, population.

The importance of reliable data means that it is essential to have an understanding of the difficulties of producing accurate results from questionnaires and experiments and in the use of sampling and there needs to be an awareness of the problems of using published statistics (secondary sources) and the importance of defining terms very carefully. The construction of tables and diagrams can help in the understanding of their appropriateness and the reliability of published diagrams. Sources of data include newspapers and magazines, television programmes, pamphlets and government publications.

The practical application of statistics can be an important element in understanding the subject, while forming the basis for course work and support for the work required in order to be successful in examinations.

How to revise

An examination involves answering questions over a few hours on what has been learnt over a year or two and is a test of the ability to extract the central points from the syllabus. However much work has been carried out during the time leading up to an examination, a period of intensive revision will be necessary. Revision should start at least six to eight weeks before the examinations and should be based on a timetable so that each topic is revised in turn with more time concentrated on 'weak' areas.

It is useful to have built up a series of notes covering the whole syllabus to provide a basis for revision. The content of these notes should be determined by individual needs for reminders of statistical methods and applications. Headings and sections, lists of formulae and methods all help in 'last minute' revision.

Examinations are based on knowledge and memory as well as understanding. In statistics this means that techniques need to be followed, formulae and definitions remembered and applications and examples prepared so that they can be used in a relevant way to illustrate and explain concepts.

Above all in preparing for a statistics examination, practice is essential, particularly of calculations and preferably under examination conditions.

How to plan for a statistics exam in 3 steps

In planning for a statistics examination it is essential to obtain certain things and to practise calculations, as follows:

Step 1   Obtain the syllabus for the examination

The syllabus will show what will be examined and how it will be examined. It is important to know the type of questions which will be asked, whether there is a choice and how many questions have to be answered. In most statistics examinations calculators can be used and papers are set assuming their use. This means that questions may include a number of calculations which would take a long time without a calculator but can be completed quickly with one.

Statistics exams seldom involve long essay questions but tend to include a variety of other types of questions, such as:

- *calculation questions*, where a calculation or a number of calculations are asked for;
- *problem-solving questions*, where a problem is posed which might involve in its solution a combination of calculations, analysis, comment and discussion;
- *interpretation questions*, where an analysis is asked for of a table, diagram or graph or of a solution to a calculation;
- *multiple-choice* or *'objective' test questions*, where several alternative answers are given and the correct one has to be ticked;
- *short answer questions*, where a two line written answer is required to what is often an interpretation question.

There is a growing tendency among examination bodies to ask a variety of types of question. Multiple-choice and short answer questions are asked in order to test the whole syllabus, while longer problem-solving questions test particular parts of the syllabus in more detail.

Step 2   Obtain the marking schemes and examiners' reports for the examination

In answering examination papers it is essential to know how marks are distributed over the questions and as far as possible for each part of a question, because this distribution will determine the length of time spent on each section of the paper.

The instructions on the examination paper will invariably indicate the distribution of marks between the questions, sometimes by stating that 'all questions carry equal marks'. In the case of some examinations the marks for each part of a question are shown on the paper, other examining boards include marking schemes in examiners' reports.

In short calculation questions most, if not all, of the marks are for a correct answer; in problem-solving questions marks are given for the various sections of the question and marks may be given for correct methods or consistent answers even when the solution is not entirely accurate; while interpretation questions will be marked on the basis of the width and depth of the comments, discussion and analysis. Multiple-choice questions are usually marked right or wrong, a mark being awarded for a correct answer. It is very, very rare for marks to be deducted for a wrong answer, or for any marks to be awarded for a 'second best' answer, and therefore it is sensible to answer all multiple-choice questions even if the answer is a guess.

Step 3   Practice

Examiners' reports point out that an examination in statistics always involves candidates in calculating some of the statistical measures which are specifically mentioned in the syllabus. It is very important to practise these calculations so that the methods are fully understood.

It is important also, to have an idea of what the answer should be to any calculation. This means that by looking at a set of figures it should be possible, with practice, to have a good idea of the solution, that is whether it will be around say one, ten, a hundred or a thousand. This will make it possible to notice immediately if a large error is made in a calculation which leads to an 'impossible' answer.

Which questions to expect in your statistics exam

In preparing for an examination, an obvious query is 'what are the most frequently asked questions?'. Trying to predict or 'spot' questions in an examination is dangerous; it is fairly safe, however, to predict topics on the basis that these are the central areas of the syllabus. Past papers show which subjects appear most frequently:

(a) GCSE examinations

The aims of GCSE syllabuses are to produce courses which will enable the achievement of the acquisition of statistical knowledge and skills; the development of an understanding of statistical methods and concepts and awareness of their power and limitations; the development of an awareness of the breadth of application of statistics and of an ability to apply and interpret statistics in everyday situations and in other disciplines.

The examinations assess a candidate's ability to recognise, recall and use statistical language and facts, perform relevant computations to appropriate degrees of accuracy, select, present and analyse data, reason logically and make statistical inferences. There are three types of paper: an objective test paper, short answer paper and a structured question paper. The GCSE boards favour questions on:

frequency distributions
classification
presentation of data through diagrams and graphs
averages, particularly the mean and median
dispersion, particularly the standard deviation and interquartile range
correlation, both product moment and rank coefficients
probability

Questions may also be asked on

quantitative/qualitative information
survey questions/sampling
maximum and minimum values
percentages and proportions
death rates
the geometric mean
z-values
index numbers
moving averages and semi-averages

Questions are less likely to be asked on a description of statistics, or in detail on survey methods, financial mathematics, Z-charts, Lorenz curves, significance tests and confidence limits, seasonal variations and the least squares method of calculating a linear trend.

(b) Business, professional and management examinations

(i) RSA papers include more questions than in the GCSE on survey methods and sampling, Z-charts and Lorenz curves, index numbers, correlation and trends. RSA papers include fewer straightforward questions on averages, dispersion and probability.

(ii) The Chartered Institute of Marketing papers have many questions on surveys and sampling as would be expected and also many questions on index numbers, correlation and trends.

(iii) Statistics papers set by the accountancy bodies and the CIMA include questions on financial mathematics, presentation, index numbers, correlation and trends. These examination papers tend to consist of long 'problem solving' questions.

(iv) GNVQ and BTEC papers are in the main set locally by colleges and therefore papers vary from centre to centre. They often include questions on financial statistics, significance tests, confidence limits, index numbers and trends as well as the areas covered in (a) above.

(v) All of these papers in (b) are more concerned with the application of statistics than the GCSE papers and in the case of (ii), (iii) and (iv) the application of statistics to particular areas of business.

Remember in the exam

Point 1: *to answer the question that is asked* and not the question that it is hoped would be asked.

Point 2: to read the instructions carefully to be sure how many questions have to be answered and which (if any) are compulsory.

Point 3: to make a timetable for the examination so that the time available is used to the best advantage (e.g. if five questions carrying equal marks are to be answered over three hours, thirty-five minutes could be allowed for each question, leaving five minutes for planning and checking).

Point 4: to answer all the required questions; it is particularly easy in questions requiring calculations to become stuck on the detail of the mathematics and waste time which would be better spent on the next question (i.e. it is easier to score nine out of twenty marks on each of two answers, than eighteen out of twenty on one).

Point 5: to make plans for questions where necessary; statistics questions are often well structured and planning can be minimal, but plans can be used for deciding which questions to answer and which to leave when there is a choice, and insuring a good and logical coverage of points in questions that require comment and discussion.

Point 6: to decide exactly what the examiner wants in the way of calculations, facts, figures, diagrams and comments. It helps to look for key words such as: describe, outline, analyse, calculate and so on, and to follow the instructions so that *the question actually asked is fully answered*.

Exam Board Addresses

Addresses of Professional Examining Boards

For syllabuses and past papers contact the
    Publications Office at the following
    addresses:

Midland Examining Group (MEG)
c/o University of Cambridge Local Examinations
    Syndicate
1 Hills Road
CAMBRIDGE
CB1 2EU
Tel. 01223 553311

Southern Examining Group (SEG)
Publications Department
Stag Hill House
GUILDFORD
Surrey
GU2 5XJ
Tel. 01483 302302 (Direct line)

**Northern Examinations and Assessment Board
    (NEAB)**
12 Harter Street
MANCHESTER
M1 6HL
Tel. 0161 953 1170
(Also shop at the above address)

**University of London Examinations and
    Assessment Council (ULEAC)**
Stewart House
32 Russell Square
LONDON
WC1B 5DN
Tel. 0171 331 4000

**Northern Ireland Council for the Curriculum,
    Examinations and Assessment (NICCEA)**
29 Clarendon Road
BELFAST
BT1 3BG
Tel. 01232 261200
Fax 01232 261234

Welsh Joint Education Committee (WJEC)
245 Western Avenue
Llandaff
CARDIFF
CF5 2YX

Scottish Examination Board (SEB)
For full syllabuses
Ironmills Road
Dalkeith
MIDLOTHIAN
EH22 1LE
Tel. 0131–663 6601

Or recent papers from the SEB's agent
Robert Gibson & Sons Ltd
17 Fitzroy Place
GLASGOW
G3 7SF
Tel. 0141–248 5674

Remember to check your syllabus number with
    your teacher!

Syllabuses and past papers for examinations
    administered by business, professional and
    management bodies can be obtained from
    the following addresses:

Association of Certified Accounts (CACA)
Syllabus from:
29 Lincoln's Inn Fields
LONDON WC2A 3EE
Tel: 0171 242 6855
Fax: 0171 396 5757
Past questions and papers from:
Student Publication Dept
1 Woodside Place
GLASGOW G3 7QS
Tel: 0141 309 4040
Fax: 0141 309 4041

Business and Technology Education Council
Central House
Upper Woburn Place
LONDON WC1H 0HH
Tel: 0171 413 8400
Fax: 0171 387 6068

Institute of Chartered Accountants
Gloucester House
399 Filbury Boulevard
CENTRAL MILTON KEYNES
Bucks MK9 2HL
Tel: 01908 668833
Fax: 01908 691165

**Institute of Chartered Secretaries and
    Administrators (ICSA)**
16 Park Crescent
LONDON W1N 4AH
Tel: 0171 580 4741
Fax: 0171 323 1132

**Chartered Institute of Management Accountants
    (CIMA)**
63 Portland Place
LONDON W1
Tel: 0171 637 2311
Fax: 0171 631 5309

Chartered Institute of Marketing (IM)
Moor Hall
COOKHAM
Berks SL6 9QH
Tel: 01628 524922
Fax: 01628 531382

Institute of Personnel and Development
IPD House
35 Camp Road
LONDON SW19 4UX
Tel: 0181 946 9100
Fax: 0181 947 2570

The Royal Society of Arts (RSA)
Progress House
Westwood Way
COVENTRY CV4 8HS
Tel: 01203 468080
Fax: 01203 470033

Contents

Acknowledgements

The author and publishers wish to thank the following for permission to use copyright material: The Associated Examining Board, The Chartered Institute of Marketing, The Institute of Chartered Secretaries & Administrators, The Northern Ireland Schools Examination Council, The Scottish Examination Board, The University of Oxford Delegacy of Local Examinations and The Southern Examining Group for questions from previous examination papers, and HMSO for permission to use a table from *Monthly Digest of Statistics* No. 429, August 1981.

The examination boards accept no responsibility for the accuracy or method in the answers given to their questions in this book.

Every effort has been made to trace all the copyright holders, but if any have been inadvertently overlooked the publishers will be pleased to make the necessary arrangement at the first opportunity.

To Gladys and Grace

First edition 1986
Reprinted (with corrections) twice
Second edition 1987
Third edition 1996

Published by
MACMILLAN PRESS LTD
Houndmills, Basingstoke, Hampshire RG21 6XS
and London
Companies and representatives
throughout the world

ISBN 0–333–64375–5

A catalogue record for this book is available from the British Library.

Printed in Hong Kong

10   9   8   7   6   5   4   3   2
05   04   03   02   01   00   99   98   97

Tim Hannagan

Statistics GCSE

MACMILLAN

Information

Objectives

By the end of this chapter the following terms should be understood:

	Date attempted	Date completed	Self-assessment
Statistics			
Primary data			
Secondary data			
Variables			
Use and abuse of statistics			
Statistical information			

Summary

This chapter explains the meaning of basic terms used in this subject such as *statistics*, *data*, *variables*, and *statistical information*.

1.1 Statistics

Statistics is concerned with scientific methods for collecting, organising, summarising, presenting and analysing data.

Data (strictly a plural word, singular 'datum', although it is now acceptable to refer to it in the singular) are things known or assumed as a basis for inference, that is for making deductions and reaching conclusions.

'Statistics' refers to:

- numerical data, information, facts;
- the study of the ways of collecting and interpreting these facts;
- the provision of numerical information to help in making decisions.

There are a number of questions to be asked about statistical data:

(i) How has the data been collected?
(ii) How has it been processed?
(iii) How accurate is it?
(iv) How far has it been summarised?
(v) How valid is it to compare one set of data with other sets?
(vi) How can the data be interpreted?

1.2 Information

Information consists of items of knowledge and it is distributed through verbal, written visual and aural media (i.e. conversations, television, radio, newspapers, posters, notices and instructions). Some information is *quantitative* in the sense that it can be measured; other forms of information are *qualitative* in the sense that differences between variables cannot be measured although they can be described.

For example: while the *length* of a piece of cloth can be measured, the *colour* of the cloth cannot be measured but can be described.

Statistics is concerned mainly with information that is quantitative.

1.3 Forms of statistics

(a) Descriptive statistics

This is the presentation of data and the calculation of descriptive measures which help to summarise data (percentages, averages, dispersion and correlation).

(b) Inductive statistics

This is the inferring of characteristics of a population on the basis of known sample results (based on probability theory).

1.4 Primary and secondary data

(a) Primary data

This is collected by or on behalf of the person or people who are going to make use of the data.

(b) Secondary data

This is 'second-hand' data, used by a person or people other than those for whom the data was collected.

Table 1.1 Primary and secondary data

	Primary data	*Secondary data*
Advantages	Information can be collected on the exact area required; it is known how the statistics have been collected and processed and their accuracy	Cheap to obtain; large quantities available with great variety on a wide range of subjects
Disadvantages	Expensive; likely to be based on a small sample; may be 'one-off' data	May be little knowledge of method of collection and processing or degree of accuracy

1.5 Secondary statistics

Secondary statistics are compiled and calculated from secondary data (e.g. percentages, averages).

1.6 Variables

Variables are characteristics of statistical data such as price, quantity, age, weight, time, which are apt to change and to assume different numerical values in different relations.

They may be:

(a) discrete variables which are measured in single units (such as people, houses, cars);

(b) continuous variables which are units of measurement which can be broken down into definite gradations (such as temperature, height, weight); and may also be:

(a) qualitative variables which are concerned with or depend on quality (such as colour, courage, ability);

(b) quantitative variables which are measurable (such as weight, height, price).

1.7 Abuse and use of statistics

(a) The abuse of statistics

'Lies, damn lies and statistics' – figures are used and can be misused to support theories, opinions and prejudices, to sensationalise, inflate, confuse and over-simplify.

(b) The use of statistics

Numerical data is used to provide a factual foundation to debates and decisions; to narrow the area of disagreement; as a method of summarising in a systematic way aspects of social and economic problems.

1.8 Where to find information

Statistical information is produced by government departments, employers' federations, trade associations, trade unions, private firms, professional institutes, public and private research organisations.

(a)   Micro-statistical information

This is produced by private firms and private organisations in the process of carrying out their business. Firms produce information on production, marketing, administration and personnel. Businesses use statisticians to provide clear and concise summaries of the firm's business activity, to carry out surveys and samples and to produce trends and forecasts, which can provide the basis for decisions.

(b)   Macro-statistical information

This is produced by the public sector relating to the country as a whole and as part of the administrative process.

1.9 Government statistics

(a)   Governments produce statistics:
- as part of the administrative process;
- because they want to monitor the effects of external factors on their policies;
- because they want to be able to measure the effects of their policies;
- because they need to be able to assess trends so that they can plan future policies.

(b)   In the UK, government statistics include a *Guide to Official Statistics* which covers a range of subjects such as:

Climate	Distribution
Population	Public Service
Vital Statistics	Prices
Social Statistics	National Income and Expenditure
Labour	Public Finance
Production	Financial and Business Transactions
Transport	Overseas Transactions

The most readily available government statistical publications in the UK are:
- *Monthly Digest of Statistics*: a collection of the main statistical series from all government departments;
- *Financial Statistics*: a monthly summary of key financial and monetary statistics;
- *Economic Trends*: a monthly commentary and selection of tables and charts providing a background to trends in the UK economy;
- *British Business*: a weekly compilation of statistics and commentary from the Departments of Industry and Trade;
- *Employment Gazette*: a monthly publication from the Department of Employment including articles, tables and charts on manpower, employment, unemployment, hours worked, wage rates, retail prices and so on;
- *Economic Briefing*: a monthly pamphlet published by the Treasury's Information Division and contains articles on economic subjects, on

government economic policy and the Treasury's assessment of the economic situation, along with tables and charts of economic indicators.

There are a number of annual publications which cover these and other areas.

- *Annual Abstract of Statistics*: which contains more series than the *Monthly Digest*;
- *Social Trends*: which brings together key social and demographic series;
- *Regional Statistics*: which provides a selection of the main regional statistics;
- *National Income and Expenditure 'Blue Book'*: which gives detailed estimates of the national accounts;
- *Family Expenditure Survey*: which shows in detail, household income and expenditure.

1.10 How to profit from official statistics

Government statistics can help firms in a variety of areas:

(a) *Marketing*, official sources can help a firm to:
- assess the market share trends in a number of product fields;
- watch the size and growth of existing and potential markets;
- count the number of potential customers, including regional patterns;
- see how people spend their money;
- check on distribution channels;
- check on price changes;
- use retail sales and stock movements to assist short-term sales forecasting;
- assess the possibility of meeting foreign competition in home markets;
- estimate world markets;
- fix quotas for area salesmen through regional statistics;
- estimate the effect of weather on business.

(b) *Buying*, official statistics can help a firm to:
- be aware of the sales trends of materials and goods;
- trace the price movements of materials.

(c) *Personnel*, official statistics help a firm to watch trends by industry and by region in aspects of unemployment, vacancies, earnings, overtime, wage rates, hours of work, industrial disputes.

(d) *Financial control*, official statistics help a firm to compare their performance with other firms in operating ratios, labour costs, company finance, replacement costs.

1.11 Conclusion

Statistical information is available in a very wide range of forms and much of it can be obtained relatively cheaply and easily. There has always to be a compromise between the statistics that are wanted and what is available. Official statistics, for example, are collected to cover activities which appear to be relevant to the administrative needs of the time. They are a by-product of

administrative processes and the figures collected for one purpose may not be suitable for another.

1.12 Worked examples

Example 1.1

Discuss the problems of using secondary data. Compare these problems with the advantages of primary data.

Solution 1.1

Secondary data is data used by a person or people other than those for whom it has been collected. For example, unemployment figures are collected mainly through the need for unemployed people to register in order to be able to claim unemployment benefits. The figures collected for this purpose are used by other people as an economic indicator to judge the performance of the economy.

The primary data is collected in connection with unemployment benefits, but this data is used on a secondary basis for a different purpose. It is for this reason that unemployment statistics do not necessarily provide a very accurate measure of unemployment in the economy. People who have not registered are not included in the statistics; this includes housewives who may not be eligible for unemployment benefit even though they become unemployed or would like a job. Many people do not register as unemployed immediately they lose their job because they expect to obtain another one in a short time.

Large amounts of secondary data (particularly government data) are collected for administrative purposes and are not entirely appropriate for other purposes. This is a good illustration of the importance of knowing how secondary data has been collected. The data could have been collected by a survey or sample, in which case it would be important to know such details as the size of the sample, its regional spread and its degree of accuracy.

Accuracy may be difficult to judge when using secondary data because of the methods of collection and the fact that secondary data will have been processed into tables and reports and some selection will have taken place from the raw data. If unemployment is considered to be the problem of people not working who are seeking work, then it has been estimated that this could be up to 20% above official figures. The collection of unemployment statistics is part of an administrative process and they are likely to be very accurate as far as they go. Where problems arise with these statistics, as with other secondary data, is in the interpretation of the tables. How far the figures represent 'true' unemployment is open to question and comparisons with other countries and other years may prove difficult because of differences in the basis on which the data is collected. For example, the rules on those people who have to register has changed over the years, most recently for men retiring at sixty with occupational pensions, and this influences the figures.

An alternative to using secondary data as information is to collect it through primary data. Primary data is collected by or on behalf of the person or people who are going to make use of the data. The advantage of primary data is that the people using it know how it has been collected, how it has been summarised and tabulated and its level of accuracy.

In theory it would be possible to carry out a survey to discover the 'true' level of unemployment. The main problem would be the cost. It would be a very large and very expensive survey. On the other hand the information published on unemployment as secondary data is cheap because it is part of an administrative process and its availability is a by-product of this fact. Primary data can be very useful where a small survey is required with a high degree of accuracy and certainty, or where a sample survey will provide the information required.

Primary data has the problem also that unless regular surveys are made it is not easy to make comparisons with other sets of data whereas the secondary data may be collected year after year. However in areas such as market research and opinion polls there will not be any secondary data and therefore primary data will have to be collected.

There are considerable problems in using secondary data, but provided these can be overcome or reduced to a level where they are relatively unimportant secondary data has the great advantage of being available on a wide range of subjects, very cheaply. Primary data can fill the gaps and provide information on a detailed level. Both primary and secondary data are important in the provision of information.

Example 1.2

Write a commentary in about 750 words on the Football League Table below, to bring out as much information as possible.

Solution 1.2

The Football League Table shows the relative position of football clubs at a particular point in the season. This is an advanced point in the season because there are 22 clubs and assuming they play each other twice they will each play a total of 42 games. All the teams have played at least 36 games and some have played 40.

The table shows a list of football clubs, the number of games they have played, the number of games they have won, drawn or lost, the number of goals for and against them and the number of points gained. For example, the top club, Liverpool, has played 38 games, won 23, drawn 9, lost 6 with 75 goals scored by them and 28 goals scored against them. They have gained 55 points. This compares with the bottom club, Bolton, which has only 24 points. The performance of Bolton is reflected in its record; it has played 40 games, won only 5, drawn 14 and lost 21, with 38 goals scored for and 72 scored against.

Liverpool is in a strong position to win the league because it has played fewer games than the clubs immediately challenging it and therefore it has more opportunities to add to its points than they have to theirs. There would appear to be two points for winning a game and one point for a draw. Liverpool has won 23 games (46 points) and drawn 9 games (9 points) for a total of 55 points. Manchester United has won 22 games (44 points) and drawn 10 games (10 points) for a total of 54 points. Assuming 42 games are played by each club to complete the season only three clubs can catch up or pass Liverpool even if it lost all its remaining games. On the same basis, Bolton cannot hope to do better on

Football League table

Football Club				Goals			
	P	W	D	L	F	A	Pts
Liverpool	38	23	9	6	75	28	55
Manchester United	39	22	10	7	61	31	54
Newcastle	40	21	9	10	66	37	51
Arsenal	37	16	14	7	48	29	46
Aston Villa	38	14	14	10	46	43	42
Southampton	39	16	9	14	56	48	41
Blackburn	37	17	7	13	49	41	41
Nottingham Forest	36	17	6	13	55	40	40
QPR	39	11	17	11	53	48	39
Middlesbrough	37	14	11	12	42	37	39
Chelsea	40	12	15	13	41	46	39
Coventry	39	16	7	16	54	61	39
Leeds	40	12	14	14	43	47	38
Tottenham	39	15	8	16	50	59	38
Sheffield Wednesday	39	11	14	14	51	60	36
Wimbledon	40	11	14	15	47	56	36
Manchester City	40	11	13	16	40	62	35
Norwich	39	11	10	18	42	56	32
Millwall	38	8	15	15	41	50	31
West Ham	40	10	8	22	42	62	28
Everton	38	8	12	18	30	57	28
Bolton	40	5	14	21	38	72	24

points than level with the two clubs immediately above it to have the lowest number of points in the League. If this was the situation and the relative positions of the clubs were then based on goal ratios Bolton and Everton would be in a weak position compared with West Ham on the evidence available, because their ratios are close to 1 goal for and 2 against while West Ham has a ratio of 2 goals for and 3 against.

It is noticeable that although there is a strong association between the number of games won and the position in the league, the clubs in the centre of the table have a varied record in this respect. Chelsea has obtained 39 points by achieving 15 draws against 12 wins, while Coventry has the same number of points with only 7 draws but with 16 wins. While Coventry has won more games than Chelsea they have also lost more. It might be possible to conclude that Coventry has played a more adventurous and risky type of football than Chelsea who may have been very defensive in their play. In fact Chelsea has conceded only 46 goals against Coventry's 61, and only scored 41 against Coventry's 54, which seems to confirm this conclusion.

The fact that goal ratios are used to decide the position of clubs in the league table when they have the same number of points, is confirmed by the fact that QPR and Middlesbrough, who have both scored more goals than had goals scored against them, are placed above Chelsea and Coventry although they all have the same number of points. Again Liverpool is in a strong position on this account compared with the clubs following them, having scored two and a half times as many goals as those scored against them.

It is interesting to note that only the top nine clubs have scored more goals than they have had scored against them. The position of the top and bottom clubs is almost directly opposite to each other. Liverpool has lost 6 games, Bolton won 5; Liverpool won 23, Bolton lost 21; Liverpool scored 75 goals, Bolton had 72 goals scored against them. As well as scoring twice as many goals Liverpool has more than twice as many points as Bolton.

The superiority of Liverpool over the other clubs is perhaps more marked than the one point lead indicates. The club has won more games than any other club, lost fewer games, scored more goals and had fewer goals scored against it. Its goal ratio is over 5 to 2 in its favour and no other club can come near to this. The club has scored an average of two goals a game which is far higher than any other club.

It would be possible to analyse the results of each club and to discuss details of goal differences against results and points. Clearly there is an association between all these factors because they are related. Points are gained by winning or drawing and to win, goals have to be scored. The total number of goals scored against equals those scored for, because a goal for one club is against another. Within the general patterns there are numerous variations which could be discussed in detail. For example, the club that has played the fewest games, Nottingham Forest, could statistically rise to third place if it won all its games and the other teams lost theirs (i.e. 6 games = 12 points + 40 = 52).

The source of the table is not given, nor is a date provided. With more information about the origins of the table and more knowledge of football it would be possible to add to the commentary at very great length.

1.13 Questions and exercises

Question 1.1

Discuss what is meant by the term 'information'. Consider the following statements on inflation:

(a) 'inflation is 6%'
(b) 'inflation is running at an annual level of 10%'
(c) 'inflation this year is running at 15%'
(d) 'the average level of inflation is 18%'.

Discuss the different meanings of these statements. Find a similar example and describe how this can illustrate the problem of the interpretation of data.

Question 1.2

Write short notes on the following:

(i)   statistics
(ii)   data
(iii) statistical information
(iv)   the abuse of statistics

(v) the use of statistics
(vi) descriptive statistics
(vii) inductive statistics
(viii) primary data
(ix) secondary data
(x) secondary statistics.

Question 1.3

Consider the kind of problems faced by a person who cannot read or write. How far are these problems similar to those of a person who cannot count or understand figures?

Question 1.4

How far is it possible to agree with the following statements?

(i) 'There are three kinds of lies: lies, damn lies and statistics'.
(ii) 'Don't be a novelist – be a statistician, much more scope for the imagination'.
(iii) 'He uses statistics as a drunken man uses a lamp post – for support rather than illumination'.

Question 1.5

Consider the importance of the various media through which information is distributed. Through which of these is statistical information included to the greatest extent?

Question 1.6

Outline two main sources of statistical information produced by government departments, describing the nature of the data contained in each publication and analysing the use of this data to private companies in a range of industrial and commercial fields.

Question 1.7

Which of the following is a quantitative variable?

A Patriotism
B Height
C Musical ability
D Health. (AEB)

Question 1.8

Which of the following defines a qualitative variable?

A Peas selected at random from a pod
B The number of good peas in a pod selected at random
C A red-headed pupil chosen at random
D The colour of a randomly chosen pupil's eyes. (AEB)

Question 1.9

Outline two main sources of statistical information with which you are familiar, one prepared by a government department and the other by some other agency. Your outline should contain sufficient detail for any colleague to learn the nature and value of the data available and to know when and how to seek the information.   (Chartered Institute of Marketing)

Question 1.10

Reports from a personnel department contained the following information on each of eleven applicants for a promotion.

A   Age next birthday
B   Height
C   Weight
D   Number of absences during last year
E   Suitability for promotion recorded as YES, NO or NOT YET.

Write down the letters corresponding to the variables which are:

(i)   qualitative;
(ii)   quantitative and discrete;
(iii)   quantitative and continuous.

(Note that in each case the correct answer may consist of more than one letter.)

(SEB)

Question 1.11

Give an example of a quantitative variable and explain how it differs from a qualitative variable.   (AEB)

Question 1.12

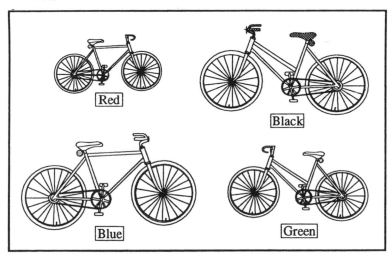

A collection of bicycles was displayed in a shop.

(a)   State a *qualitative variable* about these bicycles.

(b)   State a *continuous quantitative* variable about these bicycles.   (SEG)

Collecting Information: Surveys

| **Objectives** | By the end of this chapter the following terms and methods should be understood: |

	Date attempted	Date completed	Self-assessment
Survey design			
Survey methods			
Observation			
Interviewing			
Questionnaires			
Sampling			
Sampling methods			
Random sampling			
Quota sampling			
Panels			

| **Summary** | This chapter describes survey methods used for collecting statistical information. It explains statistical sampling techniques used in surveys. |

2.1 Introduction

If information is needed and is not readily available, it has to be collected. The collection of this primary data involves carrying out a survey or inquiry of one type or another.

A survey is an investigation with the objective of collecting information on a subject.

Surveys are carried out by:

- governments,
- market research organisations,
- research organisations,
- trade associations,
- firms.

2.2 Stages in carrying out a survey

Whether a survey covers 100% of all possible items or is a small sample survey, there will be a series of stages in carrying it out:

(a) Survey design

(i)   100% survey, e.g. Census of Population;
(ii) sample survey, e.g. Family Expenditure Survey.

(b) Pilot survey

A preliminary survey carried out on a small scale to make sure that the design and methodology of the survey are likely to produce the information required.

(c) Collection of information

The main methods are observation, interview and questionnaire.

(d) Coding

Questions are pre-coded in order that they can be easily classified and tabulated.

(e) Tabulation

After collection, information has to be classified and tabulated.

(f) Secondary statistics

Information can be summarised through the use of averages, percentages and so on.

(g) Reports

The final stage of a survey is usually to write a report on it.

Table 2.1 Survey stages

Decisions	Methods
Survey design	100% survey
	sample survey
Pilot survey	
Survey methods	observation
	interview
	questionnaire
Coding	numbering/lettering
Questions	number
	content
Summarisation	classification
	tabulation
	secondary statistics
	reports

**2.3
Survey
methods**

(a)   Observation

Watching behaviour or collecting information by looking at it, e.g. consumer behaviour, comparing prices.

• **Participant observation**

Here the observer becomes a participant in the activity being observed.

• **Systematic observation**

This is observing only those events which can be investigated without the participants knowing.

• **Mechanical observation**

This is using mechanical, electrical or electronic means to record events.

(b)   Interviewing

This is a conversation with a purpose. A 'formal' interview is a conversation between two people that is initiated by the interviewer in order to obtain information.

• **Types of interviews**

A very *formal interview* will include only set questions; an '*informal' interview* will follow a set pattern but questions will vary between interviews.

• **Purposes of interviews**

To examine attitudes and motives, and for job selection and discussions.

- Respondent (interviewee) success at interview

This will depend on:

accessibility of information to him
role expectation
motivation in answering questions
prestige carried by the interviewer.

- Interviewer success

This depends on:

the way questions are asked
extent of probing and supplementary questions
early replies setting a pattern
interviewer bias.

(c) Questionnaires

These are lists of questions aimed at discovering particular information.

- Types of questionnaire

There are:

postal questionnaires
non-postal questionnaires – used as part of an interview or completed under guidance.

- Advantages of postal questionnaires

These are:

cheap to distribute
can include large numbers of people
answers can be considered very carefully.

- Disadvantages of postal questionnaires

These are:

poor response rate
difficult to explain questions
no follow-up questions.

- Non-postal questionnaires

These usually have a limited distribution.
They may have a high response rate.

Table 2.2 Questionnaire design

Questions	Questionnaire form
Simple and clear	Clear who should complete it
Useful and relevant	Clear where answers should be recorded
Free from bias	Sufficient space for answers
Not personal or private	'Yes' and 'No' answers where possible
In a logical order	Convenience – for both respondent and
Unambiguous	survey team
Leading questions should be avoided	
Hypothetical questions are of limited value	

Table 2.3 Survey methods

Method	Advantages	Disadvantages
Observation	objective systematic mechanical	participatory selectivity interpretation chance observation
Interviewing	attitudes motives selection discussion	interviewer bias respondent expectations
Questionnaire	cheap large coverage objective	poor response rate limits on the information that can be collected

2.4 Sampling

A sample is anything less than a full survey of a population. It is usually thought of as a small part of the population, taken to give an idea of the whole. The *population* is the group of people or items about which information is being collected.

(a) Advantages of sampling

- Cost – survey of 2000 instead of 2 million;
- time – smaller survey;
- reliability – as a result of concentration on a few units;
- resource allocation – sampling enables more surveys to be carried out;
- destructive tests – since some tests destroy the product (e.g. light bulbs), there would not be any products left unless samples were used;
- compared with sampling, a full survey may be expensive, time consuming, difficult to carry out and both impracticable and unnecessary.

(b) Objectives of sampling

- To estimate certain population statistics or parameters (such as averages and proportion);
- to test a statistical theory about a population.

(c)   The basis of sampling

(i)   The law of statistical regularity

A reasonably large sample selected at random from a large population will be, on average, representative of the characteristics of the population.

(ii)   The law of the inertia of large numbers

Large groups of data show a higher degree of stability than smaller ones; there is a tendency for variations in the data to be cancelled out by each other.

  These laws are part of the central limit theorem and are ways of describing the theory of probability.

(d)   Sampling errors

- Non-sampling errors are problems involved with sample design;
- sampling errors – the difference between the estimate of a value obtained from a sample and the actual value.

(e)   Sample size

This is the number of people or units sampled.

- It is independent of the size of the population sampled.
- It does depend on the resources available and the degree of accuracy required.
- Other things being equal, a large sample will be more reliable than a small sample taken from the same population.

(f)   Sample design

Aims at avoiding bias in the selection procedure and achieving maximum precision for a given outlay of money and time.

How to design a sample
decide on the objectives of the survey,
assess the resources available,
define the sample population and the sample unit,
select a sample frame,
decide on a sample method,
choose a sampling method.

(g)   Elements in the design

(i)   The sampling population

This is the group of people, items or units under investigation.

(ii)   The sample units

These are the people or items to be sampled, clearly defined in terms of particular characteristics.

(iii)   The sample frame

This is the list of people, items or units from which the sample is taken; which should be comprehensive, complete and up-to-date to keep bias to a minimum.

(iv)   The survey method

This involves deciding on questionnaires, interviews or observations, or combinations of these methods.

(v)   Sampling methods

These fall into two categories:
random samples – simple, systematic, stratified, non-random samples – multi-stage, quota, cluster.

(h)   Bias in sampling

This consists of non-sampling errors which are not eliminated or reduced by an increase in sample size. Bias may arise from:

the sampling frame
non-response to a survey
the sample
question wording
the sample unit.

(i)   Sampling methods

(i)   Simple random sampling

In this, *each unit of the population has the same chance as any other unit of being included in the sample.*
   Characteristics:

- it is a random sample (random numbers can help to ensure this);
- it is carried 'without replacement', so that a unit selected at each draw is not replaced into the population before the next draw is made, so that a unit cannot appear more than once in the sample;
- it is 'simple' as compared with more complex methods (it is known also as 'simple' probability sampling);
- it is the standard against which other methods are evaluated;
- randomisation ensures the validity of the techniques of inference;
- it is suitable where the population is relatively small and the sampling frame complete.

(ii) Systematic sampling

This is a form of random sampling, involving a system. A name or unit is chosen at random from the sampling frame and from this chosen name or unit every *n*th item is selected throughout the list.

Characteristics:

- sufficiently random to obtain an estimate of the sampling error (sometimes known as quasi-random sampling);
- facilitates the selection of sampling units;
- not fully random and therefore there is a possibility of bias;
- particular characteristics arising in the list of names or units at regular intervals, can cause bias.

(iii) Random route sampling

An address is selected at random and every *n*th address is included after this by taking alternate left- and right-hand turns at road junctions *en route*.

Characteristics:

- quasi-random, because of a strong element of selection;
- control and checking may be difficult;
- can be quick and effective.

(iv) Stratified random sampling

In this method all the people or items in the sampling frame are divided into 'strata' (groups or categories) which are mutually exclusive. Within each stratum a simple random sample or systematic sample is selected.

Characteristics:

- within the strata the samples are random;
- particularly advantageous where there are clear strata in the population;
- problems arise when the strata are not clear.

(v) Quota sampling

Here a certain number of people with specific characteristics are interviewed.

Characteristics:

- not a random sampling method and therefore it is not possible to estimate sampling errors;
- there are problems of control and checking;
- quotas are chosen so that the overall sample reflects accurately the known population characteristics in a number of respects;
- may be the only feasible method where results are wanted quickly and there is not a suitable sampling frame for a random sample.

(vi) Cluster sampling (or area sampling)

Clusters are formed by breaking down the area to be surveyed into smaller areas a number of which are selected by random methods for survey. Units (people or households) within the selected clusters are chosen by random methods for the survey.

Characteristics:

- not a fully random sampling method, although there are elements of random sampling;
- a useful method where the population is widely dispersed;
- may be the only feasible method where there is not a suitable sampling frame and time and money need to be saved on travelling between locations and respondents.

(vii)   Multi-stage sampling

This consists of a series of samples taken at successive stages (geographical regions, towns or districts, people or households).

Characteristics:

- not a fully random sampling method, although there are elements of randomness. Random samples may be used at each stage once allowance has been made for regional and other differences;
- may be the only practical method for sampling the population of the country.

(viii)   Multi-phase sampling

Here some information is collected from the whole sample, while additional information is collected from sub-samples of the full sample.

Characteristics:

- random or non-random sampling methods may be used;
- can provide detailed information at relatively low cost.

(ix)   Replicated or interpenetrating sampling

In this method a number of sub-samples is selected from a population, rather than selecting one full sample. All the sub-samples have exactly the same design and each is a self-contained sample of the population.

Characteristics:

- random or non-random methods may be used;
- light can be thrown on non-sampling errors;
- can be expensive.

(x)   Master samples

Samples c overing the whole of a country to form the basis (i.e. a sampling frame) for smaller, local samples.

Table 2.4 Sampling methods

Sampling methods	Random or non-random	Main conditions under which a particular method might be selected
Simple	random	small population good sampling frame
Systematic	random	easy selection of sampling unit
Random route	quasi-random	speed and convenience
Stratified	quasi-random	clear strata
Quota	non-random	accurate representation of population characteristics
Cluster	non-random (elements of random)	population widely dispersed
Multi-stage	non-random (elements of random)	sampling whole population
Multi-phase	random or non-random	exposes non-sampling errors
Master samples	random or non-random	to form sampling frame
Panels	random or non-random	comparisons over time

(xi) Panels

A group of people is selected by a random sample and asked for the same information over a period of time.

Characteristics:

- results can be compared over time;
- panel 'mortality' may be high.

2.5 Worked examples

Example 2.1

'Postal questionnaires are a better method of collecting survey information than interviews.' Discuss.

Solution 2.1

Postal questionnaires and interviewing are two methods of collecting information when it is not otherwise available. A questionnaire is a list of questions aimed at discovering particular information. When it is distributed by post it can be distributed to large numbers of people relatively cheaply and quickly.

The main problem is in obtaining the return of the questionnaires. People need a strong incentive in order to persuade them to complete and return a questionnaire. The incentive may be in the form of a direct or indirect financial benefit or in the form of a non-financial benefit such as 'helping to further research' or 'mould opinion' in a particular area or subject.

In order to encourage people to complete a postal questionnaire, the questions need to be as few in number as possible, simply and clearly worded, relevant to the subject under investigation, in a logical order, not too private or personal, and unambiguous. As far as possible it should be possible to answer questions with 'yes' or 'no' or a tick or cross, it should be clear who should answer the questionnaire and it should be designed to make it easy for the respondent to complete it.

If these factors are not given due attention the response rate is likely to be poor. It is not possible in a postal questionnaire to follow up questions with supplementary questions, nor is it possible to explain what is meant by a question. Postal questionnaires are, therefore, a useful means for collecting survey information from large numbers of people providing that there is a good response rate.

The interview can be described as a conversation with a purpose, the purpose being to collect survey information. As a method of collecting information it is in many ways complementary to the postal questionnaire in the sense that it has almost the opposite advantages and disadvantages.

Interviewing takes time and, therefore, it is not possible to cover many people without incurring considerable expense. On the other hand few people refuse to be interviewed, so it is possible for the interviewer to explain the meaning of questions and ask supplementary questions. This means that it is possible to ask about people's attitudes on various issues and to consider their motives for particular behaviour.

Problems with interviews arise over the results of interviewer bias including the way questions are asked, the interaction between the interviewer and the interviewee and the kind of answers the interviewer might expect. The respondent or interviewee may not have the information that is being sought, may not know how fully questions should be answered and may not be highly motivated in answering them.

Both methods are good ways of collecting survey information. If what is required is information from large numbers of people on subjects where it is possible to set questions with 'yes' or 'no' answers, then the postal questionnaire may be the better method, particularly if there is strong motivation to return the questionnaire. A great amount of statistical information is collected by this method within organisations, industries and services. The Government obtains much of its information this way including information on, for example, personal income and liability for taxation.

If what is required is detailed information about opinions, motives and attitudes where a small sample may be useful or a small number of people are involved, the interview may be the more appropriate method for collecting survey information. It is used, often in conjunction with a set of questions, in market research, opinion polls and attitude surveys.

Example 2.2

Comment on the reasons why a sample survey may be preferred to a census to collect statistical information.

Solution 2.2

A census is a survey of all of a population, while a sample is anything less than this. It may appear to be the case that anything less than a complete survey will include only part of the information required and will be open to a high degree of error and approximation. A full survey, however, is likely to be expensive and to take a long time unless it covers a small population.

A sample, on the other hand, will be cheaper and take less time than a one hundred per cent survey. The saving in cost and time can be used to achieve a high level of reliability. Resources can be concentrated on obtaining reliable information by training field staff, making checks on the survey and in editing and analysis. Respondents may be more willing to provide detailed information if they know that they are representing the population.

If cost was not an important factor it would still be quicker to use a sample and the main reason to use a census would be to obtain greater reliability. The Population Census, for example, is used to provide large amounts of reliable information which can also provide a framework for samples on particular subjects. In many statistical investigations, in fact, a very high degree of accuracy may not be required. The size of a sample can be adjusted so that the accuracy of the results is sufficient for the needs of the survey.

Sampling will mean that errors may arise that would not occur with a census; however, provided the sampling method used is based on random selection it is possible to measure the probability of errors of any given size. The degree of sampling error will depend on the size of the sample; the larger the sample the smaller the sampling error. To reduce the sampling error to any great extent may, however, be expensive. For example, a sample of 100 with a standard deviation of 5 will have a standard error of 0.5. To halve the standard error the sample size has to be increased four times:

$$\frac{5}{\sqrt{100}} = 0.5; \quad \frac{5}{\sqrt{400}} = 0.25$$

In many circumstances a sample survey will be preferred to a census to collect statistical information because it is quicker and cheaper and its accuracy may not be any less. If accuracy is very important and there is great variability in the population, a census may be required if the resources are available. Otherwise a census is used only where there is a small population (e.g. a small group of items, or a small number of people, say within a firm), while samples are used by the government (for example for the Family Expenditure Survey), and for market research, opinion surveys, quality control and whenever statistical information is needed and is not available.

Example 2.3

Write the following question in a form suitable for inclusion in a questionnaire. 'What are your views on capital punishment, or perhaps you do not have any views?'

Solution 2.3

Please tick the appropriate box:
  Do you support capital punishment

(a) for all crimes   Yes ☐   No ☐   Don't Know ☐

(b) for some crimes   Yes ☐   No ☐   Don't Know ☐

Example 2.4

A firm employs the following people;

Management	*Sales*	*Shop floor*
100	400	4500

Explain how you would obtain a stratified sample of 150 employees.

Solution 2.4

A stratified sample is used when there are clear strata within the population to be sampled. In this case the three strata are clear. The sample size is given at 150 and the representation of each strata in the sample should be proportional to their numbers in the population.

   The total number of employees is 5000, management make up 2% of this total, sales staff 8% and shop floor 90%. In a sample of 150 the number of management staff sampled would be 3, sales staff 12 and shop floor 135.

   The people to be included in the sample for each strata could be selected either by random selection (for example, by using random numbers) or by a systematic sample method. In the latter case the first one in each strata would be selected at random, the remainder at intervals covering the number to be selected from within the strata. The sampling frame would be the wages and salaries list for the firm.

Example 2.5

A firm has approximately 1000 men and women working for it. Some work in the small manufacturing workshop, others work in the large purchasing and storage section, others in sales and marketing and a small number in management and administration. A sample of 100 employees is obtained by allocating a number to each person and selecting 100 at random.

   Explain briefly any disadvantages from which this sample might suffer.

Solution 2.5

The main disadvantage of this sample, is that it is a simple random sample and every person in the firm has an equal chance of being included. This could mean, for example, that all 100 people selected could by chance all come from the large purchasing and storage section. While this method ensures randomness, it does not ensure that all sections of the firm are represented. The population in this case is variable because people work in at least five sections within the firm and both men and women are employed.

A stratified random sample might provide a more accurate impression of the population because each gender and every section can be included in proportion to its size.

Example 2.6

Quota sampling is frequently used by organisations to obtain survey information. Explain briefly why this appears to be the case despite the weaknesses of the method.

Solution 2.6

In quota sampling the interviewer is instructed to interview a certain number of people with specific characteristics. These may include sex, age, income level and so on. The more characteristics that are introduced the more difficult the interviewer's task becomes. This is particularly the case if the interviewer is not working from a sampling frame that includes all the information he needs on it.

In fact quota sampling is often used when there is not a suitable sampling frame available and where a survey has to be completed quickly. An example would be that a market research organisation wants to obtain the views of consumers on potential consumers of a client's product, in a very short time. Interviewers may be sent to shopping centres at a certain time of the day to interview people with particular characteristics. The first people encountered and 'recognised' by the interviewer as having the necessary characteristics will be surveyed.

This is not a random sampling method and therefore it is not possible to estimate the sampling errors. Interviewer bias may be an important factor, non-response may not be recorded and the control of fieldwork may be difficult. It can be argued, however, that the greatest defects in sampling are at the interview stage and in processing the data and that the sample itself is a small source of error. If, therefore, the interviews are well conducted and the data is carefully processed, quota sampling may provide a reasonably accurate result. At the same time it does enable a market research survey to concentrate on the consumers (whether male or female, rich or poor, old or young) who are most relevant for the product under consideration.

2.6 Questions and exercises

Question 2.1

(a) Discuss, using appropriate examples, the relative advantages and disadvantages of a sample survey and a census for the collection of data.

(b) Outline the main principles to be followed when designing a questionnaire.

(RSA)

Question 2.2

Distinguish between the following terms used in sampling and survey methods:

(a) sample and population

(b)   census and survey
(c)   simple random sampling and systematic sampling
(d)   interviewer bias and interviewee bias.   (RSA)

Question 2.3

Outline the procedures employed in a national census of population.
    What uses are made of the information collected in such a census?   (RSA)

Question 2.4

Discuss the relative advantages and disadvantages of the postal questionnaire and the interview as a method of data collection.   (RSA)

Question 2.5

(a)   Discuss the relative advantages and disadvantages of the postal
        questionnaire and the interview as a means of collecting data.
(b)   Compare and contrast simple random sampling and quota sampling. (RSA)

Question 2.6

The United Nations recommended that countries should hold a national census of population at some time in the period 1980–82.

(a)   Describe the most recent population census in your country.
(b)   Discuss the uses made of the information collected in the census.   (RSA)

Question 2.7

Write notes on *three* of the following:

(i)   Questionnaire design.
(ii)   Quota sampling.
(iii)   Sampling frames.
(iv)   Stratified sampling.
(v)   Multistage sampling.   (RSA)

Question 2.8

In a questionnaire on nuclear disarmament, requiring Yes or No answers, the following question was asked 'Some people believe that unilateral disarmament will lead to world peace. Do you agree, therefore, that this country should disarm?'
    Comment briefly on the design of this question.   (AEB)

Question 2.9

It is required to obtain the views of the pupils of a school on the school magazine. It is decided to do this by means of a committee of twelve. The school consists of

600 pupils, 150 in the first year, 100 in each of the second, third and fourth years and 50 in each of the fifth, lower sixth and upper sixth years. Describe briefly how you would select such a committee by

(a) random sampling,
(b) stratified sampling,
(c) quota sampling.

(AEB)

Question 2.10

For a particular survey, a school wishes to obtain a 10% systematic sample of its pupils. Explain briefly how this can be achieved. (AEB)

Question 2.11

(a) Discuss the advantages of collecting market information by sample survey methods rather than by a complete census.
(b) What is meant by 'simple random sampling' and what are the principles upon which it depends? (Chartered Institute of Marketing)

Question 2.12

(a) Identify and explain ten guidelines you would recommend in the preparation of a good questionnaire to be used in collecting statistical data from consumers.
(b) Discuss the strengths and weaknesses to be found in using interviewers to collect data in field research. (Chartered Institute of Marketing)

Question 2.13

Using a hypothetical or real example of your own choice design a survey method for a piece of market research using multistage sampling, you should

(a) give an introduction to the market sample
(b) explain the purpose of the survey, and
(c) draft a set of clear instructions for researchers to follow, step by step, to obtain the sample units. (Chartered Institute of Marketing)

Question 2.14

(a) Explain the difference between a census and a sample survey. Give reasons why a sample survey is often preferred to a census.
(b) A proposal to close a number of small hospitals and replace them by a single large hospital has been made. As part of the evidence he is preparing for a public enquiry a local doctor wishes to find the views of the residents of one of the towns which would be affected by the proposal. Write notes advising the doctor how he might set about achieving this, assuming that both time and money will be limited. The population of the town is about 50 000. (SUJB)

Question 2.15

You are asked to prepare a questionnaire to find out whether your customers/clients are satisfied with the service your organisation provides.

(a) How would you plan and research this.
(b) List the features of a good questionnaire.
(c) Prepare a questionnaire with a minimum of ten questions.

(Chartered Institute of Marketing)

Question 2.16

(a) State briefly four rules for guidance when drafting a questionnaire for completion by the general public.
(b) Explain the circumstances under which *pilot enquiries* might be organised, and outline briefly the purposes of such enquiries.
(c) Explain what is meant by random sampling. Give an example to illustrate how bias may arise when sampling.
(d) The diagram below was drawn to illustrate the income and expenditure of a Badminton club during the season 1970–71. The area of each square was proportional to the sum of money which it represented.

(i)   Given that the expenditure in 1970–71 was £150, calculate the income in that season, giving your answer to the nearest £.
(ii)   Explain why the illustration given is likely to be misleading.
(iii) Illustrate the income and expenditure by another method which is not misleading.

(AEB)

Question 2.17

Describe *three* of the following types of sample;

(a) simple random,
(b) stratified,
(c) systematic,
(d) quota.

In each case state the conditions under which each would be used and the advantages to be gained from using them.

(RSA)

Question 2.18

A large insurance company has a head office, regional office and a number of branch offices. There is pressure from a union which has negotiating rights to introduce flexitime. (Flexitime is an alternative to working fixed hours, whereby individual employees can, within certain limits, i.e. they must work between 10 a.m. and 4 p.m., choose their hours of work subject to working a total of say, 37 hours per week.)

You are asked to conduct a survey of employees to find out their views on the introduction of flexitime.

(i)   Briefly explain how you should select a sample of employees.
(ii)   Draw up a suitable questionnaire (about 8 questions) for use with your survey.   (Institute of Chartered Secretaries and Administrators)

Question 2.19

'Quota sampling is frequently used by marketing departments to obtain survey information despite many weaknesses in the method'.

Explain carefully and fully what is meant by 'quota sampling' and discuss the above statement.   (Chartered Institute of Marketing)

Question 2.20

Explain the difference between stratified sample design and quota sample design. Discuss the advantages and disadvantages of each method with particular reference to the work of a market research department.

(Chartered Institute of Marketing)

Question 2.21

You work as a marketing assistant for Goldcare, an international company which sells luxury cars. Your marketing manager asks you to:

(a)   Write brief notes on the different methods of sampling which could be used by Goldcare.
(b)   Design a multistage sample survey showing each step of the process which would help the company improve its customer services.

(Chartered Institute of Marketing)

Question 2.22

	At Home %	In the Car %	At Work %	In the Street %	Elsewhere %
Man	81	11	9	9	7
Woman	88	5	3	5	–
Age 15–24	75	11	7	22	8
Age 65+	89	3	–	–	8

The above table shows where carry-out foods are eaten by members of the public interviewed by a research team.

(a)   Suggest a reason why the column *At Work* appears blank for the group *Age 65+*.

1

(b) By considering the *In the Street* column entries, what can you conclude? **2**
(c) Suggest why the total for the *Man* row exceeds 100% **2**

(5)

(SEB)

Question 2.23

Identify the method of sampling being used in each of the following situations, by writing the appropriate letter on the answer sheet, where

A denotes Random Sampling
B denotes Stratified Random Sampling
C denotes Quota Sampling
D denotes Systematic Sampling
E denotes Convenience Sampling.

(i) A Work Study officer used random number tables to select 20 employees to interview in a study of overtime.
(ii) In assessing the market potential of a new chocolate bar, an interviewer questioned 100 customers of a large supermarket.
(iii) In a survey into diet problems, a school doctor examined all girls in a particular school who were born during November 1970.
(iv) An audience researcher was required to interview 30 under sixteens and 40 senior citizens. (SEB)

Question 2.24

A large co-educational school comprises years one to five and a small sixth form. It is decided to carry out a survey into weekly television viewing among its pupils. A questionnaire is to be designed, a suitable sample of pupils selected and on completion of the analysis the results are to be presented in a single table summarising the findings.

(a) State briefly four rules for guidance when drafting the questionnaire.
(b) Explain what is meant by a stratified random sample. Give reasons why such a sample is to be preferred in this situation to a simple random sample.
(c) The total number of pupils in the school is 2100. The years one to five contain equal numbers of pupils and the sixth form has a quarter of the number of pupils in the fifth year. If the school decides to take a 10 per cent sample for the survey, state how many pupils should be selected from each year.
(d) Design a suitable table with which to summarise the results of the survey.

(AEB)

Question 2.25

'Young people are eating more hot take-away food. The latest survey of 15–24 year olds found that in July, of the 1024 interviewed, 86% had purchased a hot take-away meal in the previous month. A similar survey in March of the same year registered 68%.'

(a) The market research organisation responsible for the survey draw attention to the colder weather in March and suggest that their findings are all the more significant. What could be said for and against their claim that this makes their findings more significant?

(b) What factors should have been considered to ensure that the July survey was 'similar' to the March survey?

(c) The original survey asked about Chinese food, Indian food, pizzas, hamburgers and fish and chips. By combining all the statistics into the one conclusion quoted above, what information does a reader of the conclusion lose?

(d) Why is this survey by interviewing likely to be more accurate than a postal survey of 1024 young people? (SEB)

Question 2.26

A college wants to do a survey of the smoking habits of its students. Explain how you would take:

(i) a random sample of 100 students,
(ii) a stratified sample of 100 students.

Question 2.27

(a) Paul is carrying out a survey to find the most popular colour for a vehicle. He finds the colour of his mother's car and two neighbours' cars. Give *two* reasons why this sample may give a poor result.

(b) Give *two* advantages of sampling. (SEG)

The Accuracy of Information

3

| Objectives | By the end of this chapter the following terms and methods should be understood: |

	Datc attempted	Date completed	Self-assessment
Approximations			
Degrees of tolerance			
Rounding			
Error			
Calculations involving approximations and error			
Spurious accuracy			

Summary   This chapter is concerned with accuracy in statistical information and the meaning of statistical error.

3.1 Approximations

Perfect accuracy in statistical information is possible only in limited circumstances. 'One plus one equals two' is an accurate statement, but in applied areas of activity where problems have to be solved and decisions made perfect accuracy of this kind is impossible and, therefore, approximations are used.

For example: by the time the national census figures are available, the demographic statistics will have altered because of the births and deaths which have occurred in the intervening period. Although at a specific moment the population of a country is a finite figure, the actual figure available will always be an approximation because of the impossibility of counting every single person alive at that moment.

3.2 Degrees of tolerance

The degree of tolerance is the level of accuracy required in the measurement and use of particular statistics. The degree of accuracy required depends upon the type of data being measured and the uses to which it will be put. For every measurement there will be a level of tolerance beyond which inaccuracy is unacceptable.

For example: in estimating the size of an audience at a meeting, to say that there were 100 people, when there were in fact 90, might be acceptable, but to say that there were 50 or 150 might not be acceptable.

3.3 Error

'Error' in statistics means the difference between what is acceptable as a true figure and what is taken for an estimate or approximation.

For example: the population of the UK may be said to be approximately 56 million, based on the last census. If it was possible to count the population exactly at this moment (because all births, immigration, emigration and deaths were recorded at the moment they occurred), the true population might be found to be 58.3 million exactly. The error would be the difference between the approximation and the true figure: 56 million − 58.8 million = 2.8 million. This could be put in a different way by saying that the error was 5%. Error in this sense does not mean a 'mistake'. A mistake is usually involuntary and something to be avoided, while an approximation is used to improve the presentation of figures and to reflect the degree of accuracy required. The population of the UK could be counted more accurately than with a 5% error but this would involve increased time and costs.

3.4 Rounding

(a) To the nearest whole number

The convention is to round 0.5 and above to the next highest whole number and 0.499 (recurring) to the next lowest whole number.

For example: 6.5 would become 7 when rounded to the nearest whole number, 6.499 would become 6 when rounded to the nearest whole number.

(b) To the nearest even number

So that the digit preceding the final zeros in the approximate values is even and not odd.

For example: 125.4 would become 126 and 124.8 would become 124. In most circumstances this procedure does not have any advantages over rounding to the nearest whole number.

(c)   By truncation

This is the omission of the unwanted final digits.

For example: 15.268 truncated to four figures becomes 15.26, to two figures it would become 15.

This procedure produces a downward bias into the results obtained.

(d)   By significant figures

This is a rounding process by which the number of digits that are significant are stated and after that number, zeros replace other digits.

For example:

Calculated figure	Four significant figures	Three significant figures	Two significant figures
213.73	213.7	214	210
0.003 726	0.003 726	0.003 73	0.003 7
2 482 731	2 483 000	2 480 000	2 500 000
30 000	30 000	30 000	30 000
20 518	20 520	20 500	21 000

A similar process is rounding to, say, *one decimal place.*

For example:

6.438   to one decimal place   = 6.4
6.448   to one decimal place   = 6.5
6.45   to one decimal place   = 6.5
6.44   to one decimal place   = 6.4
6.5231 to one decimal place   = 6.5
6.5631 to one decimal place   = 6.6

3.5 Absolute error

This is the actual difference between an estimate or approximation and the true figure.

   For example: a housewife may expect to spend £10 on her shopping, but actually spends £12.50. The absolute error is £2.50. Another housewife expects to spend £20 on her shopping, but actually spends £22.50. Again the absolute error is £2.50.

3.6 Relative error

This is the absolute error divided by the estimate, often expressed as a *percentage*:

$$\text{Relative error} = \frac{\text{absolute error}}{\text{estimated figure}} \times 100$$

For example: $\dfrac{2.50}{10} \times 100 = 25\%$

$\dfrac{2.50}{20} \times 100 = 12\frac{1}{2}\%$

3.7 Biased, cumulative or systematic error

If in a series of items the errors are all in one direction, the result will be biased, cumulative or systematic error.

For example: if people are asked to give their ages at their last birthday, the total age of the group will be lower than the real total:

Actual ages		Approximate ages (age last birthday)
Years	Months	Years
28	6	28
25	5	25
29	2	29
27	11	27
111	0	109

The absolute error is 2 years, the relative error is 1.8%.

3.8 Unbiased or compensating error

This is when the approximation is to the nearest whole number or complete unit.

For example: if people are asked to give their ages to their nearest birthday, the total age of the group is likely to be similar to the real total.

Actual ages		Approximate ages (age at nearest birthday)
Years	Months	Years
28	6	29
25	5	25
29	2	29
27	11	28
111	0	111

3.9 Calculations involving approximations and error

Approximations can be accepted because they provide information to the level of accuracy required and in many cases, the level of accuracy possible. It is, however, useful to be clear what is meant by an approximation and to calculate the limits embraced by it.

For example: if it is known that the population of a town is 120 000 to the nearest thousand and the birth rate is 15 births per thousand to the nearest whole number; it is possible to calculate the limits of error in the statistics.

120 000 to the nearest thousand can be rewritten as $120\,000 \pm 500$
This can be written in thousands as 120 ± 0.5
15 to the nearest whole number can be rewritten as 15 ± 0.5

The greatest possible birth rate would be:

$120.5 \times 15.5 = 1867.75$ births

The lowest possible birth rate would be:

$119.5 \times 14.5 = 1732.75$ births

The number of births in the town is likely to be between these two figures:

1800.25 ± 67.5

The difference of 135 births between the two figures indicates the extent of the approximations and may be important in planning projections of the future population.

(a)   Addition

For example: add 17 ± 0.5 and 3 ± 0.01

The highest possible result is:	$17.5 + 3.01 =$	20.51
The lowest possible result is:	$16.5 + 2.99 =$	<u>19.49</u>
	Total	40.00

The mid-point is 20 ($40 \div 2$), the limits of error (the difference between 20.51 and 19.49 divided by 2) are ± 0.51.
Thus $(17 \pm 0.5) + (3 \pm 0.01) = 20 \pm 0.51$
   The error in the aggregate is the sum of the absolute errors in the component parts (0.5 ± 0.01)

(b)   Subtraction

For example: subtract 20 ± 2 from 100 ± 10

   The maximum result is the highest figure minus the lowest:

$110 - 18 = 92$

The minimum result is the lowest figure that can be obtained from 100 ± 10 minus the highest figure which can be obtained from 20 ± 2:

$90 - 22 = 68$

The mid-point $= 80$, the limits of error $= \pm 12$
Thus $(100 \pm 10) - (20 \pm 2) = 80 \pm 12$

(c)   Multiplication

For example: multiply 100 ± 2 by 20 ± 1

   The maximum possible result is obtained by multiplying the highest figure that can be obtained from 100 ± 2 by the highest figure that can be obtained from 20 ± 1:

$102 \times 21 = 2142$

The minimum possible result is obtained by multiplying the lowest figure that can be obtained from 100 ± 2 by the lowest possible figure that can be obtained from 20 ± 1:

$98 \times 19 = 1862$

The mid-point is 2002, the limits of error $= \pm 140$
Thus $(100 \pm 2) \times (20 \pm 1) = 2002 \pm 140$.

(d) Division

For example: divide 1000 ± 20 by 100 ± 1

The maximum result is obtained by dividing the minimum figure that can be obtained from 100 ± 1 into the maximum figure that can be obtained for 1000 ± 20:

$1020 \div 99 = 10.303$

The minimum result is obtained by dividing the maximum figure that can be obtained from 100 ± 1 into the minimum figure that can be obtained from 1000 ± 20:

$980 \div 101 = 9.703$

The mid-point $= 10.003$, the limits of error ± 0.3
Thus $(1000 \pm 20) \div (100 \pm 1) = 10.003 \pm 0.3$.

3.10 Spurious accuracy

This is when claims are made for a greater accuracy than in fact exists or a figure is written in such a way that it implies an accuracy greater than it really has.

For example: the statement that 'the population of the UK is 56 251 432 people' suggests that every single person has been counted and no-one has been born or died since that count. In fact it is very difficult to count every single person at any one moment and the population changes every second, and, therefore, a more accurate statement would be that 'on the 1st January 1985 the population of the UK was estimated to be 56 251 000 to the nearest 1000, based on population census returns updated by reference to OPCS statistics'.

Another example: the statement that 'about 4 million households out of a total of 18 million have a video recorder', may be summarised as '22.22% of households own video recorders'. 'About 4 million' is much more of an approximation than 22.22% and the percentage would be a better representation of the original figure if it was written as 'about 22%' or even as 'about 20%'.

3.11 Worked examples

Example 3.1

(a) Calculate the least possible value of the following expression if each of the numbers is given correct to one decimal place:

$$\frac{5.9}{2.4}$$

(b) Express the following numbers to two significant figures:
   (i)   0.0478   (ii)   6278.43
   (iii) 14.004 6   (iv)   114.004 6

Solution 3.1

(a) $\dfrac{5.85}{2.45} = 2.388$

(b) (i) 0.048   (ii) 6300
    (iii) 14   (iv) 110

Example 3.2

(a) In measuring the length of metal rods on a building site it is discovered that the first batch of rods to be delivered measure 20.5 cm in length, while the second batch measure 21.25 cm in length. Given that the first batch is estimated to be the correct length, what is the:
    (i) absolute error between the two batches,
    (ii) relative error between the two batches?
(b) If the level of tolerance in connection with the length of these rods is in fact 21 cm ± 0.75 cm, is it likely that both batches can be used?

Solution 3.2

(a) (i) absolute error $= 21.25 - 20.5$ cm $= 0.75$ cm

    (ii) relative error $= \dfrac{0.75}{20.5} \times 100 = 3.66\%$

(b) The two batches fall within the limits of tolerance and, therefore, both batches can be used:

length of rods $= 21$ cm ± 0.75; limits of tolerance $= 20.25$ cm $- 21.75$ cm.

Example 3.3

The population of a town is 250 000 to the nearest 1000, and the birth rate is 12 per thousand to the nearest whole number. Calculate the highest and lowest number of births there may be in the town during a year.

Solution 3.3

Highest number of births $= 250.5 \times 12.5 = 3131.25$
Lowest number of births $= 249.5 \times 11.5 = 2869.25$

The number of births in the town in a year is likely to be between 2869.25 and 3131.25 or 3000.25 ± 131.

Example 3.4

The 'A' Level results in a school show that 240 candidates obtained an average of 2.2 grades of E or better per candidate. If each of these figures is correct to two significant figures, what is the minimum number of grades of E or better obtained within the school?

Solution 3.4

Minimum number of candidates obtaining grade E or better = 235
Minimum average of E grades or better = 2.15
Minimum number of grades of E or better = 235 × 2.15 = 505.25

3.12 Questions and exercises

Question 3.1

(a) In measuring the quantities 400, 600 and 300 absolute errors of 5%, 7% and 12% respectively were involved. Calculate (400 ± 5% of 400) + (600 ± 7% of 600) − (300 ± 12% of 300) giving the answer in the form $x \pm y$.

Find
(i) the maximum absolute error in the answer,
(ii) the maximum relative error in the answer.

(b) If x is given as 0.05 correct to two places of decimals, which is the least

possible value of $4 + \dfrac{0.22}{x^2}$ (AEB, Additional statistics)

Question 3.2

Calculate the least possible value of the following expression if each of the numbers is given correct to one decimal place

$$\frac{9.8}{1.9}$$ (AEB)

Question 3.3

$11.6 + 13.8 + 26.1 − 10.3 = 41.2$
The four numbers on the left-hand side of this equation are known to be correct to three significant figures. The maximum possible error in the answer on the right-hand side is
A   0.05
B   0.10
C   0.15
D   0.20   (AEB)

Question 3.4

The lengths of 100 rods were measured to the nearest mm with the following results:

Length of rods (mm)	31	32	33
Frequency	10	23	67

The maximum possible value of the range of the distribution is
A   2 mm
B   3 mm

C   33 mm

D   57 mm   (AEB)

Question 3.5

The blood pressure of each of 200 men was measured to the nearest mm. The tabulated results are shown below.

Blood pressure (mm)	65–69	70–74	75–79	80–84	85–89	90–94
No. of men	8	28	54	60	32	18

Estimate the number of men with an actual blood pressure greater than 83 mm. (AEB)

Question 3.6

A headmaster announced that in recent GCE 'O' Level examinations 120 candidates from his school obtained an average of 4.1 grades of C, or better, per candidate. If each of these figures is correct to 2 significant figures, what is the minimum number of grades of C, or better, obtained within the school?   (AEB)

Question 3.7

(a)   The internal dimensions of a rectangular box are: length 25.4 cm, breadth 16.0 cm and height 9.2 cm, all figures correct to one decimal place.
Within what limits does
(i)   the length lie;
(ii) the area of the base lie;
(iii) the volume lie?
Express each dimension correct to two significant figures and use the rounded data to calculate the volume. What is the percentage error in the calculated volume due to using the rounded data? (Assume original data are exact.)

(b)   The box weighs 0.347 kg when empty and 3.951 kg when partly filled with a liquid.
Write these two weights:
(i)   correct to two significant figures;
(ii) correct to one decimal place.
(iii) Calculate the weight of the liquid using the figures corrected to one decimal place in (ii).
(iv) Calculate the weight of the liquid using the original data, and then correct your answer to one decimal place.
(v)   Which of the results in (iii) and (iv) is the more accurate?   (SUJB)

Question 3.8

An Oxfam publication states 'In many parts of Zaire, where women bear a heavy burden of manual labour, nearly half their babies die in infancy'.

(a) Does Oxfam seem to be in favour of women doing manual labour? 1
(b) What statistics would you ask to see, if you were trying to verify Oxfam's statement? 2
(c) It is known that malnutrition and disease account for 84% of all deaths among infants in a certain part of Zaire. Explain why Oxfam's claim need not contradict that statistic. 2

(5)

(SEB)

Question 3.9

A pair of scales is known to underestimate the true mass of any object with a relative error of 0.004. If the true mass of an apple is 125 grams, what will be the reading on the scales? (AEB)

Question 3.10

Each of the numbers in the expression below is given correct to two significant figures.

$$\frac{3.4 - 1.6}{8.1 + 1.8}$$

Calculate the least possible value of the expression. (AEB)

How to Use Figures: Basic Mathematics, Financial Mathematics and Vital Statistics

4

Objectives	By the end of this chapter the following terms and methods should be understood:

	Date attempted	Date completed	Self-assessment
Number systems			
Basic arithmetic			
Sequence of operations			
Simple arithmetic			
Fractions			
Decimals			
Percentages			
Powers and roots			
Proportions and ratios			
Algebra			
Levels of measurement			
Financial mathematics			
Vital statistics			

Summary	This chapter describes the main features of basic mathematics, financial mathematics and vital statistics.

4.1 Number systems

The basic vocabulary of mathematics is a number system:

(a) The *decimal system* which is based on groups of ten, such as 0–9, 10, 20, 30 . . .90; 0.1 (one-tenth), 0.01 (one hundredth) . . .

(b) The *binary system* which is based on two digits, 0 and 1. 0(zero), 1(one), 10(two), 11(three), 100(four), 101(five), 110(six), 111(seven), 1000(eight) . . .

4.2 Basic arithmetic

This is comprised of:

(a) addition (+)
(b) subtraction (−)
(c) multiplication (×)
(d) division (÷).

4.3 Sequence of operations

BODMAS or B-ODM-AS

Brackets	evaluated first
Of	
Division	} evaluated second
Multiplication	
Addition	} evaluated last
Subtraction	

If an expression contains only pluses and minuses or only multiplication and division, then the sum should be calculated by working from the left to the right.

4.4 Simple arithmetic

(i) $30 - 9 + 3 = 24$ (the working is from left to right)

(ii) $8 \times 3 - 2 = 22$ (multiplication before subtraction)

(iii) $-5 \times 3 = -15$ (a minus times a plus equals a minus)

(iv) $-5 \times -3 = 15$ (two minuses makes a plus)

(v) $4 + 7 \times 3 = 25$ (multiplication before addition)

(vi) $4(3) = 12$ (a bracket equals multiplication)

(vii) $4(3+1) = 16$ (the bracket comes first)

(viii) $(2 - 1)(7 + 5) = 12$ (brackets before multiplication)

(ix) $5 - 3 \times 4 + 5 = -2$ (multiplication before subtraction and addition)

(x) $122 \times 28 \div 7 + 60 = 548$ (multiplication and division first, working from left to right)

4.5 Fractions

These are units of measurement expressed as one whole number divided by another.

$$\text{Common fraction} = \frac{\text{Numerator}}{\text{Denominator}}$$

Proper fraction = numerator less than denominator (for example, $\frac{1}{2}$ or $\frac{3}{4}$)

Improper fraction = numerator greater than denominator (for example, $\frac{53}{10}$. This can be reduced to a whole number and proper fraction: $5\frac{3}{10}$).

(a) Addition and subtraction of fractions

$$\frac{1}{4} + \frac{1}{3} = \frac{3}{12} + \frac{4}{12} = \frac{3+4}{12} = \frac{7}{12}$$

12 is the common denominator into which both 3 and 4 can be divided.

(b) Multiplication and division of fractions

To multiply fractions the numerators are multiplied together to obtain the numerator of the answer, and the denominators are multiplied together to obtain the denominator of the answer:

$$\frac{2}{3} \times \frac{4}{12} = \frac{8}{36} = \frac{2}{9}$$

To divide by a fraction, multiply by its inverse:

$$\frac{4}{7} \div \frac{5}{8} = \frac{4}{7} \times \frac{8}{5} = \frac{32}{35}$$

To divide mixed fractions they must first be made improper (a 'mixed fraction' is one that contains whole numbers as well as fractions).

$$3\frac{2}{5} = 3 + \frac{2}{5} = \frac{15}{5} + \frac{2}{5} = \frac{17}{5}$$

$$3\frac{2}{5} \div 2\frac{4}{7} = \frac{17}{5} \div \frac{18}{7} = 1\frac{29}{90}$$

4.6 Decimals

A decimal number is one whose denominator is any power of ten: three-tenths can be written as $\frac{3}{10}$ or 0.3

The *metric system* is based on units of ten:

Length: 10 millimetres (mm) = 1 centimetre (cm)
          100 centimetres (cm) = 1 metre (m)
          1000 metres (m) = 1 kilometre (km)
Capacity: 1000 millilitres (ml) = 1 litre (l)
          1000 litres (l) = 1 kilolitre (kl)
Weight: 1000 milligrams (mg) = 1 gram (g)
          1000 grams (g) = 1 kilogram (kg)
          1000 kilograms (kg) = 1 tonne (t)

4.7 The imperial system

The *imperial system* is based on a variety of units of number:

Length: 12 inches = 1 foot
          3 feet = 1 yard
          1760 yards = 1 mile
          (1 metre = 39.37 inches or 3 feet 3.37 inches)

Capacity: 2 pints = 1 quart
              4 quarts or 8 pints = 1 gallon
              (1 litre = 1.76 pints)
Weight: 16 ounces (oz) = 1 pound (lb)
              14 pounds (lb) = 1 stone
              112 pounds (lb) = 1 hundredweight (cwt)
              20 hundredweight (cwt) = 1 ton
              (1 kilogram = 2.2 pounds)

4.8 Temperature

The freezing point of water in Celsius is at 0°, in Fahrenheit at 32°. Conversion formulae are:

$$C = \frac{5}{9}(F - 32) \text{ and } F = \frac{9}{5}C + 32$$

If F = 60° then:

$$C = \frac{5}{9}(60 - 32) = 15.55°C$$

If C = 15° then:

$$F = \frac{9}{5} \times 15 + 32 = 59°F$$

4.9 Percentages

Per cent means per hundred, so that 50 per cent is 50 per hundred, or 50 out of a hundred.

(i)   to change a fraction to a percentage, multiply by 100: $\frac{1}{4}$ equals 25%
        (25 = $\frac{1}{4} \times$ 100)

(ii)   to change a decimal to a percentage, multiply the decimal by 100:
        0.55 × 100 = 55%

(iii)   to change a percentage to a fraction, divide by 100: 50% = $\frac{50}{100}$ = $\frac{1}{2}$

(iv)   to change a percentage to a decimal, divide by 100 by moving the decimal point two places to the left: 13.96% = 0.139 6

(v)   finding a percentage can be explained by example:
        £7 as a % of £50 = $\frac{7}{50} \times$ 100 = $\frac{700}{50}$ = 14%
        5% of £4.50 = $\frac{5}{100} \times$ £4.50 = £$\frac{22.50}{100}$ = 22.5 p

4.10 Powers and roots

Multiplication is a shorthand method of representing a series of additions; a shorthand method of representing a series of multiplications is by the use of 'powers' or exponents:

$$4 \times 4 \times 4 = 4^3 = 64 \ (4 \times 4 = 16, 16 \times 4 = 64)$$

Four to the power two (4^2) is four squared, four to the power three (4^3) is four cubed. The square root of a number is that number which when multiplied by itself gives the original number:

the square root of 16 is 4 (or −4) because $4 \times 4 = 16$: $\sqrt{16} = 4$

The square root of many numbers have to be estimated and can then be calculated by trial and error or by the use of a calculator or square root tables.

For example: $\sqrt{30}$ lies between 5 (5 × 5 = 25) and 6 (6 × 6 = 36).
$$5.5 \times 5.5 = 30.25$$

With a calculator or square root tables the answer can be found to, say, four decimal places: 5.477 2 (5.477 2 × 5.477 2 = 29.999 7)
$\sqrt{300}$ lies between 15 (15 × 15 = 225) and 20
(20 × 20 = 400). 17.5 × 17.5 = 306.25. The answer is 17.32

4.11 Ratios

A ratio is a relationship between two quantities expressed in a number of units which enables comparison to be made between them.

For example: two motor cars travelling at different speeds: 60 km. per hour and 30 km. per hour, the ratio of speeds to one another is 60 : 30 or 2 : 1.

4.12 Proportions

A proportion is the amount a part of a unit makes up of the whole.

For example: If a meal costs £10 and A pays £5, B pays £3 and C pays £2, then the proportion A has paid is 50% of the total cost.

Many calculations are based on simple proportions:

For example: if a stay at a hotel costs £112 for 7 days, how much will it cost for 15 days at the same rate?

Answer: 7 days = £112, 1 day = £16 (£112 ÷ 7), 15 days = £240 (£16 × 15).

4.13 Elementary algebra

Algebra is a method of investigating the properties of numbers using general symbols. It provides a method of abbreviating information without loss of clarity or accuracy.

For example: an abbreviation for the fruit in a basket could be written as 10 As, 5 Os, 8 Bs, where A = apples, O = oranges, B = bananas. Equally these three types of fruit could be labelled x, y and z. If another basket of fruit was said to contain $15x$, $10y$ and $3z$, this could be translated as 15 apples, 10 oranges and 3 bananas.

Simple equations

$x + 6 = 8$

This means that some number plus 6 equals 8. Since 2 is the only number which when added to 6 equals 8, then x must equal 2.

If $x + 6 = 8$ Then $x = 2$

$x + x + x$ is written $3x$ and means 3 times x.

If $6x = 30$ Then $x = 5$

An algebraic formula could be:

$T = a + 2b + 5g$

where a = apples, $b = 5$, g = grapes and T is the total number of units.

If $a = 2$, $b = 5$, $g = 12$, then $T = 2 + 10 + 60 = 72$

4.14 Levels of measurement

Symmetry: a relationship between A and B also is true between B and A (if A is opposite B, B is opposite A).

Transitivity: if A = B and B = C, then A = C (if A is the same age as B, and B is the same age as C, then A must be the same age as C).

Asymmetrical: a special relationship may hold between A and B which does not hold between B and A (if A is greater than B, then B cannot be greater than A).

Unit of measurement: this can indicate the value of one number against another (20 is twice 10; there is a difference of 5 between 15 and 20; 20 divided by 5 is 4).

Table 4.1 Levels of measurement

Scales	Definition	Characteristics
Nominal	classification labelling	symmetry transitivity
Ordinal	order rank	symmetry transitivity asymmetrical
Interval	value	symmetry transitivity asymmetrical units of measurement

Interval = ordinal + nominal; ordinal includes nominal

4.15 Financial mathematics

(a) Simple interest

This is based on an arithmetic progression.

For example: if £100 is invested for 4 years at a simple interest rate of 5% per annum, at the end of 4 years the total amount accumulated would be:

£100 + £5 + £5 + £5 + £5 = £120

The formula for simple interest is: $A = P(1 + tr)$

where A is the total amount accumulated
P is the original investment
t is the time in years
r is the rate of interest (given as a decimal or a fraction).

Thus: $A = £100 (1 + 4 \times \frac{5}{100}) = £100 \times 1.2 = £120$

(b)   Compound interest

This is based on a geometric progression.

For example: if £100 is invested for 4 years at a compound interest rate of 5% per annum, at the end of 4 years the total amount accumulated would be:

original investment = £100
Year 1 = £105 (£100 + 5%)
Year 2 = £110.25 (£105 + 5%)
Year 3 = £115.76 (£110.25 + 5%)
Year 4 = £121.55 (£115.76 + 5%)

The formula for compound interest is: $A = P(1 + r)^t$
where A is the total amount accumulated
P is the original investment
r is the rate of interest
$1 + r$ is the 'common ratio'
t is the time in years.

The 'common ratio' is when the preceding number is multiplied by a fixed amount (or common ratio). The original investment is multiplied by the common ratio to the power of t, that is the number of years which the investment lasts.

Thus: $A = £100 \left(1 + \frac{5}{100}\right)^4 = £100 \times 1.2155 = £121.55$

(c)   Present values

This works in the opposite direction to compound interest.

For example: what sum of money, if invested at an annual interest rate of 5% per annum compounded annually, will give £121.55 in five years time?

The formula for present values is: $P = \dfrac{A}{(1 + r)^t}$,

where P is the original investment or the present value
A is the total amount accumulated
r is the rate of interest
t is the time in years

$$P = \frac{121.55}{\left(1 + \dfrac{5}{100}\right)^4} = £100$$

£100 is the present value (or discounted value) of £121.55 due at the end of four years, so that £100 now is equivalent to £121.55 in four years time.
[N.B. Net Present Value Tables can be used when available.]

(d)   Discounted cash flow

This involves the calculation of the present value of a series of future cash flows.

Present worth is found by calculating present values or net present values of a proposed investment.

For example: a firm has a choice between two plants, one of which costs £50 000, the other £40 000. They each have a useful life of four years. The problem is which plant the firm should purchase if the discount rate is 20%.

	Cost	Estimated annual cash flow (£)			
Plant A	−£50 000	+10 000	+20 000	+40 000	+30 000
Plant B	−£40 000	+10 000	+20 000	+15 000	+ 5 000

Plant A's net present value (in £000s):

$$-50 + \frac{10}{1.2} + \frac{20}{1.2^2} + \frac{40}{1.2^3} + \frac{30}{1.2^4} = £9.84 \text{ (in £000s)} = £9840$$

Plant B's net present value in (£000s):

$$-40 + \frac{10}{1.2} + \frac{20}{1.2^2} + \frac{15}{1.2^3} + \frac{5}{1.2^4} = £-6.69 \text{ (in £000s)} = -£6690$$

The cash flow for each year is divided by 1 plus the rate of interest (20% or 0.2) to the power of the time in years. A negative net present value for plant B shows that the return on investment is less than the current discount rate.

(e) Discounted rate of return

This is the discount rate that will give a net present value of zero.

For example: in the example in (d), Plant B will have a positive net present value (+£3200) at a discount rate of 10%, while at 11% the net present value will be just negative. The expected return on Plant B will repay the original investment of £40 000 if the firm can borrow the money at an interest rate of 10% or less.

4.16 Aids to calculation

(a) Electronic calculators and computers

These:

- are inexpensive,
- are fast,
- reduce laborious calculations ('number crunching'), and
- the fifth generation of computers are being developed to produce artificial intelligence.

(b) Logarithms (Greek for 'calculating with numbers')

Based on exponents, they are used less frequently now because of the introduction of calculators and computers. They:

- are inexpensive,
- are faster than 'manual' calculation,
- reduce laborious calculations,
- are exponents which provide a shorthand method of writing out 'multiple' multiplication,
- have been superseded by calculators and computers.

4.17 Symbols of mathematics (see Table 4.2)

Table 4.2 Symbols of mathematics

x	: a collective symbol meaning all the individual values of a variable
y	: an alternative symbol to x
$\bar{x}$ (bar x or x bar)	: a bar over a variable symbol indicates that it represents the arithmetic mean of the values of that variable
n	: the number of items in a collection of figures
Σ	: the sum of
μ ('mew')	: the population mean
Ho	: the null hypothesis
Hi	: opposite to the null hypothesis
σ (small sigma)	: the standard deviation
d	: deviation, the difference between two values
r	: coefficient of correlation
r'	: coefficient of rank correlation
$=$	: equals
$\simeq$	: approximately equals
$\neq$	: not equal to
$>$	: greater than, larger than, more than
$<$	: smaller than, less than

4.18 Vital statistics

Vital statistics are figures relating to births, marriages and deaths. *Demography* is the statistical study of life in human communities and the population in these communities depends on birth, deaths, immigration and emigration. These four factors depend on a range of other factors; so that the birth rate, for example, depends on the sex ratio, the proportion of women of child bearing age (normally considered to be between 15 and 45), the expected size of the family, the rate of illegitimate births and other social and economic factors.

(a) Crude birth and death rates

These are the total (live) births or deaths during 12 months per 1000 of the population.

$$\text{Crude birth rate} = \frac{\text{total live births} \times 1000}{\text{total population}}$$

$$\text{Crude death rate} = \frac{\text{total deaths} \times 1000}{\text{total population}}$$

For example:

Number of live births $= 750\,000$
Number of deaths $\quad= 560\,000$
Total population $\quad\;\;= 50$ million

$$\text{Crude birth rate} = \frac{750\,000 \times 1000}{50\,000\,000}$$

$$= 15 \text{ births per thousand of the population}$$

$$\text{Crude death rate} = \frac{560\,000 \times 1000}{50\,000\,000}$$

$$= 11.2 \text{ deaths per thousand of the population}$$

(b)   Standardised birth and death rates

This involves the standardisation of statistics so that like can be compared with like. Standardisation can be achieved by, for example, the use of weights.

For example: two towns may have very different age profiles. Town A may be full of young people and young families, while Town B is full of retired people.

Table 4.3   Death rates

(1)	(2)	(3)	(4)	(5)	(6)	(7)	(8)	(9)	(10)
	Town A			Town B				Numbers of expected deaths in standardised pop. if subject to mortality of Towns A and B	
Age group	Population (thousands)	No. of deaths	Death rate per thousand	Population (thousands)	No. of deaths	Death rate per thousand	Standard population	A	B
								(4) × (8)	(7) × (8)
0–9	15	45	3	5	30	6	10	30	60
10–19	15	15	1	10	10	1	5	5	5
20–29	25	50	2	10	20	2	15	30	30
30–39	20	80	4	12	84	7	20	80	140
40–49	11	110	10	23	230	10	18	180	180
50–59	8	240	30	20	200	10	20	600	200
60–69	5	120	24	15	630	42	10	240	420
70+	1	90	90	5	450	90	2	180	180
	100	750		100	1654		100	1345	1215

In order to compare, for example, the death rates of the two towns on a similar basis the death profiles of the towns can be weighted by the death profile of a standard population, such as that for England and Wales.

$$\text{Standardised death rate} = \frac{\text{total of weighted deaths} \times 1000}{\text{total population}}$$

Town A: Crude death rate $= \dfrac{750 \times 1000}{100\,000} = 7.5 \text{ per thousand}$

Town B: Crude death rate $= \dfrac{1654 \times 1000}{100\,000} = 16.54 \text{ per thousand}$

Town A: Standardised death rate $= \dfrac{1345 \times 1000}{100\ 000} = 13.45$ per thousand

Town B: Standardised death rate $= \dfrac{1215 \times 1000}{100\ 000} = 12.15$ per thousand

Although from the crude death rate it may appear that Town A is much healthier than Town B, when the standardised death rates are compared it is clear that Town B could in fact be said to be healthier than Town A. The difference in the crude rates appears to be due to the more youthful population of Town A.

4.19 Worked examples

4.1	$20 - 4 + 7$	Solution: 23
4.2	$10 \times 4 - 6$	Solution: 34
4.3	-6×3	Solution: -18
4.4	-9×-2	Solution: 18
4.5	$6 + 3 \times 4$	Solution: 18
4.6	$7(2)$	Solution: 14
4.7	$7(4 + 2)$	Solution: 42
4.8	$(4 + 2)(5 + 3)$	Solution: 48
4.9	$4 - 2 \times 6 + 4$	Solution: -4
4.10	$90 \times 20 \div 6 + 40$	Solution: 340
4.11	$\dfrac{1}{8} + \dfrac{1}{5}$	Solution: $\dfrac{13}{40}$
4.12	$\dfrac{3}{4} \times \dfrac{4}{5}$	Solution: $\dfrac{3}{5}$
4.13	$\dfrac{3}{4} \div \dfrac{4}{5}$	Solution: $\dfrac{15}{16}$
4.14	$4\dfrac{3}{5} + \dfrac{2}{3}$	Solution: $5\dfrac{4}{15}$
4.15	$4\dfrac{3}{5} \times \dfrac{2}{3}$	Solution: $3\dfrac{1}{15}$
4.16	Express $\dfrac{4}{5}$ as a decimal	Solution: 0.8

4.17   If the temperature is 70°F what is the temperature in °C?
Solution: 21.1°C

4.18   If the temperature is 25°C what is the temperature in °F?
Solution: 77°F

4.19   Express 0.49 as a percentage   Solution: $0.49 \times 100 = 49\%$

4.20 Express 25% as a fraction Solution: $\dfrac{25}{100} = \dfrac{1}{4}$

4.21 What is the square root of 25? Solution: 5

4.22 What is the ratio of apples to oranges in a basket in which there are 20 apples and 15 oranges? Solution: 20:15 or 4:3

4.23 If a journey costs £18 for 120 miles, how much will it cost for 200 miles at the same rate? Solution: 120 miles = £18, 1 mile = £$\dfrac{18}{120}$ or 15 p a mile, 200 miles = 15 p × 200 = £30.

4.24 $x + 4 = 10$. What is x? Solution: 6

4.25 $x \times 3 = 12$. What is x? Solution: 4

4.26 $3x + 14 = 23$. What is x? Solution: 3

Example 4.27

Discuss briefly why an interval scale of measurement may be used in preference to an ordinal or nominal scale.

Solution 4.27

A nominal scale of measurement provides a system of classification but does not indicate differences in value between two numbers. Hotel rooms, for example, may be numbered in order to distinguish one from another without the numbers indicating that one room is better or worse than another. A nominal scale can provide symmetry, so that if Room 6 is opposite Room 7, then Room 7 is opposite Room 6. A nominal scale also has the characteristic of transitivity, so that if Room 5 is the same size as Room 7 and Room 7 is the same size as Room 9, then Room 5 will be the same size as Room 9.

An ordinal scale of measurement provides a ranking system, putting items into a ranked order. The rooms in a hotel may be ranked in order of quality, so that Room 1 is the best room, Room 2 the second best and so on. This does not indicate value however; Room 1 is not necessarily twice as good as Room 2 or Room 10. Asymmetrical relationships can exist in the sense that if Room 1 is bigger than Room 2, then Room 2 cannot be bigger than Room 1.

The interval scale includes the characteristics of the ordinal and nominal scale but added to this it has the characteristics of units of measurement. This means that the value of one number can be measured against the value of another number. The value of 20 is twice that of 10; there is a difference of 5 between 15 and 20; 20 divided by 5 is 4. In circumstances where the relative values are important the interval scale has to be used. It is used wherever possible, because it provides more information than the other scales. If a nominal scale is used when an interval scale could be used then important information that is available may be lost.

Example 4.28

If £1000 is invested for 5 years at a simple interest rate of 10% per annum, what will be the total amount accumulated at the end of five years?

Solution 4.28

$$A = £1000 \left(1 + 5 \times \frac{10}{100} \right) = £1000 \times 1.5 = £1500$$

Example 4.29

If £1000 is invested for 5 years at a compound interest rate of 10% per annum, what will be the total amount accumulated at the end of 5 years?

Solution 4.29

$$A = £1000 \left(1 + \frac{10}{100} \right)^5 = £1000 \times (1.1)^5 = £1610.51$$

Example 4.30

What sum of money, if invested at an interest rate of 10% per annum compounded annually, will give approximately £250 in five years time?

Solution 4.30

$$P = £ \frac{250}{\left(1 + \dfrac{10}{100} \right)^5} = £\frac{250}{1.6105} = £155.23$$

Example 4.31

(a) Briefly describe the difference between simple interest and compound interest.
(b) Calculate which provides the greatest interest over three years:
    (i) £1000 at 10% simple interest for three years or
    (ii) £1000 at 9% compound interest for three years.
(c) Calculate the present value of £210 to be received in a year's time if the rate of interest payable on deposits is 10%.

Solution 4.31

(a) Simple interest is the interest paid only on the initial investment, it is calculated on the original principal for each year. Compound interest is the interest calculated on the principal plus the interest, which becomes the principal for the next year and so on, so that the interest received at the end of each year is automatically re-invested.
(b) (i) Simple interest for £1000 at 10% over 3 years =

$$£ \frac{1000 \times 10 \times 3}{100} = £300$$

(ii) Compound interest for £1000 at 9% over 3 years =

$$£1000(1.09)^3 - £1000 = £1295 - £1000 = £295$$

£1000 at 10% simple interest provides the greater interest over three years by £5.

(c) The present value is $\dfrac{£210}{1.1} = £190.90$

Example 4.32

(a) Explain the meaning of 'present value' in the context of compound interest.
(b) A company is considering buying a new plant which would allow cash savings to be realised over eight years (as shown in the table below). The cost of the new plant is £60 000 and it is expected to have a scrap value of £5000 at the end of its working life. Comment on the acceptability of this project on the basis of net present values and assuming that the forecasted cash savings are realised at the last day of the year.

Year 1	£10 000	Year 5	£13 850
Year 2	£10 000	Year 6	£13 850
Year 3	£13 850	Year 7	£13 850
Year 4	£13 850	Year 8	£12 750

Net Present Value Table (10% Discount)

Year 1	0.909	Year 5	0.621
Year 2	0.826	Year 6	0.564
Year 3	0.751	Year 7	0.513
Year 4	0.683	Year 8	0.467

Solution 4.32

(a) The 'present value' is the amount which would have to be invested now in order to receive a specified amount of money (A) after a particular period of time (t) at an interest rate ($r\%$).
(b) The net present value is £9017 and on this evidence the project is acceptable because this amount represents a figure which is greater than the cost of the new plant:

Year	Savings (£)	10% NPV values	Net Present Value (£)
1	10 000	0.909	9 090
2	10 000	0.826	8 260
3	13 850	0.751	10 401
4	13 850	0.683	9 460
5	13 850	0.621	8 601
6	13 850	0.564	7 811
7	13 850	0.513	7 105
8	12 750	0.467	5 954
8	5 000	0.467	2 335
			69 017
			60 000
		NPV	9 017

Example 4.33

Compare the use of crude death rates as against standardised death rates.

Solution 4.33

Crude death rates are not suited to comparisons because they are influenced by different age structures. In areas with large numbers of babies (under one year) and/or old people the crude death rate will be pushed upwards because these groups have a high mortality rate.

Standardisation of statistics enables sets of data to be compared. To standardise the death rate, a mortality rate that does not depend upon the age structure is used. A standard population (such as the population of England and Wales) can be used as a weighting system for the expected number of deaths in a town or region.

The standard death rate is the number of deaths per thousand which would occur in the standard population if the regional death rate is applied to this population. Thus, the standardised death rate depends only on the region's mortality rates and not on its age structure. In the examples in section 4.18 it is clear that in Towns A and B there is a marked difference between the results given by the crude death rate and the standardised death rate.

Crude death rates are useful but only provide approximate measures which determine whether or not a population will increase or decrease in the long run. For short-term comparisons in one town or area these rates may be useful because changes in the age structure may be slow to emerge. Crude death rates can be regarded as weighted arithmetic means, the weights being the actual number of people in each age group at the time. Standardised rates use the same weights for each calculation so that any differences in age structure between one region and another are eliminated.

Example 4.34

What is the crude death rate for the term to which this table relates?

Age range (years)	Population	Number of deaths
0–14	2000	40
15–34	4000	25
35–59	3000	35
60+	1000	120

A 6.0 **B** 22.0 **C** 11.0 **D** 10.0

Solution 4.34

B: $\dfrac{220 \times 1000}{10\ 000} = 22.0$

Example 4.35

What is the standardised death rate for the following term?

Age range (years)	Crude death rate	Standard population
0–14	12.0	380
15–34	5.0	470
35–39	10.0	150
60+	70.0	50

A 8.2   **B** 11.3   **C** 12.1   **D** 21.4

Solution 4.35

B: $\dfrac{11\,910}{1050} = 11.3$

4.20 Questions and exercises

Question 4.1

(a) A company borrows £100 000 on the last day of the year and agrees to repay it by four equal amounts, the repayments being made at the end of the following four years. Compound interest at 12% per annum is payable. What is the amount of each repayment?

(b) A new machine will cost £50 000 and has an expected life of 5 years. Scrap value at the end of the fifth year will be £1000. Annual depreciation is to be calculated as a fixed percentage of its current book value. What should the percentage be?

(c) £1000 is invested at 12% per annum, with interest added every quarter-end. How long will it take for the investment to amount to £3000?

Question 4.2

(a) At the beginning of each year a company sets aside £10 000 out of its profits to form a reserve fund. This is invested at 10% per annum compound interest. What will be the value of the fund after four years?

(b) A new machine is expected to last for four years and to produce year end savings of £2000 per annum. What is its present value allowing interest at 11% per annum?

(c) On 1st January, 1977 £1000 was invested. It remained invested and, on 1st January of each successive year, £500 was added to it. What sum will have accumulated by 31st December, 1981 if interest is compounded each year at 10% per annum?

(d) £20 000 is borrowed from a building society repayable over 20 years at 14% per annum compound interest. How much must be repaid over each year?

(ICMA)

Question 4.3

(a) A government advertises an issue of National Savings Certificates as '£100 becomes £154 after 5 years'. What is the effective *annual* rate of interest?

(b) A company has to choose among three mutually exclusive investments, A, B and C, each of which has a life of four years. A, B and C cost respectively £30 000, £40 000 and £35 000.

The year-end cash flows would be as follows:

	Investment A	Investment B	Investment C
		Year-end cash flows (£000)	
Year 1	15	17	20
Year 2	15	20	18
Year 3	10	13	8
Year 4	5	10	4

The cost of capital is 14%.

Using the criterion of *net present value* which one represents (i) the best investment, (ii) the worst investment?　(ICMA)

Question 4.4

In three years' time a considerable amount of the plant and machinery in your company's factory will need replacing. You estimate that a sum of £280 000 will be required for this.

(a) If you were to set aside sufficient funds now to be invested at 12% per annum compounded quarterly (i.e. every three months):
(i) what sum of money would you need, and
(ii) what is the effective annual rate of interest?
(b) If, again assuming that investments made during the three years will be at 12% per annum compounded quarterly, you decide instead to invest £4000 at the end of every quarter, what additional sum needs to be set aside now in order to provide £280 000 at the end of the three years?　(ICMA)

Question 4.5

The crude death rate of a population is the number of deaths
A in the year
B per 100 of the population at the middle of the year
C per 1000 of the population at the middle of the year adjusted to take into consideration the age structure of the population
D per 1000 of the population at the middle of the year　(AEB)

Question 4.6

What is the crude death rate for the term to which this table relates?

Age range (years)	Population	Number of deaths
0–14	4000	60
15–34	8000	56
35–59	6000	48
60+	2000	136

A 7.5　B 15.0　C 24.5　D 75.0　(AEB)

Question 4.7

What is the standardised death rate for the following term?

Age range (mean)	Crude death rate	Standard population
0–14	15.0	325
15–34	7.0	357
35–39	8.0	243
60+	68.0	75

A 7.0 **B** 8.0 **C** 14.4 **D** 24.5

(AEB)

Question 4.8

The data in the tables relate to two cities M and N in the same year.

Calculate (i)   the death rate for each age group in city M,
(ii) the crude death rate for city M,
(iii) the standardised death rate for city M.

Calculate (iv) the crude death rate for city N,
(v)   the standardised death rate for city N.

State, with reason, which city you consider offers the better chance of a long life.

Age group	City M		Standard population
	Population	Number of deaths	
0–	60 000	300	30%
18–	50 000	150	30%
45–	50 000	350	25%
65–	40 000	2400	15%

Age group	City N		Standard population
	% of population	Death rate per thousand	
0–	40%	6	30%
18–	30%	4	30%
45–	25%	8	25%
65–	5%	70	15%

(AEB)

Question 4.9

The diagram shows the assessment of hotels used by a tour operator in a certain holiday area. The table shows the number of nights spent in the various standards of hotel in the area in one season.

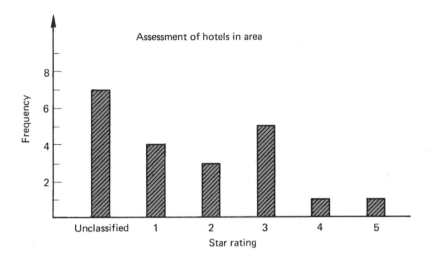

Number of nights spent in each standard of hotel in holiday area.

Type of hotel	Number of nights
Unclassified	127
1-star	61
2-star	33
3-star	48
4-star	26
5-star	15

The tour operator charges a supplement of £2.40 per star per night on all bookings.

(i)   How many hotels are used by the tour operator in this area?
(ii) Calculate the supplement per night for a 3-star hotel.
(iii) Given that 'unclassified' is rated at zero, calculate the mean star-rating of the hotels.
(iv) Calculate the mean star-rating of the season's bookings.
(v)   Which of the following gives the mean supplement per night for the season?

    A £2.40   **B** £2.40 × answer to (iii)
    C £2.40 × answer to (iv)   **D** none of these   (SEB)

Question 4.10

Age in years	Population of town X (thousands)	Death rate in town X (per thousand)	Standard population
0–34	23	0.2	50%
35–64	17	0.4	40%
over 64	10	0.8	10%

From the above table, the crude death rate per thousand of town X may be calculated as

A $\dfrac{(23 \times 0.2) + (17 \times 0.4) + (10 \times 0.8)}{50}$

B $\dfrac{(23 \times 0.2) + (17 \times 0.4) + (10 \times 0.8)}{1.4}$

C $\dfrac{(50 \times 0.2) + (40 \times 0.4) + (10 \times 0.8)}{100}$

D $\dfrac{0.2 + 0.4 + 0.8}{3}$ (AEB)

Question 4.11

The following table shows the death rates for a particular town, together with the standard population.

Age group	0–29	30–54	55–64	65 and over
Death rate (%)	0.2	0.4	0.7	3.2
Standard population	40%	30%	20%	10%

Calculate the standardised death rate. (AEB)

Question 4.12

A company producing microprocessors expects its volume of sales to increase by 20% in the coming year. If it is anticipated that the gross income will increase by 80%, find the percentage increase in the selling price of the microprocessors.

(AEB)

Question 4.13

(a) Explain briefly why standardised death rates are statistically more acceptable than crude death rates.

The table below shows the number of deaths occurring in a particular year in two towns A and B.

Age group	Town A Deaths	Town A Population	Town B Deaths	Town B Population	Standard population
0–	14	3000	22	7000	25%
20–	8	4500	18	9000	30%
40–	36	5000	42	9000	25%
60 and over	74	6000	50	2000	20%

Calculate the crude and standardised death rates per thousand for each town. Comment on your results.

(b)   In order to estimate the mean distance travelled to work by its employees a large company took a proportionate stratified sample and obtained the following results.

Employees	Sample size	Mean distance travelled (km)
Managerial	20	27.8
Skilled	200	13.6
Unskilled	75	5.8

Estimate the mean distance travelled to work by the employees.

For those travelling to work by car a car park is to be provided. Its shape is to be rectangular with sides of 100 m and 75 m respectively, these distances being measured to the nearest metre.

Calculate the maximum possible area of the car park.

The thickness of the tarmac surface of the car park is to be 5 cm, measured to the nearest centimetre.

Calculate the maximum possible number of cubic metres of tarmac needed.

(AEB)

Question 4.14

A Health Authority investigated the death rate in two towns which lie within its boundaries. The investigation produced the following data.

Age group	Town A Population	Town A Deaths	Town B Population	Town B Deaths	Standard population
0–14	45 500	100	14 000	15	24%
15–24	24 500	125	20 000	46	15%
25–44	41 500	350	26 500	177	24%
45–64	35 500	380	36 500	452	24%
65 and over	16 000	800	28 000	1897	13%

(a)   Explain *briefly* why the Authority should use Standardised Death Rates rather than Crude Death Rates.

(b)   Copy and complete the following table.

Town	Crude Death Rate/1000	Standardised Death Rate/1000
A		12.38
B	20.70	

Comment on your results.

To monitor attitudes towards the health services provided in Town *B*, the Authority decides to carry out a sample survey. A sample of those citizens *over 14 years of age* is to be taken.

(c)   State four rules that the Health Authority should keep in mind when drafting their questionnaire.

(d) Give two reasons why a sample stratified by age might be used in this situation rather than a simple random sample.
     Name another variable which might be used within each age group to further stratify the sample.

(e) If a 1% sample is to be taken, state the total sample size and how large a sample should be taken from each age group.   (AEB)

5

How to Present Figures

Objectives

By the end of this chapter the following terms and methods should be understood:

	Date attempted	Date completed	Self-assessment
Tabulations			
Frequency distributions			
Histograms			
Frequency curves			
Bar charts			
Pie charts and pictograms			
Graphs			
Break-even charts			
Z-charts			
Lorenz curves			

Summary

This chapter describes the main methods of presenting statistical information through tables, charts and graphs.

5.1 Introduction

(a)   Aims and objectives in presenting figures

- The main aim is to communicate information, and the type of presentation will, therefore, depend on the requirements and interests of the people receiving the information.
- Figures need to be arranged and presented in some way before the information contained in the data can be interpreted.

(b)   Main features

Those to consider are:

- a clear presentation of the subject matter;
- a clarification of the most important points in the data;
- consideration of the purpose of the presentation;
- consideration of the amount of detail and accuracy required;
- the use of the most appropriate method of presentation.

5.2 Methods of presentation

These can be summarised as follows:
1.   Basic Presentation
    (a)   Tabulation
    (b)   Frequency distributions
        (i)   Histograms
        (ii)   Frequency polygons
        (iii)   Frequency curves
    (c)   Reports
2.   Pictorial Presentation
    (a)   Bar charts
        (i)   The simple bar chart
        (ii)   The compound (or multiple) bar chart
        (iii)   The component bar chart
        (iv)   The percentage component bar chart
    (b)   Pie charts
    (c)   Pictograms
    (d)   Cartograms (or map charts)
    (e)   Strata charts
    (f)   Graphs
        (i)   Natural-scale graphs
        (ii)   Semi-logarithmic graphs
        (iii)   Straight-line graphs
    (g)   Other forms of pictorial presentation
        (i)   Gantt charts
        (ii)   Break-even charts
        (iii)   Z-charts
        (iv)   Lorenz curves

(a) Basic presentation

(i) Tabulation

Tables are used to facilitate the understanding of complex numerical data; data is represented in tables in order to emphasise certain features.

Tabulation involves *classification*, which is the process of relating the separate items within the mass of the data collected and the definition of various categories in the table.

Variables can be divided into:

(i) *discrete variables* which are measured in single units (such as people, houses, cars);

(ii) *continuous variables* which are units of measurement which can be broken down into definite gradations (such as temperature, height, weight).

(ii) Frequency distributions

These show the frequency with which a particular variable occurs. This involves *class intervals*, which need to be clear and unambiguous so that a particular item can be classified in only one class.

A *grouped frequency distribution* is one in which frequencies are grouped according to the number in a classification, in order to provide a summary that helps to clarify the distribution.

1. Histograms

This is a method of representing a frequency distribution diagrammatically. *A histogram consists of a series of blocks or bars each with an area proportional to the frequency.* The area of a histogram bar is found by multiplying the width of the bar (the class interval) by the height (the frequency).

For example: in the frequency distribution below (Fig. 5.1), the area of the first bar is $10 \times 5 = 50$ as compared with the area of the second bar which is $10 \times 14 = 140$.

Table 5.1 Output of machine operatives

Output (units per operative)	Number of operatives
200–209	5
210–219	14
220–229	17
230–239	29
240–249	42
250–259	21
260–269	10
270–279	2

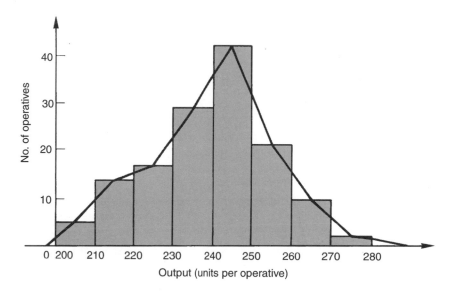

Figure 5.1 Histogram and frequency polygon

If the areas of the blocks are to maintain their proportional relationship with the frequencies, the block height and width must be changed proportionately. This means that when a grouped frequency distribution includes uneven class intervals, the area of the blocks must be kept in proportion. Figure 5.2 is drawn from the same frequency distribution but the last three class intervals have been amalgamated to make one larger class interval. Note that in Fig. 5.2 the area of the last block is:

$30 \times 11 = 330$

This compares with the area of the last three blocks in Fig. 5.1, which is:

$$10 \times 21 = 210$$
$$10 \times 10 = 100$$
$$\underline{10 \times 2\ \ =\ \ 20}$$
$$\overline{330}$$

In Fig. 5.2, the height of the last block is reduced to a third (11) of the frequency (33) and the numerical width of the block is trebled (30).

The construction of a histogram involves the following features:

- the horizontal axis is a continuous scale including all the units of the grouped class intervals;
- for each class in the distribution a block (or vertical rectangle) is drawn extending from the lower class limit to the upper limit;
- the area of this block will be proportional to the frequency of the class;
- if the class intervals are even throughout a frequency table, then the height of each block is proportional to the frequency;
- there are never gaps between histogram blocks because the class limits are the true limits in the case of continuous data and the mathematical limits in the case of discrete data.

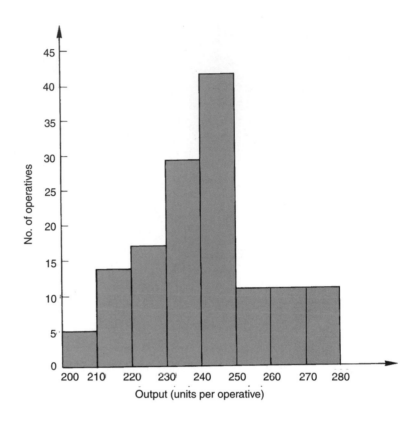

Figure 5.2 Histogram with uneven classes

2. Frequency polygons

This is a diagram which is drawn by joining up the mid-points of the tops of the histogram blocks. This is usually drawn with straight lines to form a 'many-sided figure' or polygon. In the case of the first and last class intervals, the line can be extended beyond the original range of the variable. This is because the area under the polygon should be the same as that in the histogram. Only if each triangle cut off the histogram is compensated for will this requirement be met (see Fig. 5.1).

Histograms and frequency polygons enable the properties of distributions to be examined and various forms of distribution can be compared.

3. Frequency curves

This is formed by smoothing out a histogram or frequency polygon or by using smaller class intervals or more observations to smooth out the line of the curve. The importance of the frequency curve is that it can provide a clear picture of the 'shape' of the distribution, so that distributions can be compared.

For example: see Fig. 5.3.

(iii) Reports

Reports or 'textual' reports form an early stage of presentation, produced alongside or immediately after tables have been constructed. They are often the simplest method of presenting data and the most easily assimilated. They should be accurate, concise and easy to read.

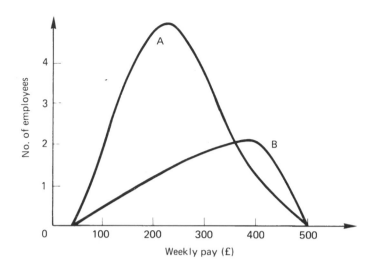

Figure 5.3 Frequency curves (weekly payments by two companies) (see page 68)

(b)   Pictorial presentation

The aim of presenting data in a pictorial form is *to make an immediate impact*, to illustrate the information and to bring out the salient points.

(i)   Bar charts

These are a form of pictorial presentation where *bars are used to provide comparison between items*. There are four types (see also Table 5.2 below).

Table 5.2   Types of bar chart

Type of bar chart	Description	Advantages	Disadvantages
Simple bar chart	Heights of bars show frequency of variable. Bars can be vertical or horizontal	Makes comparison easy; clear strong visual impact	Only simple information can be shown
Compound bar chart	Shows a number of items separately within say a year	Comparing items within say a year and items between the years	Only a few items can be included
Component bar chart	Divides an item into its component parts	Shows the division of an item into its constituent parts, while still enabling comparison between total items	Only a few parts of an item can be included
Percentage component bar chart	Bars represent 100%, the components change proportionally	Comparing the constituent parts of the total	Does not show total output

1.   The simple bar chart

Here the height or length of each bar shows the total for an item.

For example: see Fig. 5.4.

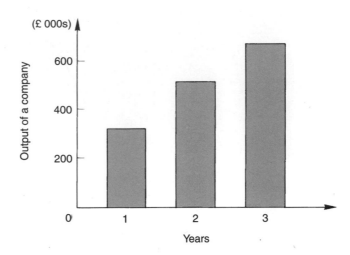

Figure 5.4 Simple bar chart

2. The compound (or multiple) bar chart

This is used for comparing the number of items within say a year, as well as comparing items between years.

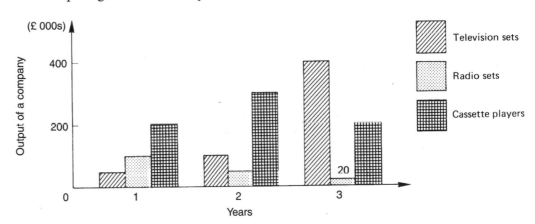

Figure 5.5 Compound or multiple bar chart

3. The component bar chart

This is useful to show the division of the whole of an item into its constituent parts.

For example: see Fig. 5.6.

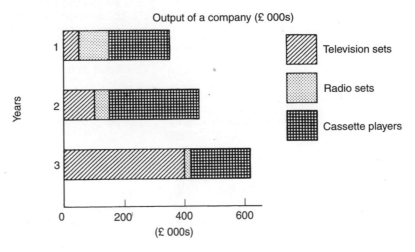

Figure 5.6 Component bar chart

4. The percentage component bar chart

This is when the bars represent 100% of an item and therefore remain the same length; the components are changed to represent the percentage they make up of the total.

For example: see Fig. 5.7.

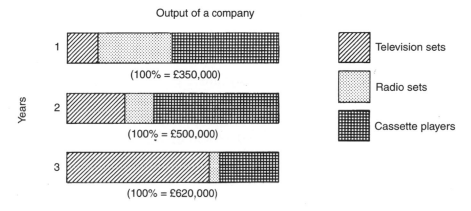

Figure 5.7 Percentage component bar chart

(ii) Pie charts

A pie chart is a circle divided into sectors to represent each item or variable. Each sector of the circle should have an area equal to the quantity of the variable.

For example: see Fig. 5.8.

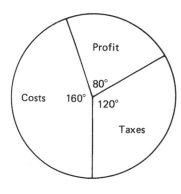

Figure 5.8 Pie chart

The pie chart in Fig. 5.8 shows the finances of a company: costs £20 m
profit £10 m
taxes £15 m

(i) costs

$$\frac{20}{45} \times 360° = 160°$$

(ii) profit

$$\frac{10}{45} \times 360° = 80°$$

(iii) taxes

$$\frac{15}{45} \times 360° = 120°$$

Comparative pie charts are used to compare two sets of data, usually two sets of the same items over time. The areas of the circle must be in proportion to the total of the data.

For example: say the totals to be represented are 30 and 45; then if 30 is represented by a pie chart with a radius of 2 cm (the area of a circle is πr^2) $r^2 = 4$ cm. 30 is represented by a circle of area $\pi 4$ square centimetres

(cm^2). 45 would be represented by a circle of area $\dfrac{\pi 4}{30} \times 45 = \pi 6$ cm^2. So

$r^2 = 6$ cm and $r = 2.4$ cm.

30 is represented by a circle with a radius of 2 cm.
45 is represented by a circle with a radius of 2.4 cm.

(iii)   Pictograms

These are *pictorial diagrams*; they are pictures to represent data.

For example: see Fig. 5.9.

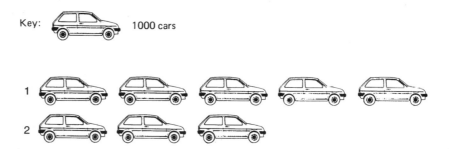

Figure 5.9 Pictogram

Comparative pictograms are pictograms which can be used to compare relationships by using symbols and pictures of different sizes. The area of the symbol should be in proportion to the quantity of the items being compared.

For example: see Fig. 5.10.

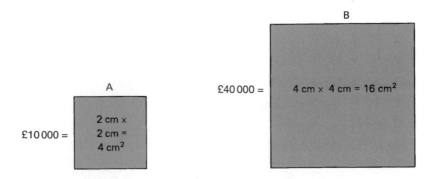

Figure 5.10 Comparative pictogram

(iv)   Cartograms (or map charts)

These are map charts or maps onto which are superimposed graphs, symbols, pictograms, flags and so on to represent various factors.

For example: salesmen use flags on a map to show outlets for their goods, and have sales areas based in geographical regions (Fig. 5.11).

Figure 5.11 Cartogram of a company's regional sales areas in England and Wales

(v) Strata charts

Each strata or layer or band is placed successively on top of the previous one (known also as layer charts or band curve graphs). Totals are cumulative, so that each element of the whole is plotted one above another.

For example: see Fig. 5.12.

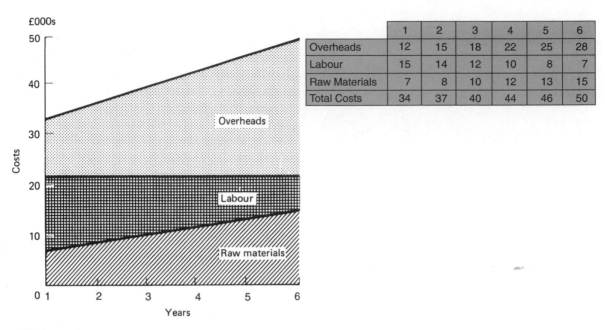

	1	2	3	4	5	6
Overheads	12	15	18	22	25	28
Labour	15	14	12	10	8	7
Raw Materials	7	8	10	12	13	15
Total Costs	34	37	40	44	46	50

Figure 5.12 Strata chart

A summary of the charts used is given in Table 5.3.

Table 5.3   Charts

Type of chart	Description	Advantages	Disadvantages
Pie chart	A circle divided into sectors to represent each item or variable	Useful where proportions are more important than the numerical values. Can provide a strong visual impact	Can only include a few variables
Comparative pie chart	Two circles used for comparison	Useful for comparison	May involve calculations of proportions which do not provide clear visual differences
Pictograms	Pictorial diagrams to represent data	Attractive, strong visual impact	Can only show simple information
Cartograms	Map charts	Strong visual impact where location is important	Can only show simple information
Strata charts	A chart in layers or stratas	Can show relative importance of items as a whole	Can only include a few variables

(vi)   Graphs

1.   Natural-scale graphs

These consist of a grid with four quadrants with zero (the origin) at the centre. Curves are drawn on the grid to illustrate the relationship between two variables

(Fig. 5.13). The *independent variable*, usually scaled on the horizontal axis, is the variable which is not affected by changes in the other variable; the *dependent variable*, usually scaled on the vertical axis, is the variable which is affected by changes in the other variable. In practice it is not always easy to decide which variable is dependent and which independent, however in Fig. 5.14 it can be agreed that while profits depend directly on sales, sales are less directly dependent on profits. The graph indicates that as sales increase profits rise or fall.

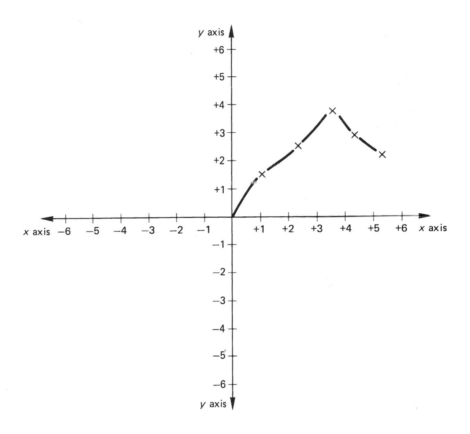

Figure 5.13 The four quadrants of a graph

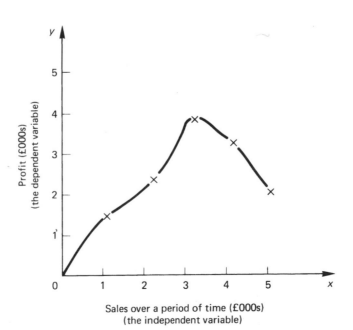

Figure 5.14 A graph

Distortion of graphs: graphs can give distorted information or provide a misleading appearance, unless the rules for drawing them are followed:

(i)   the vertical axis should always start at zero; if the scale is not in proportion this should be indicated by a broken scale (Figs 5.15 and 5.17), otherwise the result will be distorted (Fig. 5.16) in that the scale between 0 and 500 is the same as that between 500 and 600, 600 and 700, 700 and 800;

(ii)   when the method of compiling or calculating the figures under review has been changed, this should be shown by a break in the axis and in the graph (for example, when a new index number series is developed) (Fig. 5.18);

(iii) the scale for each axis should not be compressed so that the slope of the curve is artificially distorted (Figs 5.21 and 5.22).

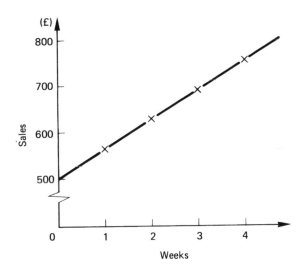

Figure 5.15 Broken scale (i)

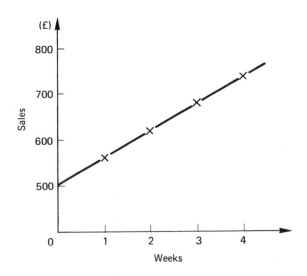

Figure 5.16 Unbroken scale

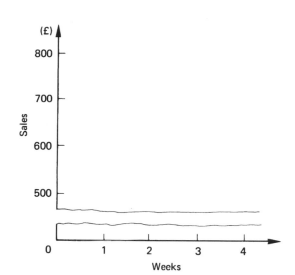

Figure 5.17 Broken scale (ii)

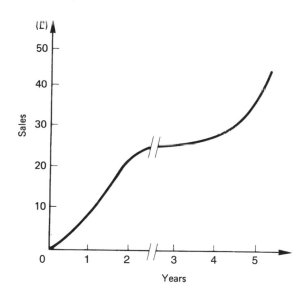

Figure 5.18 Broken curve

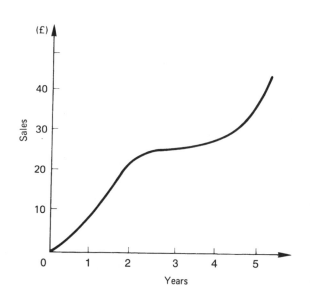

Figure 5.19 Unbroken curve

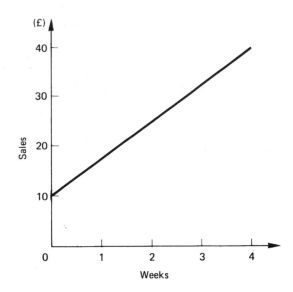

Figure 5.20 Uncompressed scale

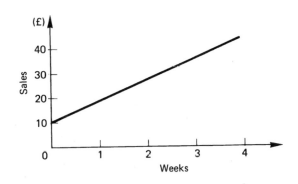

Figure 5.21 Compressed scale (i)

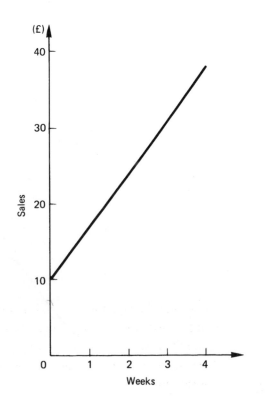

Figure 5.22 Compressed scale (ii)

2. Semi-logarithmic graphs

These are used to show the rate of change in data rather than changes in actual amounts (which are shown on natural scale graphs). They are known also as *semi-log* or *ratio* graphs. The curve at any point shows the percentage change from the last point.

For example: see Table 5.4.

Table 5.4   Semi-log graph

Years	Profit (£000s)	Increase in profit over previous years (%)	Log numbers of the profit figures
1	1000	100	3.0000
2	2000	100	3.3010
3	3000	50	3.4771
4	4000	33.33	3.6021

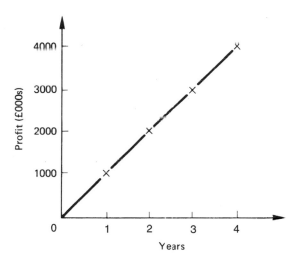

Figure 5.23 Natural scale graph

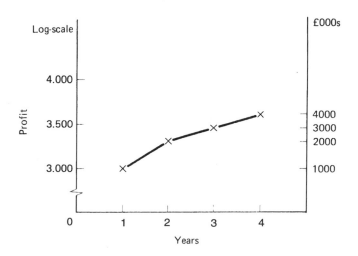

Figure 5.24 Semi-log graph

Notice that in Fig. 5.24, the log numbers are charted on the vertical axis. This graph shows that although profits are rising, they are rising at a declining rate, while the natural scale graph (Fig. 5.23) suggests a constant expansion of profits. They are both 'correct'; they simply show different aspects of the same information.

3. Straight-line graphs

These occur when there is a particular kind of arithmetical relationship between two sets of data; this is when a change in one variable is matched by a similar change in the other variable.

For example: see Table 5.5 and Fig. 5.25.

Table 5.5   Straight-line graph. Hourly paid work at £1.20 an hour

10 hours = £12	30 hours = £36
20 hours = £24	40 hours = £48

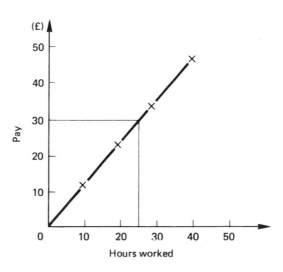

Figure 5.25 Straight-line graph

It is possible to use this graph as a ready reckoner by interpreting information: for example, 25 hours of work will earn £30.

Types of graphs are summarised in Table 5.6.

Table 5.6   Graphs

Type of graph	Description	Advantages	Disadvantages
Natural scale graph	Illustrates the relationship between one variable and another	Relationships can be seen; widely used and well understood; interpolation and extrapolation is possible	Only certain data can be shown on a graph
Semi-log graph	Shows rate of change in data	Curve shows rate of change rather than magnitude	Shows a particular relationship; can be confused
Straight-line graph	Shows relationship when there is direct variation between two variables	Possible to interpolate information and use as a ready reckoner	Shows a particular relationship

(vii) Other forms of pictorial presentation

1. Gantt charts

This usually consists of two bar charts and an indication of a period of time or scale.

For example: see Fig. 5.26. The horizontal scale shows 100% for each day, which indicates the total possible production. The top bar shows the planned production based on the variable factors in production and circumstances surrounding it. The lower bar shows the actual production achieved each day during a particular week.

	Monday	Tuesday	Wednesday	Thursday	Friday
Planned Production					
Actual Production					

Figure 5.26 Gantt chart

2. Break-even charts

This chart illustrates the profit or loss for any given output. The simplest chart shows two curves or straight lines, one showing the relationship between revenue and output, the other the relationship between cost and output. Where the two cross is the break-even point. At this output revenue covers costs, while below this output there is a loss because costs are greater than revenue and above this point there is a profit because revenue is greater than costs.

For example: see Fig. 5.27.

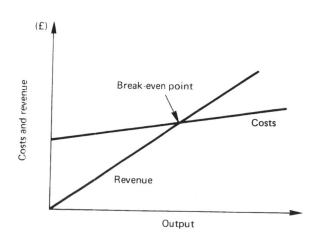

Figure 5.27 Break-even chart

3. Z-charts

This consists of three graphs plotted together on the same axes in order to compare basic data with trends:

1. the original data,

2. the cumulative total,
3. the moving annual total.

When plotted on a graph the three curves form the shape of a 'Z'. The curve of the original data shows the current fluctuations, the cumulative curve shows the position to date and the trend is indicated by the moving annual total. This chart enables the basic data to be compared with trends.

For example: see Table 5.7 and Fig. 5.28.

Table 5.7   Monthly sales

Month	Monthly sales (£) (Year 1)	Monthly sales (£) (Year 2)	Cumulative monthly total (£) (Year 2)	Moving annual total (£) (Year 2)
January	25	30	30	735
February	45	50	80	740
March	50	50	130	740
April	65	70	200	745
May	80	80	280	745
June	85	90	370	750
July	90	100	470	760
August	100	110	580	770
September	75	100	680	795
October	60	70	750	805
November	35	50	800	820
December	20	35	835	835
Total:	730	835		

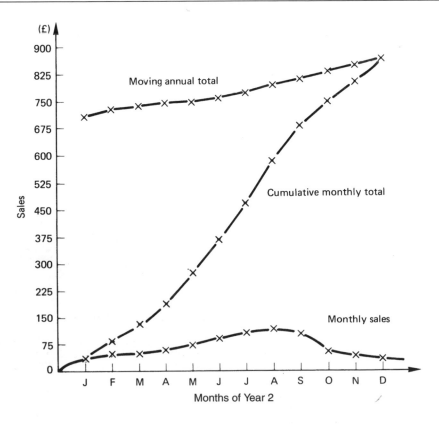

Figure 5.28 Z-chart

The moving annual total is obtained by adding a new month each time and dropping a month from the previous year (in order to do this the figures for two years are necessary).

4. Lorenz curves

This is a graphical method of showing the deviation from the average of a group of data; it is a cumulative percentage curve. It is often used to show the levels of inequality; the more equal the distribution the flatter curve. In Figs 5.29 and 5.30, if there was equality between the two variables, the 'curve' would be a straight line (i.e. the line of equal distribution). For example, the following table and figures show a comparatively high (Fig. 5.29) and low (Fig. 5.30) degree of inequality. The curves are drawn by plotting the percentage of accumulated wealth (column 5) against the percentage of the cumulative frequency of people (column 7).

Table 5.8 Accumulated wealth (i)

Income (£000s) (1)	No. of people (f) (2)	Accumulated wealth (£000s) (3)	Cumulative wealth (£000s) (4)	(%) (5)	Cumulative frequency (f) (6)	(%) (7)
Less than 5	144	32	32	16	144	48
5–9.9	54	22	54	27	198	66
10–14.9	36	24	78	39	234	78
15–19.9	24	20	98	49	258	86
20–24.9	18	24	122	61	276	92
25–29.9	15	26	148	74	291	97
30–34.9	9	52	200	100	300	100

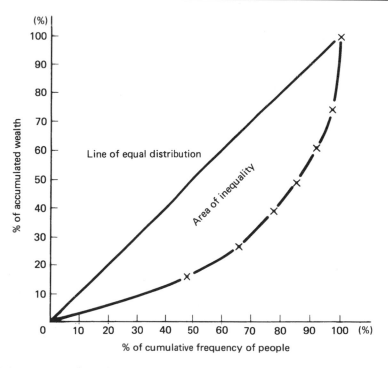

Figure 5.29 Lorenz curve (i)

Table 5.9 Accumulated wealth (ii)

Income (£000s)	No. of people (f)	Accumulated wealth (£000s)	Cumulative wealth (£000s)	(%)	Cumulative frequency (f)	(%)
Less than 5	50	25	25	12.5	50	16.66
5–9.9	46	20	45	22.5	96	32
10–14.9	45	26	71	35.5	141	47
15–19.9	39	31	102	51	180	60
20–24.9	34	22	124	62	214	71.33
25–29.9	42	31	155	77.5	256	85.33
30–34.9	44	45	200	100	300	100

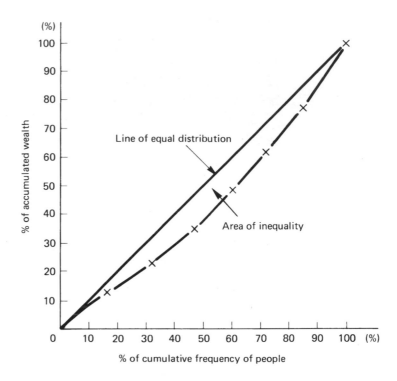

Figure 5.30 Lorenz curve (ii)

5.3 Worked examples

Example 5.1

Write short notes on the following:

(i)   the aims of the presentation of data;
(ii) classification;
(iii) report writing.

Solution 5.1

(i)   The main aim of the presentation of figures is to communicate information. The type of presentation will depend on the requirements and interests of the people receiving the information. Primary data tends to be in a 'raw' form and may consist, for example, of a pile of questionnaires or a long list of figures. This raw data needs to be presented in one way or another so that information contained in the data can be understood and interpreted.

Secondary data may be contained in government publications, company reports, books and archives from which relevant information needs to be collated and presented in a form which can be appreciated.

Further aims of presentation are to present figures clearly so that the most important points of the data are emphasised and an impact is made on people looking at the graph or chart or diagram. Company sales figures presented to a meeting of experts, for example, may require a report with tables, graphs and diagrams showing great detail. On the other hand a group of shareholders may be interested in seeing only a graph which shows whether sales are rising or falling.

(ii) Tabulation involves classification because this is the process of relating the separate items within the mass of data collected. Classification involves the definition of various categories in the table. Variables can be discrete, that is measured in single units, or continuous, which are units of measurement which can be broken down into definite gradations.

In producing a table of a frequency distribution, class intervals have to be shown clearly and unambiguously. There should not be uncertainty as to whether a unit falls into one class interval or another. Where a discrete variable is concerned it is possible to use a classification such as:

100–149   150–199   200–249

If this was written as follows:

100–150   150–200   200–250

it would not be clear as to whether 150 and 200 fell into one class interval or another. Where a continuous variable is involved, the level of approximation and rounding must be taken into account.

For example: 20 but under 40   40 but under 60

can be taken to mean that the first class includes from 20 exactly to just below 40. This could be 39.49 or 39.99, depending on the degree of accuracy required. Although 40 is written twice it should be noted that there is not any ambiguity about into which class it falls.

(iii) Reports form an early stage of presentation. After raw data has been collected a report may be written to explain how the data was collected, to highlight the main points arising from the data and to provide an interpretation of it. Before the report is written, the raw data will have been classified and tabulated to at least some extent.

Reports are often the simplest method of presenting data and may be the easiest method to understand for people not used to assimilating facts from tables, graphs or diagrams. The form that a report will take and its length will depend on the purpose for which it has been written. Reports in most newspapers, for example, usually contain few figures or tables, but may include a simple diagram; while a company report may include diagrams and tables and have a great many figures in the text.

Example 5.2

The following table shows the weekly pay of a group of part-time employees. From the table, draw a histogram and frequency polygon and comment briefly on your results.

Weekly pay of part-time employees (£)	Number of employees
0 but less than 10	5
10 but less than 20	15
20 but less than 30	22
30 but less than 40	18
40 but less than 50	10
50 but less than 60	8
60 but less than 70	2
	80

Solution 5.2   Histogram and frequency polygon

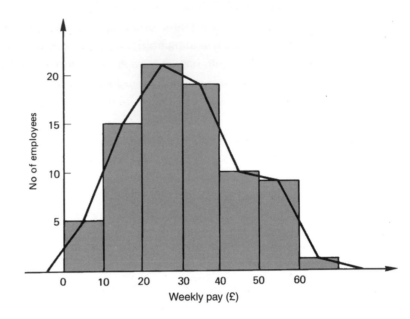

The histogram is a diagrammatic representation of the table. The width of each block is proportional to the class interval and the area of each block is proportional to the frequency. The histogram helps to illustrate the fact that the distribution is positively skewed with more of the distribution in the early class than in the later ones. This point is emphasised by the frequency polygon.

Both the histogram and the frequency polygon illustrate the fact that most of the employees earn below £50 (60 out of 80 earn between £0 and £40 and only 10 earn over £50).

Example 5.3

Comment on the differences in the two distributions in Fig. 5.3.

Solution 5.3

The frequency curves in Fig. 5.3 illustrate two distributions. The curves provide a picture of the 'slope' of the distribution and make it possible to compare the two distributions. Details of the distributions are more difficult to ascertain from the curves because the curves are formed by smoothing out histograms or frequency polygons.

The distributions show the weekly pay received by the employees of two companies. Both companies pay their employees between £50 and £500 a week. Company A has more low paid workers than Company B, with the majority of its employees receiving well under £300 a week with most of them paid around £200 a week (the modal pay). A significant number of employees in Company A are paid less than this.

In Company B the most usual pay is around £400 a week (the modal pay) with a significant number being paid above this amount. Very few employees in Company B are paid less than £100 a week or for that matter less than £200. Both companies have few employees paid close to £500 a week but Company B would appear to have around twice the number paid a little under £500 compared with Company A.

Judging by the area under the two frequency curves, it would appear that Company A has many more employees than Company B, the majority being paid at the lower end of the scale in a relatively small range between £100 and £300. Company B has a more even distribution of pay over a range from £200 to nearly £500 for the majority of its employees. Perhaps Company B consists of a highly skilled labour force with few unskilled and very young workers compared with Company A.

Without more information about the companies it is difficult to be more specific, but the two frequency curves do illustrate the differences between the companies very clearly.

Example 5.4

Illustrate the following data with appropriate diagrams or graphs. Comment briefly on your choice.

Output of a range of machinery used in a small engineering firm

| Machines | Year (output in complete units) | | | | | |
	1	2	3	4	5	6
A	500	1000	2000	3500	5000	6000
B	500	1000	1000	1500	2000	3000
C	500	600	600	600	800	900
D	500	400	400	400	200	100
Total output	2000	3000	4000	6000	8000	10 000

Solution 5.4

The data shows information over a period of six years with four different machines making up the total output. In order to illustrate this information and to make a strong visual impact, diagrams and graphs are needed to show trends over the years, the performance of the machines and the proportion that each machine makes up of total output.

Trends can best be shown on a graph while comparisons between the performance of the machines can be shown best on a compound bar chart. The proportion that each machine makes up of the total in any one year can be shown best on a pie chart or component bar chart. For these reasons the following graph and diagrams have been used to illustrate the data:

(a) Graph

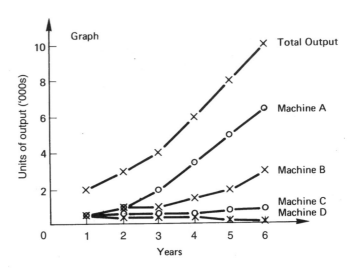

(b) Compound bar chart

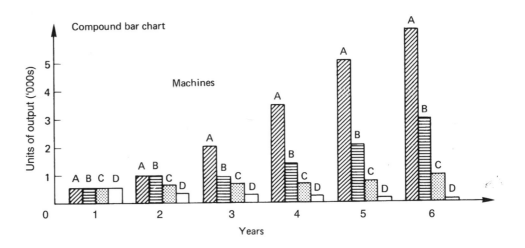

(c) Pie chart

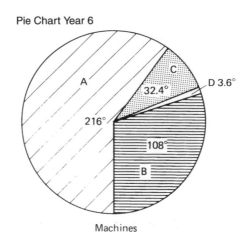

Pie Chart Year 6

A $\frac{6000}{10000} \times 360° = 216°$

B $\frac{3000}{10000} \times 360° = 108°$

C $\frac{900}{10000} \times 360° = 32.4°$

D $\frac{100}{10000} \times 360° = 3.6°$

Example 5.5

Which forms of pictorial presentation would be appropriate to illustrate the following?

(a) the individual parts of an item as proportions of the whole;
(b) the sales of butter and margarine of different brand types;
(c) Child: George   William   Henry
     No. of books owned: 20   5   2

Solution 5.5

(a) Either a pie chart or a component bar chart will illustrate the individual parts of an item as proportions of the whole. In both cases a few items only can be included. For comparison between a number of whole items, the component bar chart is clearer.

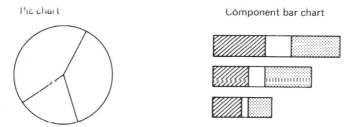

Pie chart   Component bar chart

(b) The compound bar chart or a graph can both be used to illustrate sales very clearly. If the trend of sales over a period of time is important a graph might be a clearer illustration, while for a strong visual impact the compound bar chart is good or better.

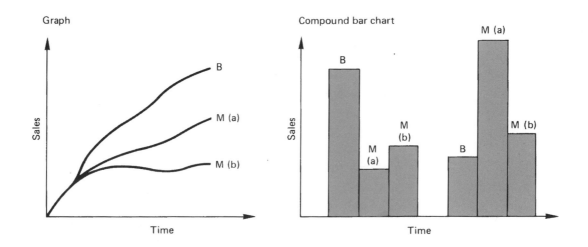

(c) A simple bar chart or a pie chart would illustrate the number of books owned by the children very clearly. The pie chart can show the number of books owned by each child as a proportion of the total number owned by the three children, while the bar chart can provide a clear visual impact and a scale.

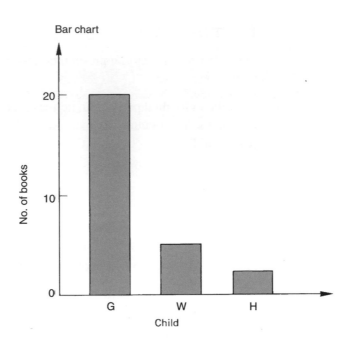

Example 5.6

Look carefully at the following graphs and analyse briefly what is wrong with them.

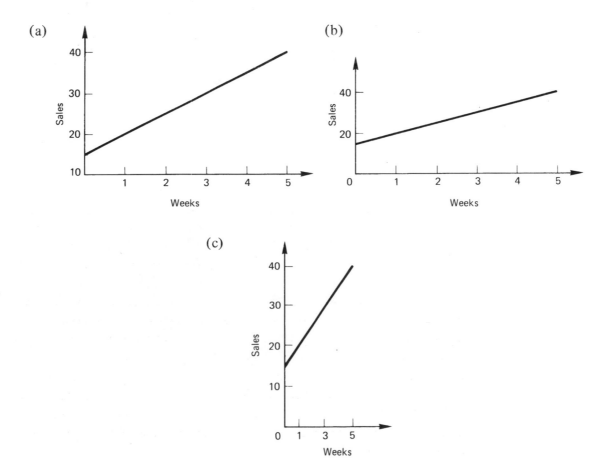

Solution 5.6

(a)   In this graph the sales scale is not shown from zero and therefore the curve of the graph appears steeper than it would if the origin was shown. This gives the impression that the sales have grown more rapidly than they have in fact.

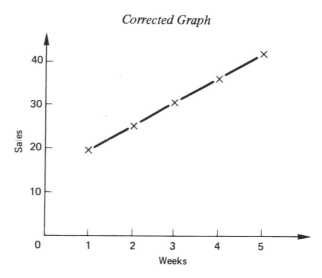

Corrected Graph

(b)   In this graph the vertical axis has been compressed so that the curve appears to be less steep than it would be if the vertical axis was the same length as the horizontal axis. This gives the impression that sales have increased more slowly than they have in fact.

(c)   In this graph the horizontal axis is compressed so that the curve is steeper than it would be if the horizontal axis was the same length as the vertical axis. This gives the impression that sales have increased more rapidly than they have in fact.

Example 5.7

Comment on the information contained in the bar charts shown in Figs 5.4–5.7.

Solution 5.7

Figure 5.4 is a simple bar chart which shows the output of a company in £ over a three year period. It shows that the output has increased from £350 000 in 1984 to £500 000 in 1985 and £650 000 in 1986. This is a steady increase of £150 000 a year, although the rate of growth is decreasing because the increase of £150 000 is based on a larger quantity each year.

Figure 5.5 is a compound bar chart which shows the output of a company divided into three items (television sets, radios and cassette players). The output of television sets has increased over the three years from £50 000 in 1984, to £150 000 in 1985 to £400 000 in 1986. The output of radio sets fell from £100 000 in 1984, to £50 000 in 1985 and £20 000 in 1986. The output of cassette players rose from £200 000 in 1984 to £300 000 in 1985 and fell back to £200 000 in 1986. While the value of the output of television sets rose rapidly during these three years, the value of the output of radios fell and of cassette players fluctuated.

Figure 5.6 is a component bar chart and shows the change in total output clearly over three years and shows the changes in the proportion which the three items make up of the total in each of the years. It is clear from this that while television sets have increased as a proportion of the value of the output, radios have decreased and cassette players have fluctuated.

Figure 5.7 is a percentage component bar chart which shows the proportions of each item of the total without showing the value of the total. The total is shown as 100% for each year. This approach emphasises the proportion that each item makes up of the total value of output and shows clearly the increased importance of television sets, the fall in importance of radios and the fluctuation in importance of cassette players. It is interesting to note that cassette players accounted for more than half of total output in 1984 and less than a third in 1986 although the actual output was the same (£200 000).

Each of the bar charts emphasises a different aspect of the same information and, therefore, they are all useful as illustrations of the data.

5.4 Questions and exercises

Question 5.1

Discuss the aims of statistical presentation. Comment on differences between presenting information to a group of specialists and to the general public.

Question 5.2

Comment, with examples, on the problems of classification.

Question 5.3

Construct a table to illustrate the following information:

'In 1801 there were 8 892 000 people in England and Wales according to information from the Office of Population Censuses and Surveys (1981). By 1851 there were 22 259 000 people in the United Kingdom, 10 855 000 males and 11 404 000 females and the population in England and Wales has risen to 17 928 000. In 1901 the UK population had risen to 38 237 00, by 1951 to 50 225 000, 1961 to 52 709 000 and 1971 to 55 515 000. It is projected that by the year 2001 the UK population will be 58 048 000.

The male population of the UK was 10 855 000 in 1851, 18 492 000 in 1901, 24 118 000 in 1951, 25 481 000 in 1961, and 26 952 000 in 1971. The female population of the UK was 11 404 000 in 1851, 19 745 000 in 1901, 26 107 000 in 1951, 27 228 000 in 1961 and 28 562 000 in 1971. The male population of the UK is expected to be 28 479 000 in the year 2001 and the female population of the UK 29 569 000 in the same year.'

Question 5.4

Draw a histogram from the data in Question 5.3. Briefly, comment on the histogram.

Question 5.5

Analyse the differences in the two distributions shown below:

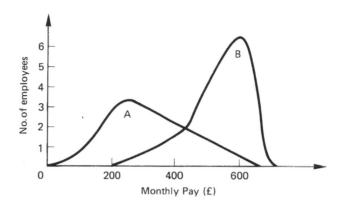

Question 5.6

Draw suitable diagrams and graphs to illustrate the data in the table for Question 5.3. Comment briefly on your choice of illustration.

Question 5.7

Discuss the advantages and disadvantages of (i) various forms of bar chart, (ii) natural scale and semi-log graphs.

Question 5.8

Draw a pie chart to illustrate the following data:
Imports into the UK: wheat   £200 million
                        sugar   £300 million
                        fruit   £100 million

Question 5.9

Discuss the problems of distortion in graphical presentation. Comment on possible uses of distortion in advertising.

Question 5.10

Compare the use of statistical presentation in the annual reports of two major companies.

Question 5.11

The pie chart shown represents the amount of time spent by a pupil on various subjects in a school during a particular week. The angles of the sectors representing Mathematics (M) and Science (S) are 60° and 120° respectively. The pupil spends an equal amount of time on Mathematics and on English (E), and twice as much time on Humanities (H) as on Languages (L). If he spends 5 hours on Mathematics per week, calculate the amount of time spent on Languages.

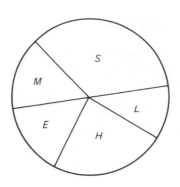

(AEB)

Question 5.12

A series of readings is being grouped into the following classes
12–
13–
14–
15–

The tally for 14.0 exactly
A must be included in the class 13–
B must be included in the class 14–
C must be included in either the 13– or the 14– class
D should be taken as $\frac{1}{2}$ in each of the 13– and 14– classes.   (AEB)

Question 5.13

The colour of the coat of a species of mammal varies from light grey to black. A biologist classifies each individual by colour using a whole number between 1 and 10.
This classification changes the variable from
A quantitative to continuous
B quantitative to discrete
C qualitative to continuous
D qualitative to discrete   (AEB)

Question 5.14

A group of school children carried out a survey on the masses of a large number of cats and dogs. The following frequency distributions result.
(a) Which type of animal has the larger average mass?
(b) Which type of animal has the smaller variation in its mass?   (AEB)

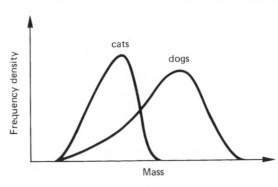

Question 5.15

For the distribution shown below determine the numbers of items having a value:
(i) less than 4; (ii) more than 3.

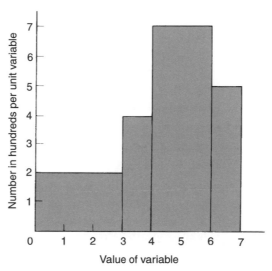

(AEB)

Question 5.16

Average daily earnings (£)	Frequency
less than 2	6
2 and less than 3	8
3 and less than 4	10
4 and less than 5	12
5 and less than 8	6

The histogram which represents the above data is A, B, C or D? (AEB)

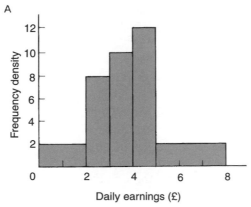

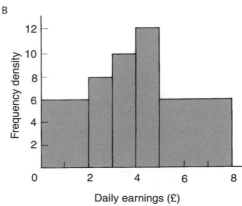

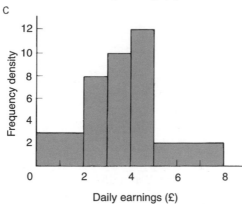

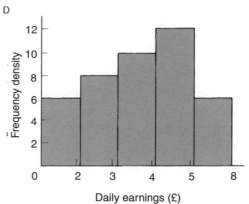

Question 5.17

Listed below are the descriptions of how various items of statistical data relating to cars were classified. For which of the following could a histogram be constructed to illustrate the data?

A The average life of cars manufactured in Great Britain in 1960 classified by the make of car

B The number of new cars registered in Great Britain in 1960 classified by the registration authority

C The number of cars manufactured in Great Britain in 1960 classified by the make of car

D The number of new cars distributed in 1960 by a large British car firm classified by the length of delay in delivery.   (AEB)

Question 5.18

The histogram below shows the distribution of distances in a throwing competition.

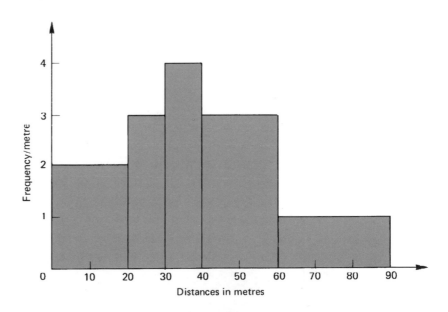

(i)   How many competitors threw less than 40 metres?

(ii) How many competitors were there in the competition?   (AEB)

Question 5.19

What features of data are clearly illustrated by a pie chart?   (SUJB)

Question 5.20

In 1978, 157.2 applications were received for driving tests in the Yorkshire traffic area, 129.5 tests were conducted, of which 66.7 were on men and the rest on women (all figures are in thousands). The corresponding figures for 1979 were 139.2 applications, 69.6 men tested and 65.2 women tested. In the East Midlands traffic area the 1978 figures were 163.9 applications, 139.9 tests, of which 68.0 were on women, and for 1979, 153.3 applications, 135.4 tests, of which 67.2 were on men. In the Eastern traffic area 39.2 men and 43.0 women were tested in 1979 when there were 102.7 applications, whereas in 1978 the figures were 103.2 applications, 88.5 tests of which 43.4 were on men.

(These data are from the Annual Abstract of Statistics 1981, HMSO)

(a)   Display the data above in a suitable table, which should also include relevant totals for the three traffic areas taken together.

(b)   Draw a diagram illustrating the change from 1978 to 1979 in the number of tests taken by men and by women in each traffic area.

(c)   Comment briefly on any notable features of the data.   (SUJB)

Question 5.21

To illustrate the sales of both condensed soups and ready-to-use soups, of different flavours, the best method would be

A   a histogram

B   a compound bar chart

C   a frequency polygon

D   a cumulative frequency polygon.   (AEB)

Question 5.22

The 'BLAND X' breakfast product was launched in December 1992. Market research shows this age profile of users in 3 European Countries.

Age group	France	Germany	Spain
0–5 yrs	39	15	41
6–10 yrs	19	30	12
11–15 yrs	28	12	13
16–20 yrs	8	15	17
20+	6	28	17

All figures are percentages.

(a)   Use suitable diagrams to show the main features of the data.

(b)   Comment on the results.

(c)   On the basis of the figures what advice would you give the advertisers?

(Chartered Institute of Marketing)

Question 5.23

A manufacturer has undertaken a large attitude survey of recent buyers of small cars in Great Britain. As part of this study, 100 recent buyers of British cars and 100 recent buyers of German cars were asked to agree or to disagree with a number of statements. One of the summary tables from a computer print-out is shown below.

Write a short report on the most significant features of these data, illustrating your analysis with simple, appropriate tables and/or diagrams.

Statements	Buyers of British cars Agree	Disagree	Buyers of German cars Agree	Disagree
British cars are:				
easy to get serviced	65	35	46	54
economical	81	19	55	45
reliable	76	24	48	52
comfortable	69	31	61	39
German cars are:				
easy to get serviced	32	68	60	40
economical	61	39	83	17
reliable	74	26	85	15
comfortable	35	65	58	42

(ICMA)

Question 5.24

You are a management accountant's assistant, employed by a company operating coach services between Backwards and Forwards. This company has researched the preferences between coach and car travel of regular travellers on this journey. One hundred regular coach users and two hundred regular car users were interviewed about a journey to Forwards. Some of the results were as follows:

Travellers' preferences on the Backwards–Forwards route

Question Answer	Which is quicker? Coach users	Car users	Which is more economical? Coach users	Car users	Which is more comfortable? Coach users	Car users
Coach	76	18	80	120	16	18
Car	14	156	10	32	71	162
About the same	7	22	9	38	11	16
Don't know	3	4	1	10	2	4

(a) What conclusions can be drawn from the data?
(b) Illustrate *two* of these conclusions with suitable charts/diagrams. (ICMA)

Question 5.25

The sales figures for GEM International are as follows:

	1991 £m	1992 £m
Jan	65	41
Feb	70	39
Mar	73	36
Apr	78	35
May	72	30
Jun	67	43
Jul	60	38
Aug	56	33
Sep	69	27
Oct	53	23
Nov	49	23
Dec	40	19

(a) Construct a *Z*-chart for this information.
(b) Write a brief report to the marketing manager commenting on the results.

(Chartered Institute of Marketing)

Question 5.26

(a) Briefly explain the uses of the Lorenz curve.
(b) Distribution of wealth in 1976 in UK is given below.
     Percentage of wealth owned by most wealthy

      1% of owners   17
      2% of owners   23
      5% of owners   35
     10% of owners   47
     25% of owners   68
     50% of owners   88
     Source: Social Trends.

    (i)   Draw a Lorenz curve
    (ii) Comment on your curve.   (RSA)

Question 5.27

The diagram below shows the number of visitors to and from Great Britain in one year.

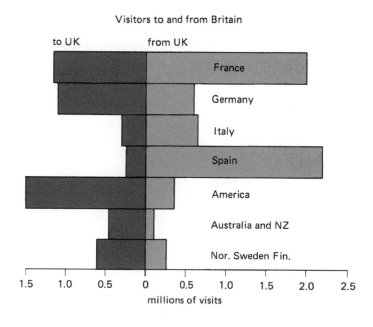

(a) Which country attracts most British visitors?
(b) From which country does Britain attract most visitors?
(c) Which countries attract more visitors from Britain than Britain attracts from them?
(d) Which country has the greatest total volume of passenger traffic to and from Britain?

(e)   Given that the total number of visits to UK was 5.4 million what would be the angle in the sector representing America, of a pie chart showing countries of origin of visitors to UK? (SEB)

Question 5.28

The incomplete pie chart represents the attendance at a concert by men, women and children. Altogether 1800 people attended the concert.

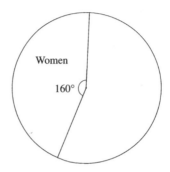

(a)   Calculate the number of women at the concert.

600 men were at the concert.

(b)   (i)   Calculate the angle needed to represent them on the pie chart.
       (ii) Use your answer to (b)(i) to *complete* the pie chart. (SEG)

Questions 5.29

The population pyramids for India and the United Kingdom show the percentage of males and females within each age group.

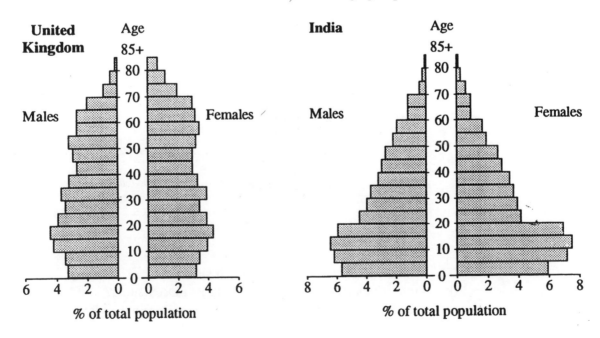

(a)   Which age group of males made up 2% of the population in the United Kingdom?

(b) (i) What age group in India accounted for the highest percentage of the population?
    (ii) Estimate what percentage of this age group were males.

(c) Estimate the percentage of females in the United Kingdom who were less than 10 years old at the time the information was collected.

(d) Give *two* comments on the population structure in these countries for people over 70 years of age. (SEG)

Question 5.30

Using data collected in a 1981 British crime survey, the percentage bar graph shown on the left was formed.

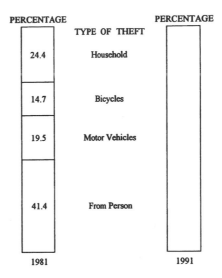

A similar survey was carried out in 1991. The results were as follows:

Type of theft	Number of thefts (in 1000s)
Household	700
Bicycles	575
Motor vehicles	510
From Person	625

Complete the percentage bar graph to show the 1991 survey results. (SEG)

Question 5.31

THE WORLD'S HEAVIEST SMOKERS

Annual cigarette consumption per country (millions). All figures are for 1991.		Daily cigarette consumption per man, woman and child. All figures are for 1991.	
China	1 617 000	Greece	7.8
USA	516 500	Japan	7.3
CIS and the Baltic States	456 000	Poland	7.3
Japan	328 300	Hungary	7.0
Brazil	156 400	Switzerland	6.5
Indonesia	146 511	Bulgaria	6.1
Germany	145 500	South Korea	6.0
Poland	102 100	Spain	5.9
France	97 100	Australia	5.6
United Kingdom	96 838	USA	5.6

United Kingdom = 4.6

(a) How many more cigarettes were smoked in the USA than in Germany during 1991?

(b) A typical smoker in the USA was given 84 cigarettes. How long would you expect these cigarettes to last?

(c) State the reason why China can be top of the consumption table and yet the consumption per person is so low that it is not recorded on that table. (SEG)

Question 5.32

On a charity collection day five people collected 10 p coins to help an old people's home.

Together they collected 7200 coins.

The pie chart represents the amounts collected by each person.

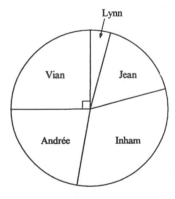

(a) The angle representing Jean's collection is 60°.
How many coins did she collect?

(b) A man gave Vian exactly half of the total money he collected.
How many coins did this man give Vian?

(c) Who collected the median amount of money?

(d) Give *one* reason why pie charts are often included in statistical reports. (SEG)

6

Summarising Data: Averages

Objectives

By the end of this chapter the following terms and methods of calculations should be understood:

	Date attempted	Date completed	Self-assessment
Arithmetic mean			
Median			
Quartiles			
Mode			

Summary

This chapter describes the summarising of data through the use of averages and methods of calculating averages and directly related statistics.

6.1 Introduction

An average:

(i) *is a measure of central location*, providing a value around which a set of data is located (e.g. the average price of a commodity is £10);

(ii) *is a measure of location*, providing an indication of the position of the data (e.g. the average price of one commodity is £10 and of another is £100);

(iii) *summarises a group of data*, providing an immediate idea about the group and distinguishing it from other groups (e.g. in terms of the price level as in (ii));

(iv) *describes data concisely* (e.g. by providing the average prices, and/or size).

The most commonly used averages are:

- the *Arithmetic Mean*: the sum of the items divided by the number of them;
- the *Median*: the value of the middle item of a distribution which is set out in order;
- the *Mode*: the most frequently occurring value in a distribution;
- the *Geometric Mean*: the nth root of the product of the distribution.

Advantages and disadvantages of these averages

Table 6.1 Averages – advantages and disadvantages

Average	Advantages	Disadvantages
Arithmetic mean	Widely used Mathematically precise Uses all the data	Distorted by extreme values May not correspond to any actual value
Median	Often an actual value Useful when a few extreme values would distort the arithmetic mean	Not widely used Gives the value of only one item
Mode	Commonly used Represents a typical item Often an actual value	People do not always realise they are using it Does not include all values More a general description than a mathematical concept
Geometric mean	Measures changes in the rate of growth	Not widely used Difficult to understand

6.2 Methods of calculating averages

(a) Calculation of the arithmetic mean

The method used for calculating the arithmetic mean depends on the type of data which is being summarised. The main types of calculation are for:

(i) unweighted and ungrouped data

(ii) a frequency distribution

(iii) a grouped frequency distribution.

(i) Calculation for unweighted and ungrouped data

$$\bar{x} = \frac{\Sigma x}{n}$$

where $\bar{x}$ (x bar or bar x) is the arithmetic mean

Σ = the sum of

x = the value of the items

n = the number of items.

(In fact $\bar{x}$ is the symbol for the arithmetic mean of a sample and μ (mu or mew) is the symbol for the arithmetic mean of the population from which samples are selected. However, $\bar{x}$ is used very widely.)

For example: if five people have £15, £17, £18, £20 and £30 respectively, the arithmetic mean is £20. That is, if £100 was shared equally between five people, they would have £20 each.

$$\bar{x} = £\frac{15 + 17 + 18 + 20 + 30}{5} = \frac{£100}{5} = £20$$

Another method of calculating the mean is to assume an average by inspection, find the deviation of the value of the items from this assumed average, sum the deviations, average them and add or subtract this from the assumed average.

For example: using the same figures as in the previous example, the average can be assumed to be £18. Deviations from the assumed mean will be:

Table 6.2 The arithmetic mean

Item (£)	Deviation from the assumed mean (£18) d_x
15	−3
17	−1
18	0
20	+2
30	+12
	−4 + 14 = +10

$$\bar{x} = £18 + \frac{10}{5} = £18 + 2 = £20$$

The formula used here is: $\bar{x} = x + \dfrac{\Sigma d_x}{n}$

where x represents the assumed mean and d_x represents the deviation from the assumed mean.

If £24 was taken as the assumed mean, the calculation would be:

Table 6.3 The assumed mean

Item (£)	d_x
15	−9
17	−7
18	−6
20	−4
30	+6
	−26 + 6 = −20

$$\bar{x} = £24 - \frac{20}{5} = £24 - 4 = £20$$

Any figure chosen as the assumed mean would give the correct answer. This method of using an assumed mean is useful because:

1. it may be a faster method of calculation than the first method, particularly with large numbers;
2. It is a useful method in other statistical calculations.

(ii) Calculation for a frequency distribution

(The 'weighted arithmetic mean' or the 'arithmetic mean of grouped data')

This is calculated by multiplying the item by the frequency or weight, adding up the products and dividing by the sum of the frequencies:

$$\bar{x} = \frac{\Sigma fx}{\Sigma f}$$

where Σ = the sum of
f = the frequency of
x = the value of the items.

With the use of the assumed mean, this becomes:

$$\bar{x} = x \pm \frac{\Sigma fd_x}{\Sigma f}$$

where x = the assumed mean
d_x = the deviation from the assumed mean
fd_x = the frequency times the deviation from the assumed mean.

For example: 25 radios stocked by a shop have the following prices (to the nearest £): two are priced at £20, 6 at £24, 10 at £25, 4 at £30, 3 at £32.

Table 6.4 The arithmetic mean of a frequency distribution

Price (to the nearest £)	Number of radios	Deviation from assumed mean ($x = 28$)	Frequency × deviation from assumed mean
	(f)	(d_x)	(fd_x)
20	2	−8	−16
24	6	−4	−24
25	10	−3	−30
30	4	+2	+8
32	3	+4	+12
	25		−70 + 20
	$\Sigma f = 25$		$\Sigma fd_x = -50$

$$\bar{x} = x \pm \frac{\Sigma fd_x}{\Sigma f}$$

$$= £28 - \frac{50}{25}$$

$$= £28 - 2$$

$$= £26$$

This shows that the average price of these 25 radios is £26. This result can be checked by making the calculation on the basis of multiplying the items by the frequencies and dividing the sum by the frequencies.

Price of the transistor radios:

Table 6.5

Price (£)	Number	Price × frequency
20	2	40
24	6	144
25	10	250
30	4	120
32	3	96
	$\Sigma f = 25$	$\Sigma fx = 650$

$$\bar{x} = \frac{\Sigma fx}{\Sigma f}$$

$$= \frac{£650}{25}$$

$$= £26$$

Both methods are equally valid; the first method, using the assumed mean, is useful as a preparation for calculations in other areas, particularly the standard deviation.

A commentary on the results of these calculations could include the following points:

The average price for this selection of radios is £26 although there are some priced at £20 and others at over £30. If this was a random sample of the price of all transistor radios then the consumer would know that £26 was likely to be a representative price for this type of radio.

(iii) Calculation for a grouped frequency distribution

(The 'weighted arithmetic mean with frequency classes')

In a grouped frequency distribution, frequencies are grouped within class intervals. The choice of class intervals is arbitrary and there is no way of knowing the distribution of frequencies within a class, and therefore it is assumed that each item within a class interval is equal to the mid-point of the class interval.

There are two methods of calculating the arithmetic mean of a frequency distribution with class intervals:

(1)   the mid-point method,
(2)   the class interval method.

(1)   The mid-point method

For example: one hundred employees of a firm are paid monthly overtime of between £20 and £50 which is distributed as shown in Table 6.6.

Table 6.6 The mid-point method

Monthly overtime pay (£)	Number of employees	Mid-points of class intervals	Deviation of mid-points from assumed mean (£37.5)	Frequency × deviation
	(f)	$(m - p)$	(d_x)	(fd_x)
20 but less than 25	11	22.5	−15	−165
25 but less than 30	15	27.5	−10	−150
30 but less than 35	16	32.5	−5	−80
35 but less than 40	18	37.5	0	0
40 but less than 45	30	42.5	+5	+150
45 but less than 50	10	47.5	+10	+100
	100			−395 + 250
	$\Sigma f = 100$			$\Sigma fd_x = -145$

$$\bar{x} = x \pm \frac{\Sigma fd_x}{\Sigma f} \qquad\qquad = £37.5 - \frac{145}{100}$$

$$= £37.5 - 1.45 \qquad\qquad = £36.05$$

(2) The class interval method

Instead of using the mid-points of the class intervals, the calculation is carried out in 'units of class interval', and this has to be allowed for in the calculation by multiplying by it.

Table 6.7 The class-interval method

Monthly overtime pay (£)	Number of employees	Deviation of classes from the assumed mean	Frequency × deviation
	(f)	(d_x)	(fd_x)
20 but less than 25	11	−3	−33
25 but less than 30	15	−2	−30
30 but less than 35	16	−1	−16
35 but less than 40	18	0	0
40 but less than 45	30	+1	+30
45 but less than 50	10	+2	+20
	100		−79 +50
$x = £37.5$			$\Sigma fd_x = -29$

$$\bar{x} = x \pm \frac{\Sigma fd_x}{\Sigma f} \times \text{class interval}$$

$$= £37.5 - \frac{29}{100} \times 5$$

$$= £37.5 - 0.29 \times 5$$

$$= £37.5 - 1.45$$

$$= £36.05$$

If the class intervals are uneven, allowance has to be made for this (Table 6.8):

Table 6.8 Uneven class intervals

Monthly overtime pay (£)	Number of employees	Deviation of class interval from assumed mean ($x = 65$)	Frequency $\times d_x$
	(f)	(d_x)	(fd_x)
40 but less than 50	10	-2	-20
50 but less than 60	14	-1	-14
60 but less than 70	16	0	0
70 but less than 80	6	$+1$	$+6$
80 but less than 100	4	$+2.5$	$+10$
	$\overline{50}$		$\overline{-34 +16}$
	$\Sigma f = 50$		$\Sigma fd_x = -18$

$$\bar{x} = £65 - \frac{18}{50} \times 10$$

$$= £65 - 3.6$$

$$= £61.4$$

Notice that the last class interval is twice as large as the previous ones. The midpoint of that class is £90 which is two and a half tens (the class interval of the other classes) from the assumed mean (£65) and therefore the deviation is 2.5.

When there are a number of unequal class intervals it may be easier to use the mid-point method.

(b) Calculation of the median

In a discrete distribution the median can be ascertained by inspection.

For example: if five people earn £60, £70, £100, £115 and £320 respectively, the median is the value of the middle item. The middle item is the third and therefore the median = £100.

The formula for finding the position of the median in a discrete series is:

The median position $= \dfrac{n + 1}{2}$

In the example above, there are five items, therefore:

The median position $= \dfrac{5 + 1}{2} = 3$

The median is the value of the third item: £100.

If there are an even number of items, the two middle items are added together and divided by two. If there are six items:

The median position $= \dfrac{6 + 1}{2} = 3.5$

Therefore the value of the median lies between item three and item four.

For example: if six people earn £60, £70, £100, £110, £115 and £320 respectively, the median equals the value of the 3.5th item:

$$M = £\frac{100 + 110}{2} = £105$$

where M = the median.

(i)   Calculation of the median with a grouped frequency distribution

There are two methods:

1.   by calculation
2.   graphically.

(1)   Calculation of the median

The median position for a continuous series is $\dfrac{n}{2}$ or $\dfrac{f}{2}$

where n = the number of units
f = the frequency.

For example: the monthly overtime pay for a group of fifty employees of a company varies between nothing and £30. It is distributed as in Table 6.9.

Table 6.9   The median

Monthly overtime pay (£)	Number of employees (f)	Cumulative frequency
0 but less than 5	3	3 people received less than £5
5 but less than 10	5	8 people received less than £10
10 but less than 15	14	22 people received less than £15
15 but less than 20	12	34 people received less than £20
20 but less than 25	10	44 people received less than £25
25 but less than 30	6	50 people received less than £30
	50	

The median position $= \dfrac{f}{2} = \dfrac{50}{2} = 25$

The overtime pay of the 25th employee is the median pay. The pay of the 25th employee falls in the class interval of £15 but less than £20, because 22 people earn up to £15 and 34 people up to £20 and the 25th person falls between these two limits. It is assumed that the number of units in the class interval is divided evenly between the number of units in the frequency. In this case 12 people share £5. The 25th employee is the 3rd person of these 12 because there are 22 people who fall within the previous class intervals:

$$M = £15 + \frac{3}{12} \times 5 = £16.25$$

where £15 is the lower class interval of the class in which the median falls and $\frac{3}{12} \times 5$ indicates that the median pay is the third out of 12 sharing £5.

Comment: in this distribution the median overtime pay is the earnings of the 25th employee which is £16.25. This divides the distribution in half, so that of the 50 employees half will earn less than £16.25 and half will earn more. In this sense the median provides a good representation of the grouped frequency distribution.

(2) Computation of the median graphically

The median is found by drawing the cumulative frequency curve or ogive and interpolating the median from this curve.

For example: using the same data as for the previous example showing the monthly overtime pay of fifty employees of a company and computing the cumulative frequency and the ogive (Table 6.10 and Fig. 6.1):

The position of $M = \dfrac{50}{2} = 25$

A horizontal line is drawn from this point (25) on the vertical axis to the ogive (cumulative frequency curve), and at the point of intersection a vertical line is dropped to the horizontal axis. This shows that the value of the median is about £16.

Note that on the horizontal axis the points are plotted at the end of the class intervals (5, 10, 15, etc.)

Table 6.10 The median calculated graphically

Overtime pay (£)	Number of employees (f)	Cumulative frequency
0 but less than 5	3	3
5 but less than 10	5	8
10 but less than 15	14	22
15 but less than 20	12	34
20 but less than 25	10	44
25 but less than 30	6	50
	50	

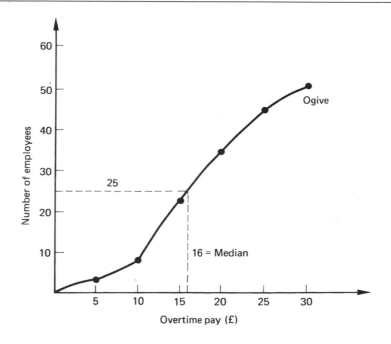

Figure 6.1 Cumulative frequency curve

(ii) Calculation of quartiles

The lower and upper quartiles and the median divide an ordered distribution into four equal parts. The method of calculating the quartiles is similar to that used for the median. It is because of these links with the median that it is usual to consider the calculation of the quartiles along with that of the median.

For example: using the same example as was used for the median (Table 6.11):

The position of the lower quartile for a continuous series (Q_1) =

$$\frac{n}{4} \text{ or } \frac{f}{4} = \frac{50}{4} = 12.5$$

The pay received by a theoretical employee lying between the 12th and 13th is the lower quartile pay. This lies in the class £10 but less than £15 which is shared by 14 employees.

Table 6.11 The quartiles

Overtime pay (£)	Number of employees (f)	Cumulative frequency
0 but less than 5	3	3
5 but less than 10	5	8
10 but less than 15	14	22
15 but less than 20	12	34
20 but less than 25	10	44
25 but less than 30	6	50
	50	

$$Q_1 = £10 + \frac{4.5}{14} \times 5$$

$$= £10 + 1.607$$

$$= £11.61$$

The position of the upper quartile for a continuous series (Q_3) =

$$\frac{3n}{4} \text{ or } \frac{3f}{4} = \frac{3 \times 50}{4} = \frac{150}{4} = 37.5$$

The pay received by a theoretical employee lying between the 37th and 38th employee is the upper quartile pay. This lies in the class £20 but less than £25, which is shared by 10 employees.

$$Q_3 = £20 + \frac{3.5}{10} \times 5$$

$$= £20 + 1.75$$

$$= £21.75$$

It is possible from these calculations to divide the distribution in the following way:

Q_1 = the 12.5th employee receiving £11.61 in overtime pay
M = the 25th employee receiving £16.25 in overtime pay

Q_3 = the 37.5th employee receiving £21.75 in overtime pay

Graphically these figures can be interpolated as shown in Fig. 6.2.

Comment: the division of this ordered distribution by the lower quartile, the median and the upper quartile makes it possible to say that:

1. half the employees are earning less than £16.25 and half more than this in overtime pay;
2. half the employees are earning between £11.61 and £21.75 in overtime pay;
3. a quarter of the employees are earning less than £11.61 and a quarter more than £21.75.

This distribution of overtime pay can be compared with similar information for previous years or for another company.

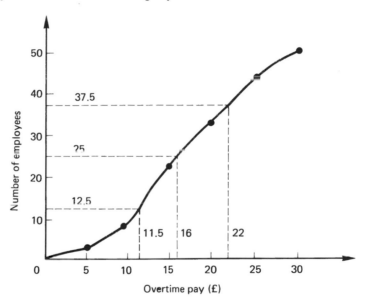

Figure 6.2 Lower and upper quartiles

(iii) Calculation of deciles and percentiles

Just as the quartiles divide an ordered distribution into four equal parts, it is possible to divide it into other equal parts. *Deciles divide a distribution into ten equal parts* and *percentiles divide a distribution into one hundred equal parts.*

The method of calculation is similar to that for quartiles:

1. Deciles

(using the distribution in Table 6.11)

The position of the first decile (D_1) $= \dfrac{n}{10}$ or $\dfrac{f}{10}$

$$= \dfrac{50}{10} = 5$$

The pay received by the fifth employee is the first decile pay. This lies in the class £5 but less than £10 which is shared by 5 employees:

$$D_1 = £5 + \dfrac{2}{5} \times 5 = £7$$

The position of the second decile (D_2) $= \dfrac{2n}{10}$ or $\dfrac{2f}{10}$

$$= \dfrac{2 \times 50}{10} = \dfrac{100}{10} = 10$$

$$D_2 = £10 + \dfrac{2}{14} \times 5 = £10.71$$

The position of the third decile (D_3) $= \dfrac{3 \times 50}{10} = 15$

$$D_3 = £10 + \dfrac{7}{14} \times 5 = £12.50$$

... and so on for $D_4, D_5, D_6, D_7, D_8, D_9, D_{10}$. The position of the deciles are 5, 10, 15, 20, 25, 30, 35, 40, 45. These divide the distribution into ten equal parts and the value of the overtime pay of the employees in these positions divides the distribution of the overtime into ten equal parts.

2. Percentiles

(using the distribution in Table 6.11)

The position of the first percentile (P_1) $= \dfrac{n}{100}$ or $\dfrac{f}{100}$

$$= \dfrac{50}{100} = 0.5$$

The overtime pay received by a theoretical employee lying below the first employee is the first percentile pay. This lies in the class £0 but less than £5, which is shared by 3 employees.

$$P_1 = £0 + \dfrac{0.5}{3} \times 5$$

$$= £0 + 0.83$$

$$= 0.83 \text{ or } 83 \text{ pence}$$

The position of the second percentile (P_2) $= \dfrac{2n}{100}$ or $\dfrac{2f}{100} =$

$$\dfrac{2 \times 50}{100} = \dfrac{100}{100} = 1$$

$$P_2 = £0 + \dfrac{1}{3} \times 5 = £1.67$$

The position of the third percentile (P_3) $= \dfrac{3n}{100}$ or $\dfrac{3f}{100} =$

$$\frac{3 \times 50}{100} = \frac{150}{100} = 1.5$$

$$P_3 = £0 + \frac{1.5}{3} \times 5 = £2.50$$

The position of the fourth percentile (P_4) $= \dfrac{4n}{100}$ or $\dfrac{4f}{100} =$

$$\frac{4 \times 50}{100} = \frac{200}{100} = 2$$

$$P_4 = £0 + \frac{2}{3} \times 5 = £3.33$$

... and so on for P_5, P_6, P_7 ... The position of the percentiles divide the distribution into a hundred equal parts and the value of the overtime pay of the employees in these positions divides the distribution of the overtime into a hundred equal parts.

(c)   Calculation of the mode

The mode is the most frequently occurring value in a distribution. In a discrete distribution the mode can be ascertained by inspection.

For example: the mode of the figures 4, 4, 5, 6, 11 is 4 because it is the most frequently occurring number.

In a frequency distribution the mode is the item with the highest frequency.

For example: the number of cars using a particular size of component is as in Table 6.12.

Table 6.12   The mode

The size of a component (cm)	The number of makes of car using the size
20	4
21	10
22	15
23	20
24	1

The mode is 23 cm because 20 is the highest frequency.

In a grouped frequency distribution the modal class is the one with the highest frequency.

For example: the monthly overtime pay of fifty employees of a company is as in Table 6.13.

Table 6.13 Modal class

Monthly overtime pay (£)	Number of employees (f)
0 but less than 5	3
5 but less than 10	5
10 but less than 15	14
15 but less than 20	12
20 but less than 25	10
25 but less than 30	6
	50

The modal class is '£10 but less than £15' because this class has the highest frequency.

Comment: The modal overtime pay for this group of employees is between £10 and £15 because this is the class interval with the greatest frequency of employees, and the largest single number of employees are paid between these amounts.

Some distributions have more than one modal class, because two (or more) classes have the same (highest) frequency. These distributions are called bi-modal, tri-modal and so on.

For example: (Table 6.14)
This is a bi-modal distribution, the modal classes are £10 but less than £15 and £20 but less than £25.

Calculating the mode for a grouped frequency distribution is impossible. Since a grouped frequency distribution does not have individual values it is impossible to determine which value occurs most frequently. It is possible to make a calculation of the mode but it is not particularly useful or meaningful to do so. Any calculation that is made will tend to reflect the 'skew' of the distribution (see Chapter 7).

Table 6.14 A bi-modal distribution

Monthly overtime pay (£)	Number of employees (f)
0 but less than 5	3
5 but less than 10	10
10 but less than 15	30
15 but less than 20	20
20 but less than 25	30
25 but less than 30	7
	100

This can be illustrated by the use of a histogram (Fig. 6.3) based on Table 6.13. A line is drawn from the top right-hand corner of the modal class rectangle or block to the point where the top of the next adjacent block to the left meets it (line A to B); a corresponding line is drawn from the left-hand top corner of the modal class block to the top of the class on the right (line C to D). Where these two lines cross a vertical line can be dropped to the horizontal axis and this will show the value of the mode (approximately £14 in the example).

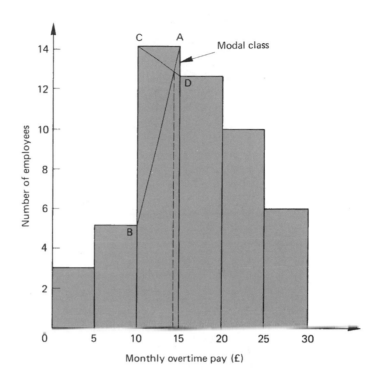

Figure 6.3 Histogram from Table 6.13

Comment: although it is possible to make this estimate of the mode, it is an approximation because the individual values are not known. Estimates of the mode are of limited use and for most purposes the modal class provides a sufficient description of this aspect of a grouped frequency distribution. It is more accurate, in fact, to say that the most usual overtime pay is between £10 and £15 rather than, it is about £14.

(d)   Calculation of the geometric mean

The geometric mean is used to measure changes in the rate of growth. It is defined as *the nth root of the product of the items in a distribution.* If there are three items it is the third root.

For example: the geometric of 3, 4, 15 = $\sqrt[3]{3 \times 4 \times 15}$ = 5.65

For example: if the price of commodity A has risen from £60 to £120, this is an increase of 100%; if the price of commodity B has risen from £80 to £100, this is an increase of 25%.

The geometric mean of these percentages is: $\sqrt{100 \times 25}$ = 50%

The arithmetic mean of these percentages is: $\dfrac{100 + 25}{2}$ = 62.5%

Whether the 'true' increase is 50% or 62% is open to argument and depends on the type of measure required.

6.3 Box and whisker diagram

A box (or box plot) diagram is used in order to display the values of the smallest observation, the largest observation, the median and the quartiles of a set of data.

In Table 6.11 and Fig. 6.2, for example, the *median* is £16.25, the *lower quartile* is £11.61, the *upper quartile* is £21.75, the *smallest observation* is £0 and the *largest* £30.00. This produces the diagram shown in Fig. 6.3.

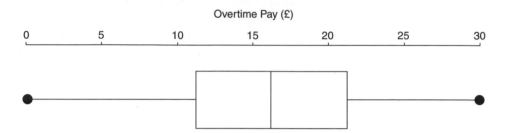

Figure 6.4 Box and whisker diagram

A scale line is used for the variable (overtime pay). The circular dots indicate the location of the smallest and largest observations. The rectangular box has its vertical sides located at the lower and upper quartiles, and the vertical line inside the box at the median.

The horizontal lines from the box to the blocks can be referred to as 'whiskers'. In Fig. 6.3, the whisker on the left is slightly larger than the one on the right, indicating that the spread of the smaller observations is greater than that of the larger observations. The median is closer to the lower quartile than to the upper quartile, which shows that the distribution is positively skewed.

6.4 Worked examples

Example 6.1

The marks of six examination candidates are 46, 38, 53, 77, 85 and 91. Find the arithmetic mean of the marks.

Solution 6.1

$$\bar{x} = \frac{46 + 38 + 53 + 77 + 85 + 91}{6} = \frac{390}{6} = 65$$

Example 6.2

The diameter of a component part on a production line is measured at intervals of time. It is found that the part measured: 2.58 cm, 2.81 cm, 2.46 cm, 3.00 cm, 2.31 cm, 2.52 cm, 2.63 cm, 2.32 cm, 2.72 cm, 2.68 cm.
Find the arithmetic mean measurement.

Solution 6.2

$$\bar{x} = \frac{2.58 + 2.81 + 2.46 + 3.00 + 2.31 + 2.52 + 2.63 + 2.32 + 2.72 + 2.68}{10} \text{ cm}$$

$$= \frac{26.03}{10} \text{ cm} = 2.603 \text{ cm}$$

Example 6.3

The profits of three companies are as follows:

Year	Company A (£)	Company B (£)	Company C (£)
1986	2 000	13 000	10 000
1987	4 000	2 000	9 000
1988	6 000	6 000	8 000
1989	9 000	2 000	6 000
1990	14 000	12 000	2 000

(i)   Calculate the annual average (arithmetic mean) profit for these companies.

(ii)   Comment on the results and on the profit figures.

(iii)   What advice would be reasonable to give to someone thinking of buying one of these companies?

Solution 6.3

(i)   Company A: $\bar{x} = \dfrac{35\,000}{5} = £7000$

Company B: $\bar{x} = \dfrac{35\,000}{5} = £7000$

Company C: $\bar{x} = \dfrac{35\,000}{5} = £7000$

(ii)   The average profit earned by these three companies over these five years is the same. Although the arithmetic mean does provide a representative figure for the profits of each company, the annual profit figures indicate that while the companies have the same average profits this does not mean that their profit record is the same.

Company A has been building up its profits over these five years at a fairly steady level. In the final year this company's profit is the highest for a year of any company.

Company B has an erratic profit record with large profits in some years and small profits in others.

Company C has steadily falling profits over the five years. The movements in profits over the five years can be illustrated by a graph:

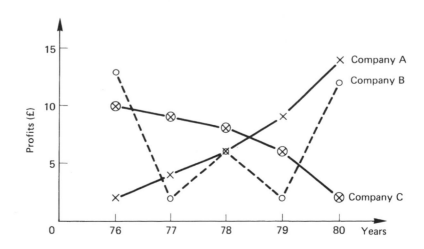

(iii)   Somebody considering buying one of these companies should look at the profit figures for the five years, and consider potential profits and the state of the markets in which the companies are working. The profit figures available show that Company A would appear at first glance to be the best one to buy. The profit figures are growing year by year and even on a percentage basis profits are expanding healthily (over 50% a year for the last three years). However, these profits might have been gained at the expense of the basic strength of the company and it could have reached the limits of its development. The company could be expensive to buy because its profits are growing.

On the other hand Company C is in need of help and revival in order to reverse the trend of falling profits. The company could be relatively cheap to take over and there could be potential for growth. However it could be a weak company, unable to compete easily in its market and therefore a risk to buy. Company B could be a good buy because it can make good profits. The risk involved would depend on the reasons for its erratic performance. If the company could be steadied it could be a good one to buy.

Without more information it is not possible to give more definite advice to a prospective buyer.

Example 6.4

Calculate the average weekly part-time wages earned by the following six people. Use the method of the assumed mean. Comment briefly on the results.

People	Part-time wage (£)	People	Weekly wage (£)
1	100	4	122
2	108	5	124
3	109	6	283

Solution 6.4

People	Part-time wage (£)	Deviation from the assumed mean (d_x) (£120)	
1	100	−20	
2	108	−12	
3	109	−11	
4	122		+2
5	124		+4
6	283		+163
		−43	+ 169 d_x = +126

$$\bar{x} = x \pm \frac{\Sigma d_x}{n} = £120 + \frac{126}{6} = £120 + 21$$

$$= £141$$

Comment: the average weekly part-time wage of these six people is £141. This is not the actual part-time wage of any of the people and five out of the six earn less than this figure. The mean is not typical of the wages and presenting this figure as an average representing this group of figures would be misleading. This illustrates that the arithmetic mean is not always the best average to use to represent data (the median would have been better for this group of figures) and that it is strongly affected by extreme values.

Example 6.5

Find the arithmetic mean of the numbers 12, 15, 13, 12, 14, 10, 11, 13, 16, 10, 12, 14, 15, 16, 14, 13, 14, 10, 12, 14.

Solution 6.5

Method I:

$$\frac{12 + 15 + 13 + 12 + 14 + 10 + 11 + 13 + 16 + 10 + 12 + 14 + 15 + 16 + 14 + 13 + 14 + 10 + 12 + 14}{20}$$

$$\bar{x} = \frac{\Sigma x}{n} = \frac{260}{20} = 13$$

Method II: these figures can be put into a table because there are a number of figures repeated.

Numbers (x)	Frequency (f)	(fx)
10	3	30
11	1	11
12	4	48
13	3	39
14	5	70
15	2	30
16	2	32
	20	260

$$\bar{x} = \frac{\Sigma fx}{\Sigma f} = \frac{260}{20} = 13$$

Example 6.6

The following table shows the diameters of a sample of washers coming off a production line:

Size (cm)	Number of washers of that size
2.2	2
2.3	8
2.4	10
2.5	30
2.6	45
2.7	5

The firm wants to advertise their washers as having an average diameter of 2.5 cm.

(i)   Calculate the arithmetic mean of the above table;
(ii)   does your result make it possible for the firm to carry out their wishes;
(iii) is the man measurement typical?

Solution 6.6

(i)

Size (cm) (x)	Number (f)	Size × number (fx)
2.2	2	4.4
2.3	8	18.4
2.4	10	24.0
2.5	30	75.0
2.6	45	117.0
2.7	5	13.5
	100	252.3

$$\bar{x} = \frac{\Sigma fx}{\Sigma f} = \frac{252.3}{100} = 2.523 \text{ cm}$$

(ii)   The result is very close to 2.5 cm and does make it possible for the company to advertise their washers as having an average diameter of 2.5 cm.

(iii)   The mean measurement is reasonably typical with most of the washers measuring 2.5 or 2.6 cm. In fact 75% of the washers measure between 2.5 cm and 2.6 cm and 85% measure between 2.4 cm and 2.6 cm.

Example 6.7

If the mean weekly income of part-time workers in Factory A is £100 and in Factory B is £200, would the combined weekly income be £150?

Solution 6.7

It would be £150 only if the number of workers in both factories were the same. To calculate the true mean it would be necessary to know the number of workers in each factory. If for example there were 2 workers in Factory B for every 5 in Factory A then:

$$\bar{x} = \frac{£100 \times 5 + £200 \times 2}{5 + 2} = \frac{£900}{7} = £128.57$$

This is a weighted arithmetic mean.
On the other hand if both factories had 100 workers, then:

$$\bar{x} = £\frac{100 \times 100 + £200 \times 100}{200} = \frac{£30\,000}{200} = £150$$

Example 6.8

The weekly overtime pay of a group of 200 employees in an engineering firm is summarised in a table as follows:

Weekly overtime pay (£)	Number of employees
80 but less than 100	20
100 but less than 120	54
120 but less than 140	63
140 but less than 160	33
160 but less than 180	18
180 but less than 200	12

(i)   Calculate the arithmetic mean weekly overtime pay of the employees;
(ii)   what does the result illustrate about the distribution of this pay?

Solution 6.8

Weekly overtime pay (£)	Number of employees (f)	Mid-point of class interval	Deviation of mid-point from assumed mean (x = £130) (d_x)	Frequency × d_x
80 but less than 100	20	90	−40	−800
100 but less than 120	54	110	−20	−1080
120 but less than 140	63	130	0	0
140 but less than 160	33	150	+20	+660
160 but less than 180	18	170	+40	+720
180 but less than 200	12	190	+60	+720
	200			−1880 +2100
				$\Sigma fd_x = +220$

$$\bar{x} = x + \frac{\Sigma fd_x}{\Sigma f} = £130 + \frac{220}{200} = £131.10$$

(ii)   The arithmetic mean is £131.10 a week. This pay falls within the third
       class, £120 but less than £140, of six classes and is less than halfway
       through the distribution £80 to £200 (halfway would be £140). Of the 200
       employees more than half (117) earn less than £140 and are in the lower
       three classes. The arithmetic mean may not be the pay earned by any
       individual employee but it does represent this group of employees quite
       well: 'the average overtime pay of this group of employees earning
       between £80 and £200 is £131.10' does provide a reasonable summary of
       the distribution.

Example 6.9

(i)   Using the same table as in Example 6.8 calculate the arithmetic mean by
       another method;
(ii)   is the result the same?

Solution 6.9

(i)

Weekly overtime pay (£)	Number of employees (f)	d_x (x = £130)	fd_x
80 but less than 100	20	−2	−40
100 but less than 120	54	−1	−54
120 but less than 140	63	0	0
140 but less than 160	33	+1	+33
160 but less than 180	18	+2	+36
180 but less than 200	12	+3	+36
	200		−94 +105
			$\Sigma fd_x = +11$

$$\bar{x} = x \pm \frac{\Sigma fd_x}{\Sigma f} \times \text{class interval}$$

$$= \pounds130 + \frac{11}{200} \times 20 = \pounds130 + 0.055 \times 20$$

$$= \pounds131.10$$

(ii)   Yes, the result is the same.

Example 6.10

The monthly overtime pay of a group of 400 employees is summarised as follows:

Monthly overtime (£)	Number of employees
0 but less than 20	300
20 but less than 60	50
60 but less than 100	40
100 but less than 160	10

(i)   Calculate the arithmetic mean;
(ii)   comment briefly on the result.

Solution 6.10

(i)

Monthly overtime (£)	Number of employees (f)	Mid-point	d_x (x = 40)	fd_x
0 but less than 20	300	10	−30	−9000
20 but less than 60	50	40	0	0
60 but less than 100	40	80	+40	+1600
100 but less than 160	10	130	+90	+900
	400			−9000 +2500
				$\Sigma fd_x = -6500$

$$\bar{x} = x \pm \frac{\Sigma fd_x}{\Sigma f} = \pounds40 - \frac{6500}{400}$$

$$= \pounds40 - 16.25 = \pounds23.75$$

(ii)   The mid-point method was chosen because of the uneven class intervals. These were uneven perhaps because most of the employees were in the lowest class and very few earned over £100. The mean of £23.25 reflects the fact that most of the employees are in the lowest class, but the figure is distorted by the higher amounts and therefore it is not very representative of the distribution when three-quarters of the employees earned between £0 and £20.

Example 6.11

(i)   Calculate the arithmetic mean of the following distribution;
(ii)   comment briefly on the result.

Solution 6.11

(i)

Monthly overtime (£)	Number of employees (f)	Deviation from x (£30) (dₓ)	fdₓ
0 but less than 20	200	−1	−200
20 but less than 40	120	0	0
40 but less than 60	70	+1	+70
60 but less than 100	10	+2.5	+25
	400		−200 +95
	$\Sigma f = 400$		$\Sigma fd_x = -105$

$$\bar{x} = £30 - \frac{105}{400} \times 20 = £30 - 5.25 = £24.75$$

(ii)   The class interval method was chosen because only the last class is uneven and using this method makes the calculation quick and easy. The mean of £24.75 is only a fair reflection of the overtime earned by these 400 employees where half earn less than £20. The mean has been 'distorted' to some extent by the extreme items.

Example 6.12

The marks of a student in five examinations were as follows: 52, 41, 63, 88, 54.

(i)   Find the median of the marks;
(ii)   comment very briefly on the result.

Solution 6.12

(i)   Arranged in order the marks are: 41, 52, 54, 63, 88

The median position $= \dfrac{n + 1}{2} = \dfrac{5 + 1}{2} = \dfrac{6}{2} = 3$

The third mark in order is 54; this is the median mark.

(ii)   This is an actual figure, the central mark achieved by this student and reasonably representative of his performance; although the mark of 88 is not well represented by the median.

Example 6.13

The marks of a student in six examinations were as follows: 52, 41, 64, 77, 82, 54.

(i)   Find the median mark;
(ii)   comment very briefly on the result.

Solution 6.13

(i)   Arranged in order the marks are: 41, 52, 54, 64, 77, 82

The median position $= \dfrac{n+1}{2} = \dfrac{6+1}{2} = 3.5$

The median lies between the third and fourth mark in order. This is

between 54 and 64 and therefore it is $\dfrac{54+64}{2} = 59$

59 is the median mark.

(ii)   The median mark is not an actual figure although it lies between two marks. It is in the central position of the marks obtained by this student and it is a fair representation of his performance.

Example 6.14

A company employing one hundred part-time employees makes the following monthly payments:

Part-time pay (£)	Number of people
10 but less than 20	10
20 but less than 30	45
30 but less than 40	28
40 but less than 50	12
50 but less than 60	3
60 but less than 70	2
	100

(i)   Calculate the median pay;
(ii)   comment on the result.

Solution 6.14

(i)

Part-time pay (£)	Number of people (*f*)	Cumulative frequency
10 but less than 20	10	10
20 but less than 30	45	55
30 but less than 40	28	83
40 but less than 50	12	95
50 but less than 60	3	98
60 but less than 70	2	100
	100	

The median position $= \dfrac{f}{2} = \dfrac{100}{2} = 50$

$$M = £20 + \dfrac{40}{45} \times 10 = £20 + 8.89 = £28.89$$

(ii)   The median pay is £28.89 which estimates the actual pay of the 50th employee, in the distribution when classified in order. This divides the distribution in half so that of the 100 employees, half will earn less than this pay and half more. In this sense the median provides a good representation of the grouped frequency distribution. However, £28 is well below the part-time earnings of some of the employees who earn up to £70.

Example 6.15

Using the data in Example 6.14, find the median graphically. Comment briefly on differences between this result and the one obtained for the previous question.

Solution 6.15

Part-time pay (£)	Number of people (f)	Cumulative frequency
10 but less than 20	10	10
20 but less than 30	45	55
30 but less than 40	28	83
40 but less than 50	12	95
50 but less than 60	3	98
60 but less than 70	2	100
	100	

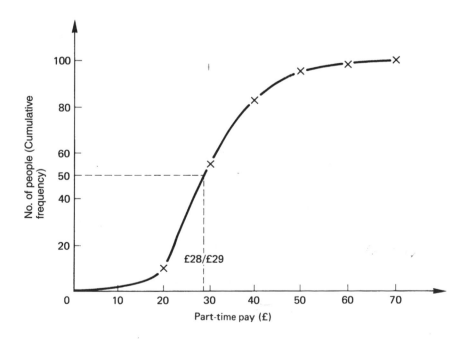

The position of $M = \dfrac{100}{2} = 50$

The median can be computed as approximately £29, this result is similar to that achieved by calculation. A more detailed graph would have provided a more exact result.

Example 6.16

The marks of pupils in seven examinations were as follows: 46, 52, 41, 63, 88, 54, 64. The median mark is 54.

(i)   Find the lower and upper quartiles and
(ii)   comment very briefly on the result.

Solution 6.16

(i)   Arranged in order the marks are: 41, 46, 52, 54, 63, 64, 88.

The lower quartile position $= \dfrac{n+1}{4} = \dfrac{7+1}{4} = \dfrac{8}{4} = 2$

The second mark in order is 46, this is the lower quartile mark.

The upper quartile position $= \dfrac{3(n+1)}{4} = \dfrac{3 \times 8}{4} = \dfrac{24}{4} = 6$

The sixth mark in order is 64, this is the upper quartile mark.

(ii)   In both cases these are actual figures, the second and sixth marks achieved by this student. The marks are divided equally by Q_1, M and Q_3, 46, 54, 64. They are reasonably representative of the student's performance, although the top mark (88) is not well represented.

Example 6.17

The marks of another student in eight examinations are as follows: 40, 46, 52, 41, 63, 88, 54, 64, 67. The median mark is 54.

(i)   Find the lower and upper quartile and
(ii)   comment very briefly on the result.

Solution 6.17

(i)   Arranged in order the marks are: 40, 41, 46, 52, 54, 63, 64, 67, 88.

The lower quartile position $= \dfrac{n+1}{4} = \dfrac{9+1}{4} = \dfrac{10}{4} = 2.5$

The lower quartile is the mark between the second and third mark in

order $= \dfrac{41+46}{2} = \dfrac{87}{2} = 43.5$

The upper quartile position $= \dfrac{3(n+1)}{4} = \dfrac{3 \times 10}{4} = \dfrac{30}{4} = 7.5$

The upper quartile is the mark between the seventh and eighth mark in

order $= \dfrac{64+67}{2} = \dfrac{131}{2} = 65.5$

The lower quartile mark is 43.5, the upper quartile is 65.5 marks.

(ii) In neither case are these marks actual marks achieved by the student. With the median mark they divide the scores into four equal sections and are reasonably representative of the student's performance, although the top mark (88) is not well represented.

Example 6.18

A company employing one hundred part-time employees makes the following monthly payments:

Part-time pay (£)	Number of people (f)
10 but less than 20	10
20 but less than 30	45
30 but less than 40	28
40 but less than 50	12
50 but less than 60	3
60 but less than 70	2
	100

(i)   calculate the lower and upper quartile;
(ii)   interpolate the results on a graph and include the median;
(iii) comment on the results.

Solution 6.18

(i)

Part-time pay (£)	Number of people (f)	Cumulative frequency
10 but less than 20	10	10
20 but less than 30	45	55
30 but less than 40	28	83
40 but less than 50	12	95
50 but less than 60	3	98
60 but less than 70	2	100
	100	

$$\text{The lower quartile position} = \frac{f}{4} = \frac{100}{4} = 25$$

$$Q_1 = £20 + \frac{15}{45} \times 10 = £20 + 3.33 = £23.33$$

$$\text{The upper quartile position} = \frac{3f}{4} = \frac{3 \times 100}{4} = 75$$

$$Q_3 = £30 + \frac{20}{28} \times 10 = £30 + 7.14 = £37.14$$

(ii)

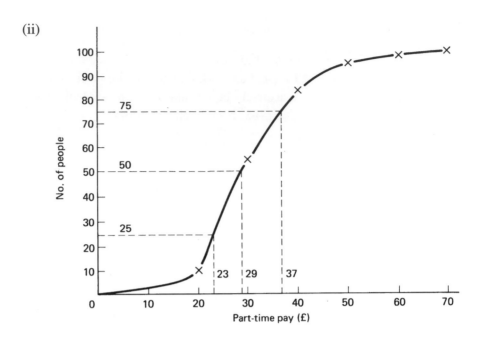

(iii)   The lower quartile pay is £23.33, the median pay (as calculated in Example 6.14) is £28.89 and the upper quartile pay is £37.14. These three pay points divide the distribution into four equal parts. The lowest quarter of the 100 employees earn between £10 and £23.33; the upper quarter earn between £37.14 and £70; the middle half of the 100 earn between £23.33 and £37.14. This summary provides a fair representation of the distribution in which most of the people earn towards the lower end of the pay scale, with 55 people earning less than £30.

Example 6.19

Complete the examples of the calculation of deciles in Section 6.2(b) (Table 6.11). Draw a graph and include the deciles. Comment briefly on the results.

Solution 6.19

$D_1 = £7$	$D_4 = £14.29$	$D_7 = £20.50$	$D_{10} = 30$
$D_2 = £10.71$	$D_5 = £16.25$	$D_8 = £23$	
$D_3 = £12.50$	$D_6 = £18.33$	$D_9 = £25.83$	

The position of $D_4 = \dfrac{4n}{10} = \dfrac{4 \times 50}{10} = 20$

$$D_4 = £10 + \frac{12}{14} \times 5 = £14.29$$

The position of $D_5 = \dfrac{5n}{10} = \dfrac{5 \times 50}{10} = 25$

$$D_5 = £15 + \frac{3}{12} \times 5 = £16.25$$

The position of $D_6 = \dfrac{6n}{10} = \dfrac{6 \times 50}{10} = 30$

$D_6 = £15 + \dfrac{8}{12} \times 5 = £18.33$

The position of $D_7 = \dfrac{7n}{10} = \dfrac{7 \times 50}{10} = 35$

$D_7 = £20 + \dfrac{1}{10} \times 5 = £20.50$

The position of $D_8 = \dfrac{8n}{10} = \dfrac{8 \times 50}{10} = 40$

$D_8 = £20 + \dfrac{6}{10} \times 5 = £23$

The position of $D_9 = \dfrac{9n}{10} = \dfrac{9 \times 50}{10} = 45$

$D_9 = £25 + \dfrac{1}{6} \times 5 = £25.83$

The position of $D_{10} = \dfrac{10n}{10} = \dfrac{10 \times 50}{10} = 50$

$D_{10} = £25 + \dfrac{6}{6} \times 5 = £30$

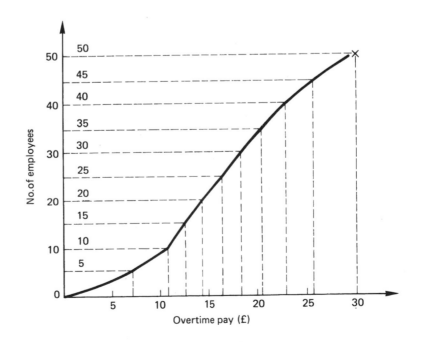

Deciles		
Position		Values (£)
D_1	5	7
D_2	10	10.71
D_3	15	12.50
D_4	20	14.29
D_5	25	16.25
D_6	30	18.33
D_7	35	20.50
D_8	40	23
D_9	45	25.83
D_{10}	50	30

The result of the calculations and the graph show the division of the distribution into ten equal parts. It is possible to say that the lowest 10% of employees earn overtime pay of £7 or less while the top 10% earn over £25.83; and whereas the lowest 20% earn less than £10.71, the top 20% earn more than £23. The 20% in the centre of the distribution (D_5 and D_6) earn between £16.25 and £20.50. These figures can be compared with national overtime rates, or rates for other companies or rates for previous years.

Example 6.20

What is the modal weight of the following sacks of potatoes:

1. 52 kilos
2. 55 kilos
3. 54 kilos
4. 55 kilos
5. 55 kilos
6. 54 kilos
7. 53 kilos
8. 52 kilos

Solution 6.20

The modal weight is 55 kilos because this is the weight that occurs most frequently.

Example 6.21

What is the mode in the following distribution?

The weight of bunches of grapes	The number of bunches of this weight
$\frac{1}{2}$ kilo	6
1 kilo	20
$1\frac{1}{2}$ kilos	15
2 kilos	7
$2\frac{1}{2}$ kilos	4

Solution 6.21

The mode is 1 kilo because more bunches of grapes are of this weight than any of the other weights.

Example 6.22

What is the modal class of the following distribution?

The length of a component (cm)	Number of engines using this size
2 but less than 3	3
3 but less than 4	8
4 but less than 5	15
5 but less than 6	2

Solution 6.22

The modal class is 4 cm but less than 5 cm because this is the size of component used in more engines than any other size.

Example 6.23

What is the modal class of the following distribution?

The length of a component (cm)	Number of engines using this size
2 but less than 3	3
3 but less than 4	8
4 but less than 5	15
5 but less than 6	2
6 but less than 7	7
7 but less than 8	12
8 but less than 9	15
9 but less than 10	1

Solution 6.23

This is a bi-modal distribution with two modal classes: 4 cm but less than 5 cm and 8 cm but less than 9 cm. Both of these sizes of components are used in more engines than any other size and in an equal number of engines.

Example 6.24

Using the table in Example 6.22 use a histogram to show the value of the mode. Comment briefly on the result.

Solution 6.24

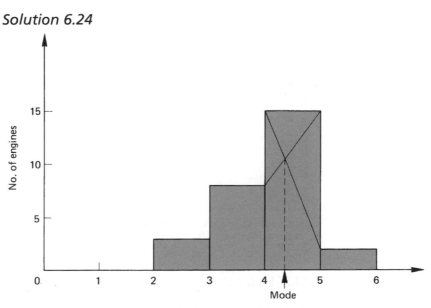

The modal class is 4 cm–5 cm and the mode is approximately 4.4 cm. This is the most frequently used size of component.

Example 6.25

A businessman buys a shoeshop and decides to keep the shop running although he does not know much about shoes. He looks at the sales ledger and discovers that against every sale the price of the shoes is noted along with the name and code number of the shoe and the size. How can the use of the mode help him in his decisions about buying stock for the shoeshop?

Solution 6.25

He will want to stock the most popular shoes in the most popular sizes and therefore he will look at the most frequently occurring shoe type and size. For example, he might find from the records that shoes have been sold in the following sizes and quantities over the last six months:

Shoe sizes	Men's	Women's
1	—	—
2	—	2
3	—	12
4	2	42
5	7	65
6	21	68
7	38	15
8	43	2
9	35	—
10	12	—
11	10	—

The modal size of shoes will be 8 for men and 6 for women. Therefore the businessman may decide to stock most of these sizes and of sizes close to the modes. The same will be true of other characteristics of the shoes, he will be guided by the mode.

Example 6.26

Find the geometric mean of 2, 5, 8, 10, 12.

Solution 6.26

$$\text{GM} = \sqrt[5]{2 \times 5 \times 8 \times 10 \times 12} = \sqrt[5]{9600}$$
$$= 6.26$$

Example 6.27

Given that $xyz = 512$, the geometric mean of xyz is:

A 64   B 8   C $\sqrt{52}$ D 104

Solution 6.27

$\text{GM} = 8 \ (\sqrt[3]{512} = 8)$

Answer: B

Example 6.28

If x is the geometric mean of 4 and 16, the arithmetic mean of three numbers 4, 16 and x is:

A 20 **B** 16 **C** 9.3 **D** 12

Solution 6.28

x is the geometric mean of 4 and 16

$$GM = \sqrt[2]{4 \times 16} = \sqrt{64} = 8$$

Therefore $x = 8$

$$\bar{x} = \frac{4 + 16 + 8}{3} = \frac{28}{3} = 9.3$$

Answer: C

Example 6.29

A student achieves marks of 80, 76, 93, 82 and 96 in five subjects. Find the arithmetic mean of the marks.

Solution 6.29

85.4

Example 6.30

A jeweller stocks a range of gold bracelets; they are priced as follows: £24, £86, £94, £102, £110, £112, £115, £245. Find the mean price of these bracelets and comment briefly on how far the result represents the prices of the ranges.

Solution 6.30

(to calculation only)

£111

Example 6.31

The mean annual salary paid to all employees in a company is £20 000. The mean annual salaries paid to male and female employees of the company are £20 800 and £16 800, respectively. Calculate the percentages of males and females employed by the company.

Solution 6.31

80% men and 20% women

Example 6.32

The profits of three companies are as shown:

Year	Company A (£)	Company B (£)	Company C (£)
1988	100 000	30 000	150 000
1989	90 000	45 000	20 000
1990	77 000	70 000	102 000
1991	71 000	102 000	48 000
1992	62 000	143 000	80 000

Calculate the annual mean profit for these three companies. Comment on the results and discuss the advice that would be reasonable to give to someone thinking of buying these companies.

Solution 6.32

(to calculation only)

Company A £80 000, Company B £78 000, Company C £80 000

Example 6.33

The weight of a component part on a production line is measured at intervals. It is found to vary as follows:

Item	Weight (g)	Item	Weight (g)
1	4.20	6	4.15
2	4.09	7	4.16
3	4.14	8	4.13
4	4.16	9	4.12
5	4.19	10	4.17

Calculate the mean weight of the components and comment briefly on the result.

Solution 6.33

(to calculation only)

4.15 g

Example 6.34

Calculate the average weekly wage earned by the following group of people. Comment briefly on the result.

People	Weekly wage (£)
A	120
B	170
C	180
D	204
E	296

Solution 6.34

(to calculation only)

£194

Example 6.35

If the mean weekly wage of workers in one factory is £360 and in another factory is £440, is the mean wage of the two factories combined £800?

Solution 6.35

It depends on the number of workers in the factories. The mean would be £800 only if there were the same number of workers in each factory.

Example 6.36

The monthly commission earned by 500 employees in an insurance company is summarised in the table below.

(i) Calculate the arithmetic mean monthly commission of these employees,

(ii) what does the result illustrate about the distribution of these wages?

Monthly commission (£)	Number of employees
Less than 500	10
500 but less than 600	15
600 but less than 700	25
700 but less than 800	5
800 but less than 900	35
900 but less than 1000	98
1000 but less than 1100	106
1100 but less than 1200	100
1200 but less than 1300	88
1300 but less than 1400	10
1400 but less than 1500	5
1500 and above	3

Solution 6.36

(to calculation only)

£1036.60

Example 6.37

Calculate the arithmetic mean of the following table of weekly overtime pay. Comment briefly on the result.

Monthly overtime (£)	Number of employees
0 but less than 10	40
10 but less than 20	148
20 but less than 30	62
30 but less than 40	30
40 but less than 50	20

Solution 6.37

(to calculation only)

£19.73

Example 6.38

The marks of nine students in an examination were as follows: 36, 44, 50, 52, 53, 62, 65, 66, 91

(i)   Find the median mark,
(ii)   comment briefly on the result.

Solution 6.38

(to calculation only)

53

Example 6.39

The marks of a student in his GCE 'O' Level examinations were as follows: 41, 49, 52, 58, 60, 86.

(i)   Find the median mark,
(ii)   comment briefly on the result.

Solution 6.39

(to calculation only)

55

Example 6.40

The table below shows the age distribution of heads of families in a country in 1984.

(i)   Find the median age,
(ii)   why is the median a more suitable average than the mean in this case?

Age of head of family (years)	Number (millions)
Under 25	
25 but less than 30	2.22
30 but less than 35	4.05
35 but less than 40	5.08
40 but less than 45	10.45
45 but less than 55	9.47
55 but less than 65	6.63
65 and over	5.82

Solution 6.40

(to calculation only)

45.1 years

Example 6.41

Using the table of data in Example 6.40 find the median graphically. Comment briefly on differences between this result and the one obtained for the previous question.

Solution 6.41

(to calculation only)

Approx. 45 years

Example 6.42

The table shows the percentage distribution of the total income of males in a business section of a capital city in 1995.

(i) Find the median income for the data and
(ii) comment on the result.

Income (£)	%
Under 10 000	17.2
10 000 but less than 20 000	11.7
20 000 but less than 30 000	12.1
30 000 but less than 40 000	14.8
40 000 but less than 50 000	15.9
50 000 but less than 60 000	11.9
60 000 but less than 100 000	12.7
100 000 and above	3.6

Solution 6.42

(to calculation only)

£36 080

Example 6.43

The marks of a student in nine examinations were as follows:
36, 44, 50, 52, 53, 62, 65, 66, 91

The median mark is 53, find the lower and upper quartile marks and comment briefly on the results.

Solution 6.43

(to calculation only)

47, 65.5

Example 6.44

A company employing 100 people on a part-time basis makes the weekly payments shown in the table below. Calculate the median pay, lower and upper quartile pay and comment on the results.

Weekly pay (£)	Number of people
Less than 100	10
100 but less than 120	12
120 but less than 140	30
140 but less than 160	25
160 but less than 180	10
180 but less than 200	8
200 and above	5

Solution 6.44

(to calculation only)

138.66, 122, 158.4

Example 6.45

Using the table in Example 6.44 find the median, lower and upper quartiles graphically. Comment briefly on differences between this result and the one obtained for the previous question.

Solution 6.45

(to calculation only)

Approx. 139, 122, 158

Example 6.46

What is the modal weight of the following group of men:

Men	Weight (lb)	Men	Weight (lb)
1	160	6	164
2	162	7	166
3	169	8	162
4	163	9	160
5	162	10	169

Solution 6.46

162 lb

Example 6.47

What is the mode of the following distribution?

The weight of sacks of potatoes (kilos)	Number of sacks
50	2
51	6
52	9
53	11
54	22
55	28
56	15
57	14
58	7
59	3

Solution 6.47

55 kilos

Example 6.48

What is the modal class of the following distribution?

The length of a component (cm)	Number of engines
15.2 but less than 15.22	102
15.22 but less than 15.32	108
15.32 but less than 15.42	143
15.42 but less than 15.52	424
15.52 but less than 15.62	468
15.62 but less than 15.72	444

Solution 6.48

15.52–15.62 cm

6.5 Questions and exercises

Question 6.1

Using the table in Example 6.48 draw a histogram and show the value of the mode. Comment briefly on the result.

Question 6.2

A company takes over a sweet factory. This is a new line of production for the company. How could the mode help the company in making decisions about the future production of the factory?

Question 6.3

Analyse the differences between the various measures of central tendency and discuss the circumstances in which each would be used.

Question 6.4

One hundred people estimated the number of sweets contained in a bottle, and the following table shows the distribution of their estimates.

Estimate	32	33	34	35	36	37	38	39	40
Frequency	2	6	4	21	32	15	10	7	3

Calculate the mean value of the estimated number of sweets in the bottle. (AEB)

Question 6.5

The mean value of 24 observations is 5.0 and the mean value of 18 of these observations is 4.2. Calculate the mean value of the remaining 6 observations.

(AEB)

Question 6.6

The mean of the ten numbers 5, 6, 7, 8, . . ., 14 is 9.5. Write down the mean of

(a)   the ten numbers 5.7, 6.7, 7.7, 8.7, . . ., 14.7,
(b)   the ten numbers 10.1, 12.1, 14.1, 16.1, . . ., 28.1.   (AEB)

Question 6.7

A set of numbers is changed by first multiplying by 10 and then adding 4 to each number. If the mean of the new set of numbers is 24, find the mean of the original set of numbers.   (AEB)

Question 6.8

Which of the following frequency distributions have the same mean value?

I	Variable	10	11	12	13	14
	Frequency	25	27	29	27	25

II	Variable	8	10	12	14	16
	Frequency	25	27	29	27	25

III	Variable	10	11	12	13	14
	Frequency	250	270	290	270	250

A   **I** and **II** only
B   **I** and **III** only
C   **II** and **III** only
D   **I**, **II** and **III**
Estimate the median yield.   (AEB)

Question 6.9

Name a statistical average that can easily be estimated from a cumulative frequency curve. (AEB)

Question 6.10

The median number of inhabitants per house in a certain street is found to be $3\frac{1}{2}$. Which of the following statements must be true?

I   There is an even number of houses in the street
II   There are as many houses with 3 or less inhabitants as there are with 4 or more

A   **I** only
B   **II** only
C   Both **I** and **II**
D   Neither **I** nor **II** (AEB)

Question 6.11

The table below shows the number of telephone calls per day received by a certain company over the 250 working days of a given year. Determine the median of this distribution.

No. of calls per day	30	31	32	33	34	35	36 and over
No. of days	82	67	34	31	19	12	5

(AEB)

Question 6.12

For the frequency distribution shown below the vertical at A divides the total area into two equal parts. State the usual name given to the value of the variable at A. (AEB)

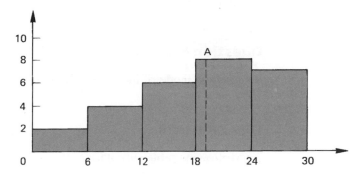

Question 6.13

From a large set of measurements the following results were obtained:

1st decile	6th decile	9th decile
143	189	203

Which of the following statements about the data must be true?
- **I**   10% of the measurements are greater than 203
- **II**   half of the measurements lie between 143 and 189

A **I** only
B **II** only
C Both **I** and **II**
D Neither **I** nor **II**   (AEB)

Question 6.14

The table below shows the masses of 100 men measured to the nearest kilogram.

Mass (kg)	45–54	55–64	65–74	75–84	85–94	95–104
Number of men	12	23	25	20	16	4

Estimate the modal mass.   (AEB)

Question 6.15

The distribution of the diameters of 200 ball bearings is shown below.

Diameter (mm)	5.90–5.94	5.95–5.99	6.00–6.04	6.05–6.09	6.10–6.14
No. of ball bearings	12	47	82	38	21

Estimate the value of the 80th percentile.   (AEB)

Question 6.16

The number of fish caught by each of twenty fishermen on a particular day was as follows: 6, 0, 1, 0, 3, 0, 4, 5, 1, 1, 0, 0, 0, 12, 2, 2, 1, 9, 0, 1. What is the median number of fish caught by a fisherman?   (SUJB)

Question 6.17

What is the mode of the data in Example 6.11?   (SUJB)

Question 6.18

The following table summarises the results of a survey on wages.

	Annual wages of 100 women						
Wage: Over	£ 800	1000	2000	3000	4000	6 000	10 000
Up to	1000	2000	3000	4000	6000	10 000	20 000
Frequency	3	20	22	18	23	12	2

(i)   Write down the modal class of this distribution
(ii) Construct a histogram to illustrate the distribution.   (WJEC)

Question 6.19

Draw, on graph paper, a cumulative frequency polygon to illustrate the wages data in Question 6.18.
Deduce from your diagram

(i)   the median wage
(ii)   the 80th percentile wage
(iii) the proportion of the women earning more than £7500 per annum.

Calculate an estimate of the arithmetic mean of the wages of the 100 women.
What proportion of the women earn more than the arithmetic mean?
Would you consider the arithmetic mean or the median as being the more apt as a measure of the 'average wage'? Give reasons for your answer.   (WJEC)

Question 6.20

Give an example of circumstances in which the mode might be preferred to the arithmetic mean as a measure of central tendency.   (SUJB)

Question 6.21

The masses of a sample of beads, measured correct to the nearest gram, are tabulated below.

Mass (g)	4	5	6	7	8
Frequency	1	3	9	5	3

Treating mass as a continuous variable, estimate the modal mass.   (AEB)

Question 6.22

Calculate the geometric mean of 4, 16 and 27.   (AEB)

Question 6.23

The geometric mean of 4 and 9 is x. Calculate the arithmetic mean of 3, 5, 18 and x.   (AEB)

Question 6.24

The population of a city was 40 000 in 1963 and 90 000 in 1983. Use the geometric mean to estimate the population in 1973.   (AEB)

Question 6.25

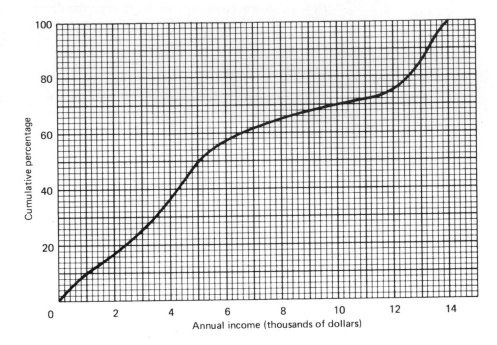

The diagram above shows a cumulative percentage distribution of annual incomes in a certain country.

(a) Using this diagram, find
   (i)   the median income;
   (ii) the interquartile range of annual incomes;
   (iii) the percentage of the population with an annual income of $10 000 or more.
(b) A politician claims that 10% of the population are below the 'poverty line'. From the above diagram, what annual income corresponds to the 'poverty line'?   (SEB)

Question 6.26

Since getting a compact disc player for her birthday, Rachel has bought nine discs. She noticed that each disc had a different playing time. Rachel made a table showing the minutes of playing time for each of her discs:

Time in minutes	76	52	78	60	65	45	78	55	67

(a) What is the range of the playing times?
(b) Calculate the mean playing time of the discs.
(c) Rachel buys four more compact discs which have a total playing time of 204 minutes. Calculate the new mean playing time of Rachel's collection.
                                                                              (SEG)

7

Summarising Data: Dispersion

Objectives

By the end of this chapter the following terms and methods of calculation should be understood:

	Date attempted	Date completed	Self-assessment
Dispersion			
Skewed distributions			
Range			
Interquartile range			
Standard deviation			
Normal curve			
Scaling			
Variance			

Summary

This chapter describes the summarising of data through the use of measures of dispersion and methods of calculating these measures and directly related statistics

7.1 Introduction

Data can be summarised and compared by *measures of dispersion* (*deviation* or *spread*). Distributions are not only clustered around a central point, but also spread out around it. *It is possible, therefore, to summarise a distribution of data by using an average and a measure of dispersion. The average provides an indication of location, the measure of dispersion provides an indication of the spread or deviation around this location.*

The frequency distributions may be symmetrical (in that the items are spread equally on either side of the average), or may be 'skewed' so that the peak of the distribution is displaced to the left ('positively skewed') or right ('negatively skewed'). In a symmetrical distribution (Fig. 7.1) the mean, median and mode are equal; in skewed distributions (Figs 7.2 and 7.3) the mode is located at the highest point while the median usually lies between the mode and the mean.

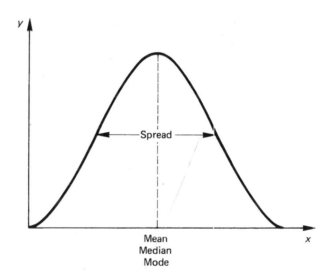

Figure 7.1 Bell-shaped (or normal) distribution

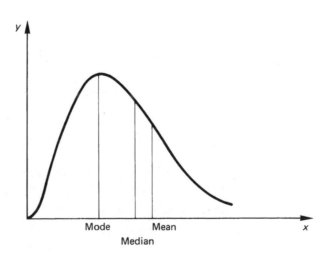

Figure 7.2 Positively skewed distribution

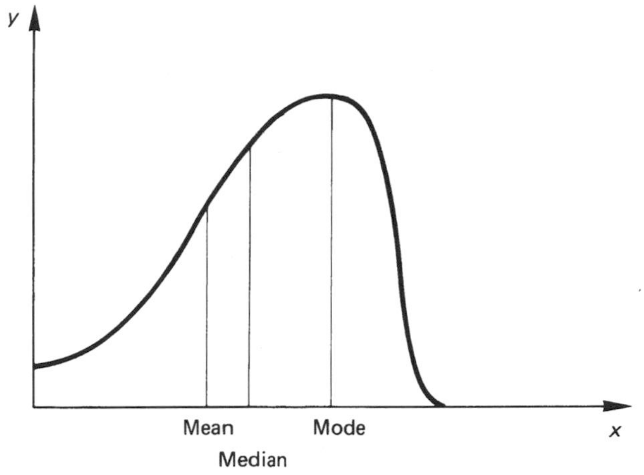

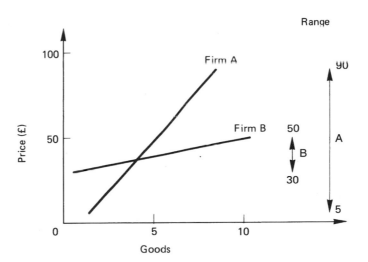

Figure 7.3 Negatively skewed distribution

7.2 Measures of dispersion

(a) Range

The highest value in a distribution minus the lowest. *For example* see Fig. 7.4:

Figure 7.4 Range

(b) Interquartile range

The difference between the upper quartile and the lower quartile ($Q_3 - Q_1$). In Table 6.11 $Q_1 = £11.61$
$Q_3 = £21.75$

The interquartile range $= £21.75 - £11.61 = £10.14$

The interquartile range of the overtime pay of these fifty employees is £10.14. This includes the central 50% of the employees or the middle range of overtime pay. Another group of employees could have an interquartile range of overtime pay of £30. This would indicate a more widely spread range of pay than the first group.

The semi-interquartile range $= \dfrac{Q_3 - Q_1}{2}$

In the example this would be $\dfrac{£21.75 - 11.61}{2} = \dfrac{£10.14}{2} = £5.07$

The interquartile range and the semi-interquartile range can be arrived at by using the ogive as in Fig. 6.2.

(c) Mean deviation

The arithmetic mean of the absolute difference of each value from the mean.
For example:

Table 7.1 The mean deviation

Value	Deviation ($\bar{x} = 9$)	
5	−4	
6	−3	
8	−1	
11	+2	Total deviations $= 18$ (ignoring the signs)
17	+8	
	−8 +10	Mean deviation $= \dfrac{18}{5} = 3.6$

In a frequency distribution, to calculate the mean deviation it is necessary to find the arithmetic mean first (Table 7.2).

Table 7.2 The mean deviation of a frequency distribution

Item	Value	Frequency	Value × frequency	Deviation of value from mean ($\bar{x} = 8$)	Deviation × frequency
1	5	2	10	3	6
2	6	3	18	2	6
3	8	5	40	0	0
4	10	4	40	2	8
5	12	1	12	4	4
		15	120		24

$$\bar{x} = \frac{120}{15} = 8 \qquad \text{Mean deviation} = \frac{24}{15} = 1.6$$

(d) Standard deviation

The dispersion or deviation of items around the arithmetic mean. It is 'standard' both because it is standardised for all values of n and because it is very useful both practically and mathematically.

Formula for calculation: σ (S or S.D.) $= \sqrt{\left(\dfrac{\Sigma(d_x)^2}{n}\right)}$

(or $\sqrt{\left(\dfrac{\Sigma(x - \bar{x})^2}{n}\right)}$ where x is the item and $\bar{x}$ is the mean)

where σ represents the standard deviation,
$\Sigma(d_x)^2$ represents the sum of squared deviations from the mean,
n is the number of items (f in a frequency distribution).

For example:

Table 7.3 The standard deviation

Family	Weekly expenditure on transport (£)	Deviation from arithmetic mean ($\bar{x} = 20$) (d_x)	Deviation squared ($d_x)^2$
1	15	−5	25
2	25	+5	25
3	26	+6	36
4	20	0	0
5	14	−6	36
			122

$$\sigma = \sqrt{\left(\frac{\Sigma(d_x)^2}{n}\right)} = \sqrt{\left(\frac{122}{5}\right)} = \sqrt{24.4} = £4.9$$

Formula for the calculation of the standard deviation of a grouped frequency deviation:

$$\sigma = \sqrt{\left(\frac{\Sigma fd_x^2}{\Sigma f}\right)} - \sqrt{\left(\frac{\Sigma fd_x}{\Sigma f}\right)^2} \times \text{class interval}$$

where f = the frequency

d_x = the deviation from the assumed mean

or

$$\sigma = \sqrt{\left(\frac{\Sigma fd^2}{N}\right) - \left(\frac{\Sigma fd}{N}\right)^2}$$

where N = the total number of cases

For example:

Table 7.4 The standard deviation of a grouped frequency distribution

Expenditure (£) (x)	Number of households (f)	Deviation of classes from class of assumed mean (d_x) (45)	Frequency × deviations from assumed mean (fd_x)	Frequency × deviation from assumed mean squared (fd_x^2)
0 and under 10	2	−4	−8	32
10 and under 20	6	−3	−18	54
20 and under 30	12	−2	−24	48
30 and under 40	15	−1	−15	15
40 and under 50	18	0	0	0
50 and under 60	20	+1	+20	20
60 and under 70	17	+2	+34	68
70 and under 80	8	+3	+24	72
80 and under 90	2	+4	+8	32
	100		−65 + 86 = + 21	341

$\Sigma f = 100$ $\quad\quad \Sigma fd_x = +21$ $\quad\quad \Sigma fd_x^2 = 341$

$\bar{x} = 45 + \dfrac{21}{100} + 10 = 45 + 2.1 = £47.10$

$$\sigma = \sqrt{\left(\frac{341}{100}\right) - \left(\frac{21}{100}\right)^2} \times 10$$

$$= \sqrt{3.41 - 0.0441} \times 10$$
$$= \sqrt{3.3659} \times 10$$
$$= 1.835 \times 10 = £18.35$$

(i) Interpretation of standard deviation

The standard deviation shows the dispersion of values around the arithmetic mean. The greater the dispersion the larger the standard deviation.

It has been calculated that with a normal curve (i.e. a bell-shaped, symmetrical distribution) it is possible to mark off the area under the curve into certain proportions. Approximately 68% of the items in the distribution will lie within one standard deviation on either side of the arithmetic mean; within two standard deviations (or 1.96 standard deviations) on either side of the mean will lie approximately 95% of the items; and within three standard deviations on either side of the mean will lie approximately 99% (in fact 99.74% or nearly all) of the items. These proportions make it possible to arrive at a fairly clear picture of a distribution if the arithmetic mean, the standard deviation and the number of items are known (see Fig. 7.5).

The further away a distribution is from the normal curve the more difficult it becomes to interpret the standard deviation accurately.

For example: with a mean of £20, a standard deviation of £5 and 500 items in the distribution, it is possible to draw the curve in Fig. 7.6.

1σ on either side of $\bar{x}$ = 68% or approx. 340 out of 500
2σ on either side of $\bar{x}$ = 95% or approx. 475 out of 500
3σ on either side of $\bar{x}$ = 99% or approx. 495 out of 500

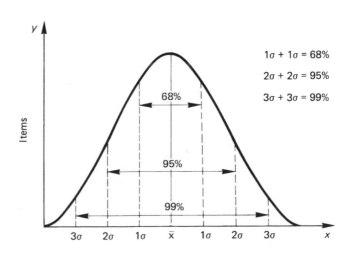

Figure 7.5 Standard deviation and the normal curve

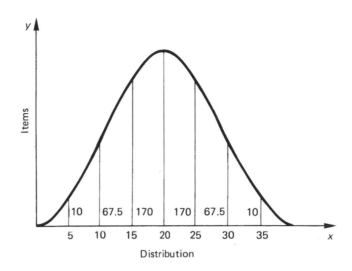

Figure 7.6 Standard deviation and a distribution

(ii) Scaling and adjusting

The standard deviation and the mean can be used to adjust or scale a set of figures.

For example: the mean and the standard deviation of a set of examination marks are 50 and 8 respectively. The marks are adjusted so that the mean and the standard deviation become 60 and 12 respectively. To find the adjusted or scaled mark corresponding to an original mark, the distance in proportions of the standard deviation is calculated.

The mark of 60 is $1\frac{1}{4}$ standard deviations from the mean on the original scale $(50 + 8 + 2)$. $1\frac{1}{4}$ standard deviations on the new scale would be $60 + 12 + 3 = 75$. An original mark of 60 would be adjusted, therefore, to a new mark of 75. This can be illustrated by drawing the normal curves for the original distribution and the adjusted distribution (see Fig. 7.7).

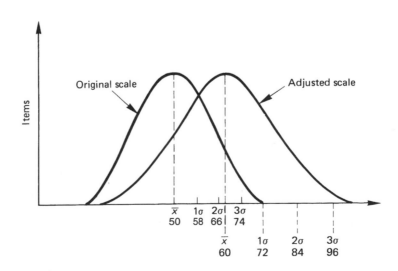

Figure 7.7 Adjusted scale

(e) Variance

This is the square of the standard deviation (σ^2). For example: The variance of the following numbers:

103, 105, 108, 110, 114 is 14.8 (see Table 7.5).

Table 7.5 The variance

Item	Deviation from mean ($\bar{x} = 108$) (d_x)	(d_x2)
103	-5	25
105	-3	9
108	0	0
110	$+2$	4
114	$+6$	36
	$-8 + 8$	74

$$\text{Variance} = \frac{74}{5} = 14.8$$

$$\sigma = \sqrt{\frac{74}{5}} = \sqrt{14.8} = 3.847$$

For example: The variance of a frequency distribution is as shown in Table 7.6.

Table 7.6 The variance of a frequency distribution

Value	Frequency	Value × frequency	d_x	fd_x	fd_x^2
9	1	9	-5	-5	25
12	3	36	-2	-6	12
14	2	28	0	0	0
16	3	48	$+2$	$+6$	12
19	1	19	$+5$	$+5$	25
	10	140			74

$$\bar{x} = \frac{140}{10} = 14$$

$$\text{Variance} = \frac{74}{10} = 7.4$$

(f) Coefficient of variation

The standard deviation divided by the mean. This is a measure of relative variability which can be used when it is desirable to compare several groups with respect to their relative homogeneity in instances where the groups have very different means. In these circumstances it might be misleading to compare the absolute magnitudes of the standard deviations and it might be more relevant and of greater interest to look at the size of the standard deviation relative to the mean.

The formula for the coefficient of variation (V) is:

$$V = \frac{\sigma}{\bar{x}}$$

If $\sigma = 5$ and $\bar{x} = 2.5$, $V = 2$

Measures of dispersion are summarised in Table 7.7.

Table 7.7 Measures of dispersion

Measures of dispersion	Description	Usually used with:	Advantages	Disadvantages
Range	Highest value minus lowest	Mode or perhaps the mean	Everyday measure, clear, does not depend on number of items	Provides limited information, can be 'distorted' by extreme items
Interquartile range and semi-interquartile range	Difference between the upper and lower quartiles	Median	Not influenced by extreme items	Provides limited information
Mean deviation	Arithmetic mean of the absolute difference of each value from the mean	Mean	Uses all the values in a distribution	Seldom used
Standard deviation	Dispersion of items around the arithmetic mean	Mean	Uses all the values in a distribution, used in sampling and in other mathematical areas	Difficult to understand, not an everyday measure
Variance	Square of the standard deviation	Mean	Uses all the values in a distribution	Difficult to understand
Coefficient of variation	Standard deviation divided by the mean	Mean	A measure of relativity for comparing distributions	Difficult to understand

7.3 Worked examples

Example 7.1

Draw examples of symmetrical distributions and compare these with skewed distributions in relation to the position of the averages.

Solution 7.1

(a) Symmetrical distributions:

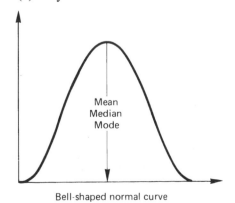

Bell-shaped normal curve

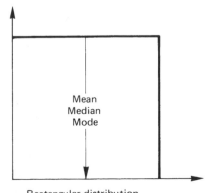

Rectangular distribution

(b)   Skewed distributions:

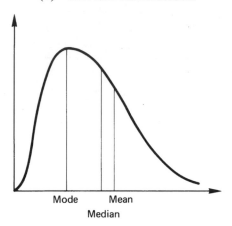

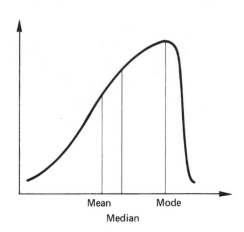

| Positively skewed distribution | Negatively skewed distribution |

In the case of the symmetrical distributions (a) the mean, median and mode are the same, that is in the centre of the distribution. In the case of the skewed distributions (b) the mean, median and mode are not the same. With a positively skewed distribution the mean is usually higher (or further along the x axis) than the median, which is higher than the mode. With a negatively skewed distribution the mean is lower (or not as far along the x axis) than the median, which is below the mode.

For example:

a symmetrical distribution:

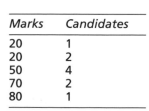

Marks	Candidates
20	1
20	2
50	4
70	2
80	1

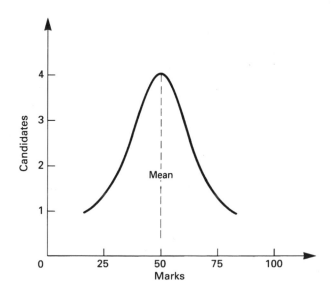

$$\bar{x} = \frac{500}{10} = 50 \text{ marks}$$

Median = 50 marks (4 candidates)

Mode = 50 marks (4 candidates)

A positively skewed distribution:

Size of components (cm)	Number of makes of cars using this size
1	25
2	17
3	14
4	4
5	2
	62

$\bar{x} = 12.4$ (cars)

Median $= 14$ (cars)

Mode $= 25$ (cars)

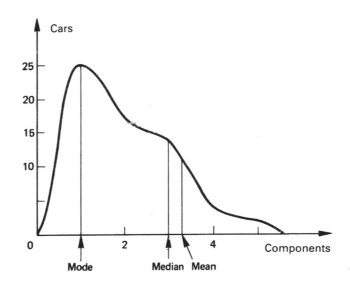

The mode is greater than the median which is greater than the mean.

If the values (number of makes of cars) in this distribution were reversed, the value of the averages would remain the same but their position would be as follows:

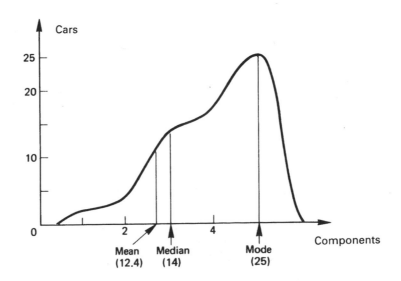

Example 7.2

Find the range of the following observations:
11, 2, 15, 3, 4, 18, 12, 14, 8, 16

Solution 7.2

The range is the highest value minus the lowest value:
$18 - 2 = 16$

Example 7.3

A shoe shop has shoes for men priced from £9 to £38. The price range of men's shoes is:

A £20   **B** £29   **C** £38   **D** £47

Solution 7.3

B (£29)   £38 − £9 = £29

Example 7.4

A sample of 45 items had a semi-interquartile range of 15 and an upper quartile of 40. The lower quartile of the sample is:

A 5   **B** 10   **C** 15   **D** 30

Solution 7.4

B (10) $Q_3 = 40$, $Q_1 = 10$, the semi-interquartile range =

$$\frac{40 - 10}{2} = 15$$

Example 7.5

Calculate the semi-interquartile range and the median of the following distribution of wages of part-time employees.
Comment briefly on the results.

Wages (£)	No. of employees
100 but less than 110	5
110 but less than 120	8
120 but less than 130	15
130 but less than 140	20
140 but less than 150	16

Solution 7.5

Wages (£)	No. of employees	Cumulative frequency
100 but less than 110	5	5
110 but less than 120	8	13
120 but less than 130	15	28
130 but less than 140	20	48
140 but less than 150	16	64

Position of $Q_1 = \dfrac{f}{4} = \dfrac{64}{4} = 16$

Position of $Q_3 = \dfrac{3f}{4} = \dfrac{3 \times 64}{4} = \dfrac{192}{4} = 48$

Position of $M = \dfrac{f}{2} = \dfrac{64}{2} = 32$

$Q_1 = £120 + \dfrac{3}{15} \times 10 = £120 + 2 = £122$

$Q_2 = £130 + \dfrac{20}{20} \times 10 = £130 + 10 = £140$

$M = £130 + \dfrac{4}{20} \times 10 = £130 + 2 = £132$

The semi-interquartile range $= Q_3 - Q_1 = \dfrac{£140 - 122}{2} = \dfrac{£18}{2} = £9$

The semi-interquartile range is £9 and the median is £132. The median divides a distribution in half and in this distribution half the employees earn more than £132 and half earn less. The relatively small interquartile range indicates a fairly high concentration of wages amongst the middle fifty per cent of employees. £18 covers this middle fifty per cent of a distribution spread over £50 (£100 to £150). The median is close to the centre of this range in a negatively skewed distribution.

Example 7.6

Calculate the mean deviation of the following observations:
2   2   4   4   6   7   7   8

Solution 7.6

The arithmetic mean $= 40 \div 8 = 5$
Deviations from the arithmetic mean $= 3 \quad 3 \quad 1 \quad 1 \quad 1 \quad 2 \quad 2 \quad 3$
Total deviations $= 16$
Mean deviation $= 16 \div 8 = 2$

Example 7.7

Calculate the mean deviation of the following distribution:

Value of the variable	2	3	4	5	6
Frequency	6	3	6	3	6

Solution 7.7

Value (x)	Frequency	x × f	Deviation of V from $\bar{x}$	Deviation × frequency
2	6	12	2	12
3	3	9	1	3
4	6	24	0	0
5	3	15	1	3
6	6	36	2	12
	24	96		30

$$\bar{x} = \frac{96}{24} = 4 \qquad MD = \frac{30}{24} = 1.25$$

Example 7.8

The marks of a student in his first eight examinations had an arithmetic mean of 40 and a mean deviation of 15. In his last two examinations, the student's marks were 20 and 60.

What is the mean deviation for all ten examinations?

A 7.5   **B** 15   **C** 16   **D** 20

Solution 7.8

$\bar{x} = 40$ for eight examinations
MD = 15 for eight examinations
Total marks for 8 examinations $= 8 \times 40 = 320$
Total marks for 10 examinations $= 320 + 80 = 400$
$\bar{x}$ for 10 examinations $= 400 \div 10 = 40$
Total deviation of marks from $\bar{x}$ for 8 examinations $= 120 \; (120 \div 8 = 15)$
Total deviation of marks from $\bar{x}$ for 10 examinations $= 120 + 20 + 20 = 160$
$$MD \text{ for 10 examinations} = \frac{160}{10} = 16$$
Answer: C

Example 7.9

The weekly wages of the part-time employees of a small manufacturing company have a mean of £120 and a standard deviation of £25. If these employees each receive a rise of £10 per week, what will be

(i)   the mean
(ii)   the standard deviation, of the new weekly wage?

Solution 7.9

The mean = £130 (£120 + £10)
The standard deviation = £25

    The standard deviation will be the same as before the wages rose because the 'spread' or deviation of wages has not changed. If previously most employees' wages fell between £70 and £170 most will now fall between £80 and £180.

Example 7.10

Company A pays its employees an average weekly wage of £300 with a standard deviation of £5, while Company B pays its employees £330 with a standard deviation of £40. Compare the pay scales of the two companies.

Solution 7.10

Company B pays its employees on average £30 more a week than Company A but its distribution of wages is much wider. In Company A most employees (approximately 95%) will receive between say £290 and £310 while in Company B the comparable spread could be between £250 and £410. It would be possible to be paid very much less in Company B than Company A or very much more. At the very extreme it is possible that a few people in Company B could be paid as little as £210 or as much as £450 while in Company A the dispersion is unlikely to be greater than between £285 and £315. These figures are all based on the assumption that the distribution of wages in both cases is spread symmetrically around the mean and approximates to the normal curve. If the distributions are skewed the examples given will be less likely.

(a) Example 7.11

The weekly expenditure on transport of a number of households is shown in the following table. Calculate the arithmetic mean expenditure and the standard deviation. Comment briefly on the results.

Weekly expenditure on transport (£)	No. of families
0 but less than 10	4
10 but less than 20	5
20 but less than 30	5
30 but less than 40	4
40 but less than 50	2
	20

Solution 7.11

Expenditure	No. of families (f)	(d_x) (25)	(fd_x)	(fd_x^2)
0 but less than 10	4	−2	−8	16
10 but less than 20	5	−1	−5	5
20 but less than 30	5	0	0	0
30 but less than 40	4	+1	+4	4
40 but less than 50	2	+2	+4	8
	20	0	−5	33

$$\bar{x} = £25 - \frac{5}{20} \times 10 = £25 - 2.5 = £22.50$$

$$\sigma = £\sqrt{\left(\frac{33}{20}\right) - \left(\frac{-5}{20}\right)^2} \times 10 = £\sqrt{1.65 - 0.0625} \times 10$$

$$= £\sqrt{1.5875} \times 10 = £1.26 \times 10$$
$$= £12.60$$

The arithmetic mean of this distribution is £22.5, which is the average expenditure of these twenty households on transport. The standard deviation is £12.60, and this means that the two standard deviations on either side of the mean include the expenditure of all the families.

Example 7.12

What is the variance of the following data?
120, 122, 125, 128, 130

Solution 7.12

Item	Deviation from assumed mean	Deviation squared
120	−5	25
122	−3	9
125	0	0
128	+3	9
130	+5	25
		68

$$\bar{x} = \frac{625}{5} = 125$$

$$\text{Variance} = \frac{68}{5} = 13.6$$

Example 7.13

Calculate the variance of the distribution below:

Value of the variable	3	4	7	9	10
Frequency	2	3	2	2	1

Solution 7.13

Value	Frequency	$V \times f$	Deviation of value from $\bar{x}$ (d_x)	fd_x	fd_x^2
3	2	6	−3	−6	18
4	3	12	−2	−6	12
7	2	14	+1	+2	2
9	2	18	+3	+6	27
10	1	10	+4	+4	16
	10	60			75

$$\bar{x} = \frac{60}{10} = 6$$

$$\text{Variance} = \frac{75}{10} = 7.5$$

Example 7.14

Nails in a box are measured and various statistical measures are calculated. The longest nail and the shortest nail are then removed and the measures recalculated. Which one of the following is necessarily unchanged?

A   arithmetic mean   **C** range
B   standard deviation   **D** median

Solution 7.14

D, the median, because all the other measures are influenced by extreme items.

Example 7.15

The monthly wages of 100 part-time employees of a company are tabulated below. Calculate

(i)   the median,
(ii)   the lower quartile,
(iii)   the upper quartile, and
(iv)   the semi-interquartile range.

Draw a graph to illustrate this data and use the graph to estimate the wages of the forty-fifth and fifty-fifth employee.

Monthly wages (£)	Employees
400–425	10
425–450	12
450–475	20
475–500	33
500–525	15
525–550	10

Solution 7.15

Monthly wages (f)	Employees (f)	Cumulative frequency
400 but less than 425	10	10
425 but less than 450	12	22
450 but less than 475	20	42
475 but less than 500	33	75
500 but less than 525	15	90
525 but less than 550	10	100

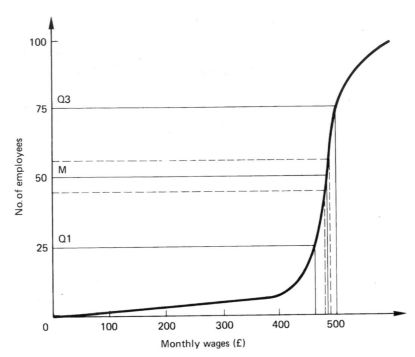

Forty-fifth employee = £475 approx.
Fifty-fifth employee = £485 approx.

$$\text{Position of } Q_1 = \frac{100}{4} = 25$$

$$\text{Position of } Q_3 = \frac{3 \times 100}{4} = 75$$

$$\text{Position of } M = \frac{100}{2} = 50$$

$$Q_1 = £450 + \frac{3}{20} \times 25 = £450 + 3.75 = £453.75$$

$$Q_3 = £475 + \frac{33}{33} \times 25 = £475 + 25 = £500$$

$$M = £475 + \frac{8}{33} \times 25 = £475 + 6.06 = £481.06$$

$$\text{The semi-interquartile range} = \frac{Q_3 - Q_1}{2} =$$

$$£\frac{500 - 453.75}{2} = £\frac{46.25}{2} = £23.13$$

Example 7.16

The following table shows the results of information collected by a company selling consumer products directly to retailers.

Number of orders taken in a month	Number of salesmen
0 and under 10	1
10 and under 20	4
20 and under 30	6
30 and under 40	5
40 and under 50	4

Calculate the range, the mean, the standard deviation and the coefficient of variation. Comment briefly on how far these measures help to interpret the information the company has collected.

Solution 7.16

No. of orders	No. of salesmen (f)	(d_x) (25)	(fd_x)	(fd_x^2)
0 and under 10	1	−2	−2	4
10 and under 20	4	−1	−4	4
20 and under 30	6	0	0	0
30 and under 40	5	+1	+5	5
40 and under 50	4	+2	+8	16
	20		−6 +13	29
			$\Sigma fd_x = +7$	

$$\bar{x} = 25 + \frac{7}{20} \times 10 = 25 + 3.5 = 28.5$$

$$\sigma = \sqrt{\frac{29}{20} - \left(\frac{7}{20}\right)^2} \times 10 = \sqrt{1.45 - 0.12} \times 10 = \sqrt{1.33} \times 10$$

$$= 1.153 \times 10 = 11.53$$

Coefficient of variation $= \dfrac{\sigma}{\bar{x}} = \dfrac{11.53}{28.5} = 0.4$

Range $= 50 - 0 = 50$

The mean indicates the location of the central value of the distribution within the range. There is a range of from 0 to 50 orders taken by any one salesman in a month, the average number being 28.5. The performance of the salesmen can be compared with this average. Most of the salesmen fall within two standard deviations of the arithmetic mean in the number of orders they have taken (5 to 50 orders) and this can be compared with the results of other months and other companies. The coefficient of variation can be compared also with other months to see if the performance of the salesmen changes to any extent.

Example 7.17

Which of the following distributions can be described as negatively skewed?

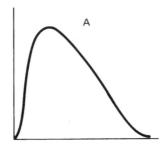 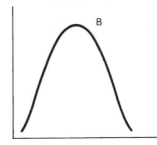 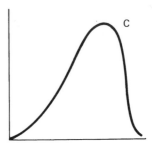

Solution 7.17

C

Example 7.18

Find the range of the following observations:
10, 5, 8, 7, 16, 20, 4, 15, 9, 14

Solution 7.18

16

Example 7.19

A sample of 25 items has a semi-interquartile range of 10 and an upper quartile of 30. The lower quartile is:
A 10　　　**B** 15　　　**C** 25　　　**D** 30

Solution 7.19

A

Example 7.20

Calculate the semi-interquartile range and the median of the following distribution of overtime pay. Comment briefly on the result.

Overtime pay (£)	Number of employees
100 but less than 105	2
105 but less than 110	3
110 but less than 115	12
115 but less than 120	8
120 but less than 125	5

Solution 7.20

(to calculation only)

M = £114.17, Semi-interquartile range = £2.53

Example 7.21

Calculate the mean deviation of the following observations:

2, 2, 2, 4, 4, 6, 6, 6

Solution 7.21

Mean = 4, MD = 1.5

Example 7.22

Calculate the mean deviation of the following distribution:

Value of variable	1	3	5	7	9
Frequency	3	4	6	4	3

Solution 7.22

Mean = 5, MD = 2

Example 7.23

Calculate the standard deviation of the following distribution:

Value of variable	1	3	5	7	9
Frequency	3	4	6	4	3

Solution 7.23

Standard deviation = 2.53

Example 7.24

The weekly wages of the part-time employees of a small manufacturing company have a mean of £60 and a standard deviation of £10. If these employees each receive a rise of £10 per week, what will be

(i)   the mean,
(ii)   the standard deviation, of the new weekly wage?

Solution 7.24

(to calculation only)

Mean = £70, Standard deviation = £10

Example 7.25

The mean and the standard deviation of a set of examination marks are 50 and 10 respectively. The marks are adjusted so that the mean and the standard deviation become 60 and 12 respectively. Find the adjusted mark corresponding to an original mark of 40.

Solution 7.25

Example 7.26

Calculate the mean and the standard deviation of the following grouped frequency distribution.

Overtime pay (£)	Number of employees
100 but less than 110	2
110 but less than 120	5
120 but less than 130	10
130 but less than 140	4
140 but less than 150	1

Solution 7.26

Mean = £123.60, Standard deviation = £9.65

Example 7.27

What is the variance of the following numbers?
101, 103, 105, 108, 111

Solution 7.27

12.64

Example 7.28

Calculate the variance of the following distribution:

Value	10	11	15	20	24
Frequency	1	2	4	2	2

Solution 7.28

Mean = 16.36, $V = 22.7$

7.4 Questions and exercises

Question 7.1

For the type of distribution shown above it is necessarily true that

    I   the mean is equal to the median

    II   the standard deviation is equal to the mean deviation

A   **I** only

B   **II** only

C   Both **I** and **II**

D   Neither **I** nor **II**   (AEB)

Question 7.2

Sketch a frequency distribution for which the median is greater than the mode.

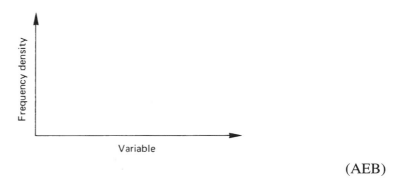

(AEB)

Question 7.3

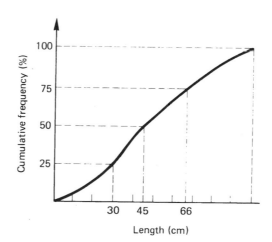

The above cumulative frequency curve is obtained from a set of lengths. The semi-interquartile range is

A   15 cm

B   18 cm

C   21 cm

D   36 cm   (AEB)

Question 7.4

A group of six observations has an arithmetic mean of 4.5 and a mean deviation of 1.4. When two further observations are taken the arithmetic mean and the mean deviation remain the same as before. Find the values of the two further observations.   (AEB)

Question 7.5

Calculate the mean deviation of the following numbers:

| 5 | 6 | 7 | 8 | 9 | 12 | (AEB) |

Question 7.6

The mean and standard deviation of a set of raw examination marks are 45 and 10 respectively. The marks are scaled so that the mean and standard deviation of the scaled marks are 50 and 16 respectively. Calculate the raw mark corresponding to a scaled mark of 66. (AEB)

Question 7.7

Which of the following measures of dispersion of the values in a large sample would be unaffected by doubling the largest value – the range, the semi-interquartile range or the standard deviation? (AEB)

Question 7.8

A large number of apples are all weighed individually. The heaviest and the lightest apples are removed, and replaced by an even heavier apple and an even lighter apple respectively. Name

(a) a measure of dispersion which will remain unchanged,
(b) a measure of dispersion which will change. (AEB)

Question 7.9

Five samples of a chemical product showed the following percentages of a given impurity 1.22, 0.96, 1.14, 1.20, 1.03. Calculate their standard deviation. (AEB)

Question 7.10

The three numbers x, y and 20 are such that their mean is 20 and the mean deviation is 6. If y is greater than x what is the value of x? (AEB)

Question 7.11

A set of raw marks is transformed by adjusting the mean and the standard deviation to new values. If raw marks of 40 and 44 become scaled marks of 50 and 56 respectively, the value of the ratio

$$\frac{\text{standard deviation of the raw marks}}{\text{standard deviation of the scaled marks}} \text{ is}$$

A $\frac{2}{3}$
B   1
C $1\frac{1}{2}$
D $2\frac{1}{4}$ (AEB)

Question 7.12

Calculate the variance of the numbers 5, 9, 10, 12, 14. Hence, or otherwise, write down the variance of

(a) 25, 45, 50, 60, 70
(b) 40, 60, 65, 75, 85. (AEB)

Question 7.13

Calculate the variance of the following numbers:
103, 105, 108, 111, 113 (AEB)

Question 7.14

Calculate the variance of the distribution shown:

Value of variable	9	12	14	16	19
Frequency	1	3	2	3	1

(AEB)

Question 7.15

Calculate the variance of the following numbers:
7, 11, 13, 19, 16, 4 (SUJB)

Question 7.16

The largest of a number of observations is replaced by an even larger observation. Name a measure of dispersion which would be

(i) affected,
(ii) unaffected. (AEB)

Question 7.17

Construct a frequency table of the number of letters per word for the following quotation of thirty words.

 'In the case of tied marks, the convention of giving the arithmetic mean mark to each equal item will be used. The correction for tied marks will not be required.'

Illustrate this frequency table graphically. Use your table to find, for the number of letters per word,

(i) the arithmetic mean,
(ii) the standard deviation, correct to three significant figures,
(iii) the median,
(iv) the upper and lower quartiles,
(v) the mean deviation from the median. (AEB)

Question 7.18

Which of the following represents a negatively skewed distribution?

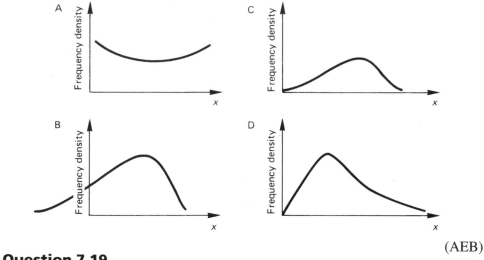

(AEB)

Question 7.19

Some of the following numerical measures can take both positive and negative values, while others are always non-negative:
arithmetic mean, coefficient of skewness, range, mode, standard deviation, variance.
Write down *three* which can take both positive and negative values. (SUJB)

Question 7.20

One hundred seeds of the same variety of flower were sown on the same day. Six months later, the heights of the surviving eighty plants were measured accurately. The data obtained are given below:

Height (cm)	Number of plants
Less than 4.20	0
Less than 4.40	6
Less than 4.50	14
Less than 4.60	28
Less than 4.65	39
Less than 4.70	52
Less than 4.80	69
Less than 5.00	80

(i) Using 2 cm to represent 0.1 cm of height and 2 cm to represent 10 plants, draw a cumulative frequency curve of the data. Use your graph to find, for the height of the plants,
(a) the median, (b) the lower quartile, (c) the upper quartile, (d) the semi-interquartile range.

(ii) Use your graph to estimate the number of plants of height 4.75 cm or more which you would expect to obtain six months after sowing 4000 seeds of the same type under the same conditions as before.

(iii) Using 2 cm to represent 0.1 cm of height and 2 cm to represent 50 plants per cm, illustrate the distribution of heights by a histogram.

Hence or otherwise estimate the modal height. (AEB)

Question 7.21

One hundred children are given a Mathematics test which is marked out of 20. The results obtained are shown below.

Marks	Number of children
9	1
10	1
11	3
12	5
13	8
14	13
15	19
16	24
17	14
18	10
19	2

(a) For this distribution calculate
   (i)   the mode,
   (ii) the median.
(b) Show that the mean mark scored is 15.23. Explain why the mean, mode and median are not equal.
(c) Calculate the lower quartile, upper quartile and semi-interquartile range for this distribution.

The standard deviation of the mathematics scores was 1.41. The same children were then given a History test which was marked out of 50. The mean score in History was 32.71 with a standard deviation of 3.21.
David scored 16 in Mathematics and 32 in History.

(d) Convert both these scores to a scale which has a mean of 100 and a standard deviation of 15.
(c) State the subject in which David produced his better performance.   (AEB)

Question 7.22

A physiotherapist records the time (to the nearest minute) spent at each session with each of her patients over a period of several weeks. The following grouped frequency distributions summarise the data for two of her patients.

Time (minutes)	Number of sessions	
	Patient A	Patient B
5– 9	3	1
10–14	8	5
15–19	21	f
20–24	14	25
25–29	10	7
30–34	3	4
35–39	1	0

(a) Calculate the mean and the standard deviation of the times spent with patient A.

(b)   Unfortunately the physiotherapist cannot remember how many sessions of length 15–19 minutes she spent with patient *B*. She does, however, remember that the mean time spent with this patient was 21 minutes. Show that the frequency she cannot remember, denoted by *f* in the table, was 13.

(c)   The physiotherapist found that the mean time spent with a third patient during 50 sessions was 20 minutes. Calculate the overall mean time spent with these three patients.   (AEB)

Question 7.23

A farmer records the number of eggs he collects from his hens over a 150 day period. The frequency distribution of the eggs collected is shown below.

Number of eggs:	15	16	17	18	19	20	21	22	23	24	25
Number of days:	1	2	4	6	9	13	18	22	35	30	10

What is the modal number of eggs collected per day? Calculate

(a)   the median number of eggs collected per day,
(b)   the mean and standard deviation of the number of eggs collected per day.

Draw a line diagram to illustrate the data given in the table. Comment on the shape of your diagram.   (AEB)

Question 7.24

(i)   In a certain factory, the mean and the standard deviation of the wages during the first week of June 1980 were £80 and £5 respectively. Given that the basic wage was £65 per week and the fixed rate of overtime was £2 per hour, calculate the mean and the standard deviation of the number of hours overtime worked by the employees.

(ii)   Under a wage claim submitted by the Union, the mean and the standard deviation of the wages would have become £90 and £6 respectively. Calculate the basic wage and the overtime rate claimed by the Union.

(iii) The employers offered a basic wage of £69 and an overtime rate of £2.80 per hour. Calculate the mean and the standard deviation of the wages under the employers' proposal.

(iv)   Compare the total wage bills under the two schemes.

(v)   State which employees, if any, would prefer the employers' scheme.

(vi)   Suggest a possible reason why the employers preferred their scheme to that proposed by the Union.

(vii) The following week, 28 employees worked 8 hours overtime, 19 employees worked 9 hours overtime while the remaining 3 employees worked 10 hours overtime. Calculate the mean and the standard deviation of the number of hours overtime for that week.   (AEB)

Question 7.25

The following table shows the length of time spent by a motor engineer in repairing faults on motor vehicles.

Time (minutes)	Number of repairs
0–	21
30–	45
60–	29
90–	12
120–	6
150–	4
180–	2
210–240	1

(a)   Using 2 cm to represent 30 minutes and 2 cm to represent 10 repairs, plot the cumulative frequency curve corresponding to the above distribution.

(b)   Use your graph to determine the median, lower quartile, upper quartile and semi-interquartile range.

Estimates of the mode, mean and standard deviation for this distribution are 47.4, 65.5 and 40.3 respectively.

(c)   By considering the relative magnitude of the median, mean and mode, comment on the skewness of the distribution.

A coefficient of skewness can be estimated using

$$\text{Coefficient of Skewness} = \frac{3(\text{Mean} - \text{Median})}{\text{Standard Deviation}}$$

(d)   Evaluate this coefficient for this distribution   (AEB)

Question 7.26

(a)   Discuss what is meant by an *average* with respect to a statistical distribution.
Give *four* examples of different ways of determining an average and how they are calculated. Give examples of where each might be appropriate.

(b)   Discuss what is meant by a *measure of dispersion* of a distribution.
Give *two* examples of different ways of determining a measure of dispersion that relate to two different averages and how they are calculated. Give examples of where each might be appropriate.   (ICSA)

Statistical Decisions

8

Objectives

By the end of this chapter the following terms and methods of calculation should be understood:

	Date attempted	Date completed	Self-assessment
Estimation			
Probability			
Statistical event			
Tree diagram			
Normal curve			
Standard normal distribution			
Sampling distribution of the mean			
Standard error			
Sample accuracy			
Significance tests			
Confidence limits			

Summary

This chapter describes aspects of statistical decisions and methods of calculating probability, the standard normal deviation, standard error, sample accuracy and significance tests.

8.1 Introduction

It can be argued that most decisions are made on a qualitative rather than a quantitative basis. Statistics can support decisions, provide evidence and narrow the area of disagreement.

For example: in buying a car, the number of people to be carried in the car and the maximum price that can be afforded are both pieces of data which can reduce discussion to cars of a certain seating capacity within a particular price range.

Used in this process are methods and techniques such as statistical estimation and the theory of probability.

8.2 Estimation

This is concerned with finding a statistical measure of a population from the corresponding statistic of the sample.

For example: whether the arithmetic mean of a sample is a good estimate of the arithmetic mean of the population.

8.3 Probability

The probability of an event is the proportion of times the event happens out of a large number of trials.

For example: the probability of tossing a head when throwing a coin would be 1 in 2 or $\frac{1}{2}$ or 0.5 or 50%.

(a) Event

An event is an occurrence. Tossing a head is an event. A failure is also an event, so that not tossing a head is an event.

(b) Empirical definition of probability

This is based on experimental data. If a coin is tossed ten times out of which there are seven heads, the empirical probability is $\frac{7}{10}$ or 0.7. As the number of tosses increases, the ratio between heads and tails will become more stable or approach a limit. This limit coincides with the value derived from the 'classical' definition of probability.

(c) Classical definition of probability

$$\text{Probability} = \frac{\text{The number of ways the event can happen}}{\text{The total number of outcomes to the experiment}}$$

(d) Sample space

This is the set of possible outcomes to an experiment.

For example: Rolling a die: sample space, S = (1, 2, 3, 4, 5, 6)
                        Tossing a coin: sample space, S = H, T

A coin is tossed twice and the sequence of heads and tails observed: S = HH, HT, TH, TT

(e)   Measuring probability

The most useful measure involves relating how often an event *will normally occur* to how often it *could* occur – and expressing this relationship as a fraction. If a coin is tossed 1000 times then normally 500 heads will be obtained. So the probability of tossing a head is measured as $\frac{500}{1000} = \frac{1}{2}$.

In the case of a pack of cards, the ace of spades will be drawn normally once in 52 draws, so the probability of drawing the ace of spades is $\frac{1}{52}$.

When an event is absolutely certain to happen the probability of its happening is 1. When an event can never happen the probability of it happening is 0. All probabilities therefore have a value between 0 and 1 (see Fig. 8.1). This is true only when each outcome is equally likely.

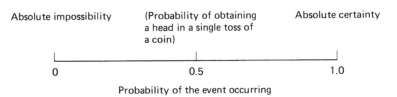

Figure 8.1 Probability

For example: a die is rolled; what is the probability of an even score?
The sample space, S = 1, 2, 3, 4, 5, 6 (the sample space is the total number of possible outcomes). The way the event can happen (the number of even scores): 2, 4, 6 (or three ways).

$$P = \frac{3}{6} = \frac{1}{2}$$

For example: a bag contains 5 blue balls, 3 red balls and 2 black balls. A ball is drawn at random from the bag. The problem is to calculate the probability that it will be (a) blue, (b) red or (c) not black.

Answer: (a) P(blue) $= \dfrac{5}{10} = 0.5$

(b) P(red) $= \dfrac{3}{10} = 0.3$

(c) P(black) $= \dfrac{2}{10} = 0.2$

P(not black) $= 1 - 0.2 = 0.8$

The probability that the ball will be blue is 0.5 (they constitute half the balls in the bag), that it will be red is 0.3 and that it will not be black is 0.8 (the total number of balls minus the number of black balls/the other two probabilities added together).

(f)   Mutually exclusive events

(or complementary events)

Two events are said to be mutually exclusive if the occurrence of one of them excludes the occurrence of the other, i.e. only one can happen.

For example: if a coin is tossed and a head appears uppermost, the tail cannot appear uppermost.

If three events are mutually exclusive then the probability of any one event occurring is the sum of the individual probabilities. If A, B and C represent the three events and P the probability of occurrence, then P(A or B or C) $= P$(A) $+ P$(B) $+ P$(C).

For example: a bag contains 4 red marbles, 2 white marbles and 4 blue marbles. What is the probability of (i) drawing a red marble, (ii) not drawing a red marble?

(i) $$P = \frac{\text{number of red marbles}}{\text{total number of marbles}} = \frac{4}{10} = \frac{2}{5}$$

(ii) $$P = \frac{\text{number of blue and white marbles}}{\text{total number of marbles}} = \frac{6}{10} = \frac{3}{5}$$

(The probability of not drawing a red marble is the complement of the probability of drawing red marbles.) With mutually exclusive events, the cases must equal 1 that is, $\frac{2}{5} + \frac{3}{5} = 1$.

(g) Independent events

Two or more events are said to be independent if the occurrence or non-occurrence of one of them in no way affects the occurrence or non-occurrence of the others.

For example: if A and B represent the result 'heads' in two successive tosses of a coin, then the events are independent, since the second toss cannot be influenced by what happens before.

When two events, A and B, are independent, the probability that they will both occur is given by: P(A and B) $= P$(A) $\times P$(B)
The answer is the product of the individual probabilities, no matter how many of them there may be.

For example: if the probability that three successive tosses of a biased coin will produce three heads is $\frac{1}{64}$, the probability that one toss of the same coin will produce heads is $\frac{1}{4}(\frac{1}{4} \times \frac{1}{4} \times \frac{1}{4} = \frac{1}{64})$.

(h) Conditional events

(or combined events)

Two or more events are said to be conditional when the probability that event B takes place is subject to the proviso that A has taken place, and so on. This is usually written P_A(B). P_B(A) would be the other way around, the assumption being that B had taken place first.

The probability that one of these events will occur is given by:
P(A or B) $= P$(A) $+ P$(B) $- P$(A $\times$ B).
The reason for subtracting P(A $\times$ B) is because A and B are not necessarily mutually exclusive, and therefore both events might occur.

For example: the probability of a firm failing through shortage of capital is 0.6 and the probability of failing through shortage of orders is 0.5.
$P(A \text{ or } B) = 0.6 + 0.5 - 0.3 = 0.8$

(i) Tree diagrams

These are used to reduce the need to produce a complete sample space for complicated combinations.

For example: What is the probability of drawing two aces from a pack of 52 cards (replacing the first card before drawing the second).
The probability of the first card drawn being an ace is $\frac{1}{13}$ ($\frac{4}{52} = \frac{1}{13}$) (see Fig. 8.2).

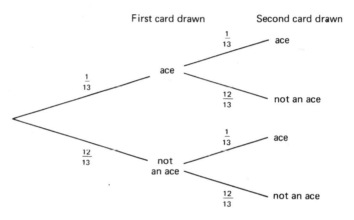

Figure 8.2 Tree diagram (i)

The probability of not drawing an ace is $\frac{12}{13}$. The replacement of the first card means that the probabilities remain the same for the second draw. If this experiment was repeated a great number of times $\frac{1}{13}$ of the experiments would produce an ace on the first draw. Out of these experiments, $\frac{1}{13}$ would produce a second one. In other words $\frac{1}{13}$ of $\frac{1}{13}$ of the experiments would be expected to produce two aces.

$$P(\text{the probability of drawing two aces}) = \frac{1}{13} \times \frac{1}{13} = \frac{1}{169}$$

For example: A bag contains 4 red balls and 5 blue balls. A second bag contains 2 red balls and 5 blue balls. If a ball is taken at random from each bag, find the probability that both balls are red.

The probability that both balls are red $= \dfrac{4}{9} \times \dfrac{2}{7} = \dfrac{8}{63}$ (see Fig. 8.3).

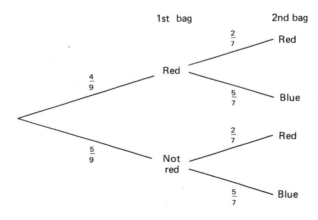

Figure 8.3 Tree diagram (ii)

8.4 The normal curve

The normal curve is a bell-shaped symmetrical distribution whose shape depends on the values of the mean and the standard deviation. Typical distributions include those in sampling theory (the sampling distribution of the mean), in intelligence tests, examination results and in biological data (height and weight for example).

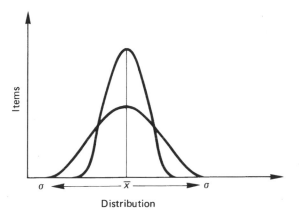

Figure 8.4 Normal curve

A normal curve may be very tall or very flat as shown in Fig. 8.4: on both these curves the arithmetic mean is shown in the centre, but the distributions around the mean are different. As has been seen already in Chapter 7, the areas under any normal curve can be calculated (see Table 8.1 and Fig. 8.5).

Table 8.1 Areas under the normal curve

68%	1σ on either side of the mean
95%	2σ on either side of the mean
99%	2.58σ on either side of the mean
99.74%	3σ on either side of the mean

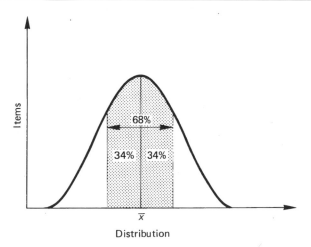

Figure 8.5 Areas under the normal curve

(a) The standard normal distribution

This is a way of stating an actual value in terms of its standard deviation from the mean in units of the standard deviation. This value is called a z value.

$$z = \frac{\text{the value} - \text{the mean}}{\text{the standard deviation}} = \frac{x - \bar{x}}{\sigma}$$

where x = any particular value.

For example: a distribution with a mean of 400 cm and a standard deviation of 20 cm will have 400 cm at 0 and the 400 − 20 and 400 + 20 values lying at the −1σ and +1σ points (Fig. 8.6).

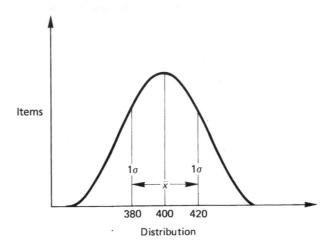

Figure 8.6 Normal curve and standard deviation

The z value of 360 cm would be

$$z = \frac{360 - 400}{20} = \frac{-40}{20} = -2$$

The 360 cm value lies two standard deviations below the mean of the distribution. This means that approximately 47.7% of the area under the curve lies between 360 cm and 400 cm (the mean). This is found from the area tables ($z = 2$, area $= 0.4772$ or 47.7%).

(b) The binomial and Poisson distributions

These are probability distributions which are similar to frequency distributions except that probabilities are used instead of frequencies.

A *binomial distribution* is concerned with two items (hence its name), such as the probability that the event occurs and the probability that the event does not occur.

The *Poisson distribution* provides a good approximation to the binomial distribution.

Both distributions are discrete, while the normal distribution is continuous, and the normal distribution can be used as an approximation to them provided a correction is made for this fact.

8.5 Sampling

If a sample is selected at random from a population, there is a good chance (or probability) that it will represent the population from which it is drawn and therefore provide evidence for decision making.

(a) The sampling distribution of the mean

If a large number of samples are taken from a population which is normally distributed, most of the sample means will be the same or very similar, although some will by chance be above or below other means. If all these means are graphed they will look like a normal curve and the average of these means will be the best estimate of the population mean.

(b) Standard error

This is the standard deviation of the sampling distribution of the mean. It provides an indication of the extent to which the sample means deviate from population means.

$$\text{Standard Error (S.E.)} = \frac{\text{Standard deviation of the sample}}{\sqrt{\text{Sample size}}}$$

$$= \frac{\sigma}{\sqrt{n}}$$

where n = sample size.

If a single sample is taken from a population, 19 times out of 20 (or 95% of the time), the sample mean will be within two standard errors of the true mean of the population.

(c) The accuracy of a sample

This depends on the sample size (not on the population size) and the variability of the characteristics measured.

For example: A sample of 100 with a standard deviation of 5 will have a standard error of:

$$\text{S.E.} = \frac{\sigma}{\sqrt{n}} = \frac{5}{\sqrt{100}} = \frac{5}{10} = 0.5$$

A sample of 400 with a standard deviation of 5 will have a standard error of:

$$\text{S.E.} = \frac{5}{\sqrt{400}} = \frac{5}{20} = 0.25$$

To halve the standard error in the original sample, the sample size has to be increased four times.

8.6 Significance tests

The aim of significance tests is to reveal whether or not the difference between a belief or hypothesis and the result of a random sample taken to test the hypothesis, could be reasonably ascribed to chance factors operating at the time the sample was selected.

Statistical significance is said to exist when the difference between an hypothesis and a random sample result cannot be explained as being due to chance alone. The 'null hypothesis' is the assumption that there is no difference between the hypothesis and the sample result.

For example: If the theory is that a group of employees receive an average wage of £130 a week, the null hypothesis (Ho) is that the population mean (μ:

pronounced 'mew') is £130. The opposite theory (Hi) is that it is not £130.

Ho : μ = £130 (the population mean is £130)

Hi : $\mu \neq$ £130 (the population mean is not £130)

A random sample is taken and the results show:

$n = 100$ $\bar{x}$ = £123 σ = £30

If the population mean is £130, then 95% of the means of all samples will fall within two standard errors of this figure. If the sample mean, £123, is not within two standard errors of £130, then the population mean is probably not £130 unless the sample mean is the one in twenty that is one-sided.

$$\text{S.E.} = \frac{\sigma}{\sqrt{n}} = \frac{30}{\sqrt{100}} = \frac{30}{10} = 3$$

The *critical values* are the population mean, plus or minus two standard errors:

$$\begin{aligned} \text{Critical values} &= £130 \pm 2 \times 3 \\ &= £130 \pm 6 \\ &= £124 \text{ to } £136 \end{aligned}$$

The sample mean (£123) does not lie within the critical values; therefore Ho (the null hypothesis) is rejected at the 5% level of significance. The difference between the assumed population mean (£130) and the sample mean (£123) can be said to be significant. There is evidence to suggest that the population mean is not £130 a week.

If the sample mean had fallen within the critical values then Ho would be accepted at the 5% level and the difference between μ and $\bar{x}$ would not be significant. It would mean that there was evidence to suggest that the population mean could be £130 a week.

At the 1% level of significance, between 99% and 100% of the items lie within three standard errors of the population mean.

$$\begin{aligned} \text{Critical values} &= £130 \pm 3 \times 3 \\ &= £130 \pm 9 \\ &= £121 \text{ to } £139 \end{aligned}$$

At this level of significance the null hypothesis is accepted. However, by widening the critical values there is an increased probability of a Type II error.

Type I error is rejecting Ho when it is in fact true.

Type II error is accepting Ho when it is in fact false.

It is important that the level of significance (1% or 5% or another level) is decided before data is collected or calculations are made in order to avoid the possibility of manipulating the level to produce a particular result.

8.7 Confidence limits

Confidence limits involves constructing an interval that will, at specific levels of probability, include the population mean.

For example: a random sample taken from the weekly wages of a group of employees provides the following results:

$n = 100, \bar{x} = £20, \sigma = 20$

$$\text{S.E.} = \frac{20}{\sqrt{100}} = \frac{20}{10} = 2$$

95% confidence limits (for the unknown population mean)

$$= \bar{x} \pm 2 \times \text{S.E.}$$
$$= £20 \pm 2 \times 2$$
$$= £20 \pm 4$$
$$= £16 \text{ to } £24$$

There is a 95% chance (approximately) that this range will include the unknown population mean (μ).

With a sample size of 400 and the same results:

$$\text{S.E.} = \frac{20}{\sqrt{400}} = \frac{20}{20} = 1$$

$$95\% \text{ confidence limits} = £20 \pm 2 \times 1$$
$$= £18 \text{ to } £22.$$

8.8 Worked examples

Example 8.1

A bag contains 20 white balls, 10 red balls and 10 blue balls. A ball is drawn at random, replaced, and a second ball is drawn at random. Find the probability that:

(i)   both balls are red,
(ii) the first ball is white and the second ball is blue,
(iii) both balls are white or blue.

Solution 8.1

(i) $\dfrac{10}{40} \times \dfrac{10}{40} = \dfrac{100}{1600} = \dfrac{1}{16}$

(ii) $\dfrac{20}{40} \times \dfrac{10}{40} = \dfrac{200}{1600} = \dfrac{1}{8}$

(iii) $\dfrac{30}{40} \times \dfrac{30}{40} = \dfrac{900}{1600} = \dfrac{9}{16}$

Example 8.2

In a period of petrol shortage the probability that any filling station will have petrol for sale is 0.25. On one particular journey five filling stations are passed. On the assumption that these are independent events, calculate the probability that:

(i)   they will all have petrol,
(ii) none will have petrol,
(iii) at least one will have petrol,
(iv) the first one will have petrol, but none of the others will.

Solution 8.2

(i) $\dfrac{1}{4} \times \dfrac{1}{4} \times \dfrac{1}{4} \times \dfrac{1}{4} \times \dfrac{1}{4} = \dfrac{1}{1024}$

(ii) $\dfrac{3}{4} \times \dfrac{3}{4} \times \dfrac{3}{4} \times \dfrac{3}{4} \times \dfrac{3}{4} = \dfrac{243}{1024}$

(iii) $1 - \dfrac{243}{1024} = \dfrac{781}{1024}$

(iv) $\dfrac{1}{4} \times \dfrac{3}{4} \times \dfrac{3}{4} \times \dfrac{3}{4} \times \dfrac{3}{4} = \dfrac{81}{1024}$

Example 8.3

The probability that two successive tosses of a biased coin will produce two tails is $\frac{1}{25}$. The probability that one toss of the same coin will produce heads is:

A $\dfrac{1}{50}$ **B** $\dfrac{1}{625}$ **C** $\dfrac{1}{5}$ **D** $\dfrac{1}{12.5}$

Solution 8.3

C: $\dfrac{1}{5} \left(\dfrac{1}{5} \times \dfrac{1}{5} = \dfrac{1}{25} \right)$

Example 8.4

If two dice are thrown and the total score is noted it follows that:

(i)   there are 11 possible different totals,
(ii) each possible total is equally possible,
(iii) some totals are more likely than others.

A (i) and (ii) only   **C** (ii) and (iii) only
B (i) and (iii) only   **D** (i), (ii) and (iii)

Solution 8.4

B: (i) and (iii)

Example 8.5

How many different ways are there of picking 4 books from a shelf containing 12 books?

Solution 8.5

11 880: $(12 \times 11 \times 10 \times 9)$

Example 8.6

Two fair six sided dice are thrown simultaneously. Determine the probability that the sum of the scores is:
(i) 4   (ii) 5   (iii) 8

Solution 8.6

(i) $\dfrac{3}{36} = \dfrac{1}{12}$ (ii) $\dfrac{4}{36} = \dfrac{1}{9}$ (iii) $\dfrac{7}{36}$

Example 8.7

What is the probability of tossing a head when throwing a coin?
A 1   **B** $\frac{1}{2}$ **C** 4   **D** 2

Solution 8.7

B: $\frac{1}{2}$

Example 8.8

A bag contains 3 blue balls, 2 red balls and 1 black ball. A ball is drawn at random from the bag. Calculate the probability that it will be (a) blue (b) red (c) black.

Solution 8.8

(a) $P(\text{blue}) = \dfrac{3}{6} = \dfrac{1}{2}$

(b) $P(\text{red}) = \dfrac{2}{6} = \dfrac{1}{3}$

(c) $P(\text{black}) = \dfrac{1}{6}$

Example 8.9

A bag contains 3 blue balls, 2 red balls and 1 black ball. A ball is drawn at random from the bag. Calculate the probability that it will not be (a) blue (b) red (c) black.

Solution 8.9

(a) $P(\text{not blue}) = 1 - 0.5 = 0.5$
(b) $P(\text{not red}) = 1 - 0.33 = 0.67$
(c) $P(\text{not black}) = 1 - 0.167 = 0.83$

Example 8.10

What is the probability that one toss of a biased coin will produce heads if the probability of a biased coin tossed three times producing heads is $\frac{1}{27}$.

Solution 8.10

$$\frac{1}{3} \times \frac{1}{3} \times \frac{1}{3} = \frac{1}{27} \text{ so } P = \frac{1}{3}$$

Example 8.11

If a firm supplies orders on time 80% of the time, what is the probability of the firm not meeting an order on time?

Solution 8.11

$1 - 0.8 = 0.2$ or 20%

Example 8.12

A bag contains 6 red balls, 3 white balls and 2 blue balls. What is the probability of (i) drawing a red ball, (ii) not drawing a red ball?

Solution 8.12

(i) $P = \dfrac{6}{11}$

(ii) $P = \dfrac{5}{11}$

Example 8.13

A bag contains 5 red balls and 7 blue balls. A second bag contains 3 red balls and 4 blue balls. If a ball is taken at random from each bag, find the probability that both balls are red.

Solution 8.13

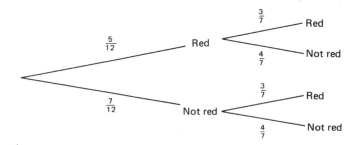

The probability that both balls are red $= \dfrac{5}{12} \times \dfrac{3}{7} = \dfrac{15}{84}$

Example 8.14

A bag contains 8 white balls and 10 black balls. A second bag contains 4 white balls and 10 black balls. If a ball is taken at random from each bag, find the probability that the ball taken from the first bag is white and the other black.

Solution 8.14

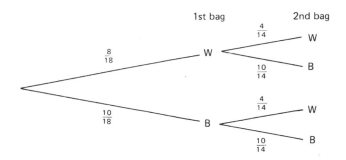

The probability of the first bag producing a white ball and the second bag a black ball is

$$\frac{8}{18} \times \frac{10}{14} = \frac{80}{252} = \frac{20}{63}$$

Example 8.15

Five cards numbered 1, 2, 3, 4, 5, are placed in a box. Two cards are drawn, the first not being replaced before the second is drawn. Find the probability that both cards are even.

Solution 8.15

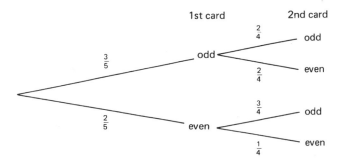

The probability that both cards are even $= \dfrac{2}{5} \times \dfrac{1}{4} = \dfrac{2}{20} = \dfrac{1}{10}$

(N.B. The sample space for the second draw is reduced by one, from 5 to 4, and the first draw either reduces the number of odd numbers left or the number of even numbers. If the first card drawn is even, the number of even cards for the second draw is reduced to 1.)

Example 8.16

A bag contains 4 red balls and 5 blue balls. A second bag contains 2 red balls and 5 blue balls. If a ball is taken at random from each bag, find the probability that both balls are red.

Solution 8.16

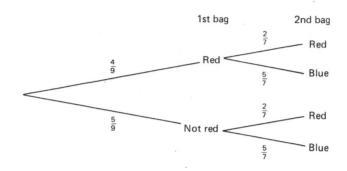

The probability that both balls are red $=$

$$\frac{4}{9} \times \frac{2}{7} = \frac{8}{63}$$

Example 8.17

A distribution has a mean of 100 cm and a standard deviation of 5 cm. Show this on a normal curve in units of the standard deviation and show the 90 cm and 86 cm value on the curve.

Solution 8.17

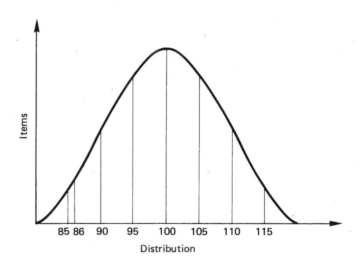

$$z = \frac{90 - 100}{5} = \frac{-10}{5} = -2$$

In the z table, 2 $=$ the area 0.4772 or 47.72%.

Approximately 47.72% of the distribution will lie between 100 cm and 90 cm and approximately 95% of the distribution will lie between 90 cm and 110 cm.

$$z = \frac{86 - 100}{5} = \frac{-14}{5} = -2.8$$

In the z table 2.8 $=$ the area 0.4974.

Approximately 49.74% of the distribution will lie between 100 cm and 86 cm.

Example 8.18

Calculate the standard error of a sample including 2500 respondents with a standard deviation in the responses of 25.

Solution 8.18

$$\text{S.E.} = \frac{25}{\sqrt{2500}} = \frac{25}{50} = 0.5$$

Example 8.19

It is thought that a large group of workers receive on average weekly wages of £200 each. A random sample is taken including 400 employees. The average wage is found to be £195 with a standard deviation of £40.

Does the result of the sample suggest that the average wage is £200, at the 5% or the 1% level of significance?

Solution 8.19

Ho : $\mu = £200$
Hi : $\mu = £200$

$$\text{S.E.} = \frac{\sigma}{\sqrt{n}} = \frac{40}{\sqrt{400}} = \frac{40}{20} = 2$$

The critical values (the population mean, plus and minus two standard errors)
= £200 ± 2 × 2
= £200 ± 4
= £196 to £204

The sample mean (£195) does not lie within the critical values, therefore Ho is rejected at the 5% level of significance. The difference between the assumed mean and the sample mean can be said to be significant. There is evidence to suggest that the population mean is not £200.

As the 1% level of significance 99% of the items lie within three standard errors of the population mean.

Critical values = £200 ± 3 × 2
= £200 ± 6
= £194 to £206

At this level of significance the null hypothesis is accepted. There is evidence to suggest that the population mean could be £200 because the sample mean does fall within the critical values.

Example 8.20

A random sample taken from a group of employees to discover the cost of transport provides the following results. The sample includes 225 employees and their transport costs are found to average £10 a week with a standard deviation of £7.50. Is this result likely to be a good indicator of the average transport costs of all the employees?

Solution 8.20

$n = 225, \bar{x} = £10, \sigma = £7.50$

$$\text{S.E.} = \frac{7.50}{\sqrt{225}} = \frac{7.50}{15} = 0.5$$

The 95% confidence limits (for the unknown population mean μ)
$$= £10 \pm 2 \times 0.5$$
$$= £10 \pm 1$$
$$= £9 \text{ to } £11$$
There is a 95% chance that this range will include the unknown population mean.

Example 8.21

The probability that two successive tosses of a biased coin will produce two heads is $\frac{1}{16}$. The probability that one toss of the same coin will produce heads is

(AEB)

A $\dfrac{1}{256}$ **B** $\dfrac{1}{32}$ **C** $\dfrac{1}{8}$ **D** $\dfrac{1}{4}$

Solution 8.21

D

Example 8.22

A bag contains six balls each of which is either white or black. One ball is taken out, and not replaced. A second ball is then taken out. The probability that they are both the same colour is $\frac{4}{6}$. Which one of the following numbers represents the number of black balls originally in the bag.

(AEB)

A 3   **B** 4   **C** 5   **D** 6

Solution 8.22

C

Example 8.23

How many different ways are there of picking 3 books from a shelf containing 13 books?

(SUJB)

Solution 8.23

$13 \times 12 \times 11 = 1716$

Example 8.24

A chain is made of ten links. For each link the probability of breaking under a load of 60 kg is 0.1. What is the probability of the chain not breaking under a load of 60 kg?

(SUJB)

Solution 8.24

$(0.9)^{10} = 0.349$

Example 8.25

The blood pressure of each of 200 men was measured to the nearest mm. The tabulated results are shown below.

Blood pressure (mm)	65–69	70–74	75–79	80–84	85–89	90–94
No. of men	8	28	54	60	32	18

Estimate the number of men with an actual blood pressure greater than 83 mm.

(AEB)

Solution 8.25

62

8.9 Questions and exercises

Question 8.1

The following data refers to the journey time to work of 100 office workers, all of whom work in the same office block. The journey times are measured to the nearest minute.

Journey time (minutes)	Number of office workers
1–10	0
11–20	4
21–30	8
31–40	18
41–45	18
46–50	22
51–60	20
61–70	6
71–80	3
81–90	1

Using 2 cm to represent 10 minutes and 2 cm to represent 10 office workers plot the cumulative frequency curve corresponding to the above distribution. Use your graph to determine:

(a) The median, lower quartile, upper quartile and semi-interquartile range of the journey time to work.

(b) The 58th percentile and the percentile corresponding to a journey time to work of $43\frac{1}{2}$ minutes.

All the office workers arrive at 9.00 a.m. and leave at 5.00 p.m. and the homeward journey takes the same time as the journey to work. If a worker is chosen at random from these 100 office workers state the probability that the worker left home before 8.15 a.m. What is the probability that any worker chosen at random would arrive home by 5.30 p.m.?

(AEB)

Question 8.2

Three classes each contain thirty children of whom 12, 15 and 20 respectively are boys. One child is selected at random from each of these classes. What is the probability that at least one of the three children selected is a girl. (AEB)

Question 8.3

A bag contains 1 red, 2 white and 3 blue beads. Two beads are drawn at random without replacement. Calculate the probability that the two beads are of the same colour. (AEB)

Question 8.4

Three fair six-sided dice are tossed simultaneously. Determine the probability that the sum of the scores is (a) 18, (b) 4. (AEB)

Question 8.5

Of the eight football teams that have qualified for the quarter final draw of a certain competition, five are English, two are Scottish and one is Welsh. The names of the eight teams are put into a hat and are to be drawn at random, the first match will be between the first two names drawn. Calculate the probabilities that this match will involve:

(i)   two English teams;
(ii)   two teams from the same country;
(iii)   teams from different countries;
(iv)   the Welsh team. (WJEC)

Question 8.6

The length of a sample of sixty components taken from the output of a production line were measured accurately and the results are tabulated below.

Length (cm)	3.160–	3.180–	3.190–	3.195–	3.200–	3.210–	3.220–	3.230–
Number of components	4	9	21	11	9	4	2	0

(i)   Illustrate the above data by a histogram.
(ii)   Construct a cumulative frequency table for the data.
(iii)   Taking 2 cm to represent 5 components and also to represent 0.01 cm construct a cumulative frequency curve for the data.
(iv)   Use your curve to estimate
        (a) the median length
        (b) the lower quartile
        (c) the upper quartile
        (d) the semi-interquartile range.

(v)   The tolerance limits specified for the component are 3.200 ± 0.020 cm. Estimate the percentage of the output which is acceptable.

(vi)   A component is taken at random from the sixty components. Calculate the probability that its length is less than 3.190 cm.

(vii) Two components are taken simultaneously and at random from the sixty components. Calculate the probability that the length of both components are each greater than 3.210 cm. Give your answer correct to two significant figures.   (AEB)

Question 8.7

A bag contains 6 red, 9 white and 5 green discs. If 3 discs are drawn together at random from the bag, calculate the probability that;

(a)   all discs are green,
(b)   none of the discs are green,
(c)   at least one disc is green,
(d)   the discs are all different colours.   (AEB, Additional Statistics)

Question 8.8

A company has ten independent telephone lines. At any instant the probability that any particular line is engaged is $\frac{1}{5}$. State the mean number of free telephone lines. Calculate for any instant, correct to three significant figures, the probability that

(a)   all the lines are engaged,
(b)   at least one line is free,
(c)   exactly two lines are free.   (AEB, Additional Statistics)

Question 8.9

Find the following probabilities, either directly or using an appropriate approximate method. If you use an approximate method, justify its use.

(a)   Probability that in seven throws of a fair six-sided die whose faces are labelled 1 to 6 at least two throws give a 1 or a 2.
(b)   The probability that in a group of 500 randomly selected people at least two have a birthday on March 1 (ignore leap years).
(c)   The probability than in 100 tosses of a fair coin at least 60 heads are obtained.   (AEB, Additional Statistics)

Question 8.10

Responses of patients to a certain drug may be assumed to be normally distributed with mean 77 units, standard deviation 11 units. What is the probability that a response lies between 60 units and 100 units?

The drug is administered to 60 patients. Find the probability that the mean response is less than 75 units. What assumption do you need to make to obtain this probability?

A new drug is tested on 50 volunteer patients and their mean response is found to be 78 units. Assuming that the variance of responses to the new drug is the same as that of responses to the original one, test the hypothesis that the mean response to the new drug is 77 units. (AEB, Additional Statistics)

Question 8.11

Explain what you understand by the terms the null hypothesis and alternative hypothesis, when used in the context of an hypothesis test. A test in mathematics, devised by the local Schools Inspector, was taken by a random sample of ten pupils from school A and a further independent random sample of ten pupils from school B. Their marks, out of 20, are given in the table below.

	Marks									
School A	3,	15,	14,	18,	10,	3,	5,	8,	9,	10
School B	4,	18,	10,	15,	14,	16,	5,	9,	12,	6

Assuming that these samples came from normal distributions with the same standard deviation of 5 marks, test the hypothesis that the two distributions have the same mean. (AEB, Additional Statistics)

Question 8.12

(a) Part 1 of the examinations of the Institute of Chartered Secretaries and Administrators consists of two modules. The subjects of Module 1 are (i) Communication, (ii) General Principles of Law. The subjects of Module 2 are (i) Principles of Economics, (ii) Statistics. A student attempts part 1 of the examinations of the Institute of Chartered Secretaries and Administrators, i.e. he takes Modules 1 and 2. He considers that his chances of passing Communication is 0.7, General Principles of Law is 0.6, Principles of Economics is 0.8 and Statistics is 0.9. Assuming that the probability of his passing one subject is independent of the probability of his passing the other 3 subjects, find the probability:
   (i)   that he passes part 1,
   (ii) that he fails all four examinations,
   (iii) that he passes just one module, i.e. passes either Module 1 or Module 2.
(b) Another student attempts Module 3. If the probability of passing this module is constant and equal to 0.6, find the probability that the student passes Module 3 at the third attempt. (ICSA)

Question 8.13

The table below relates to the number of employees in the mechanical engineering industry in Great Britain in 1978.

	Male	Female
Managerial, administrative	221 310	93 830
Chargehands	36 890	320
Craft operatives	285 210	2 080
Apprentices	40 940	280
Other	196 860	48 050

(a) How many men were employed in mechanical engineering?

(b) What is the probability that a male chosen at random is a chargehand?

(c) What is the probability that an employee chosen at random will be a woman?

(d) What is the probability that an apprentice chosen at random is male? (SEB)

Question 8.14

A potter knows that only one out of five vases of a certain design is passed as suitable for firing.

Answer the following questions by writing on the answer sheet the appropriate letter **A**, **B**, **C**, **D** or **E**.

(i) The probability that a vase chosen at random will be rejected is

$$\textbf{A} \ \frac{1}{6} \quad \textbf{B} \ \frac{1}{5} \quad \textbf{C} \ \frac{1}{2} \quad \textbf{D} \ \frac{4}{5} \quad \textbf{E} \ \frac{5}{6}$$

(ii) The probability that two vases chosen at random will both be accepted for firing is

$$\textbf{A} \ \frac{1}{25} \quad \textbf{B} \ \frac{2}{25} \quad \textbf{C} \ \frac{1}{4} \quad \textbf{D} \ \frac{8}{25} \quad \textbf{E} \ \frac{16}{25}$$

(iii) The probability that exactly one out of three vases chosen at random will be rejected is

$$\textbf{A} \ \frac{4}{125} \quad \textbf{B} \ \frac{12}{125} \quad \textbf{C} \ \frac{16}{125} \quad \textbf{D} \ \frac{48}{125} \quad \textbf{E} \ \frac{64}{125} \qquad \text{(SEB)}$$

Question 8.15

Three boxes each contain 10 cards. All the ten cards in each box show pictures of various fruits; 4 show an orange, 3 a lemon, 2 a banana and 1 an apple. If one card is drawn at random from each box, calculate the probability of drawing 2 bananas and 1 apple. (AEB)

Question 8.16

The letters of the word PERMUTATION are written, one letter on each of eleven cards. The cards are shuffled, placed face downwards on a table and then two cards are turned over. Calculate, giving your answers in their lowest terms, the probability that

(a) both cards will be T's

(b) there will be at least one vowel. (AEB)

Question 8.17

In a certain large primary school it was found that the weekly pocket money of pupils was normally distributed with a mean of 86p and a standard deviation of 18p. Calculate

(i) the amount of pocket money corresponding to a z-value of -0.6, *correct* to the nearest penny;

(ii)   the z-value corresponding to £1 per week pocket money;
(iii) the percentage of pupils receiving more than £1 per week pocket money;
(iv) the percentage of pupils who receive between 75p and £1 pocket money per week.   (SEB)

Question 8.18

A poultry farmer fattens 200 turkeys for Christmas. The following table shows the distribution of the oven-ready weights of these turkeys, measured to the nearest 0.1 kg.

Weight (kg)	Number of turkeys
3.5–4.4	2
4.5–4.9	6
5.0–5.4	20
5.5–5.9	54
6.0–6.4	59
6.5–6.9	25
7.0–7.9	22
8.0–9.4	10
9.5–11.4	2
Total	200

(a)   Using 2 cm to represent 20 turkeys and 2 cm to represent 1 kg, plot the cumulative frequency curve corresponding to the above distribution.
(b)   Use your graph to estimate the median, lower quartile, upper quartile and semi-interquartile range of the weights.
(c)   The farmer advertises his turkeys for sale and classifies them as small, medium and large. The top 15% are classified as large and the bottom 30% as small. Estimate the weight ranges of his small, medium and large turkeys to the nearest 0.1 kg.
(d)   If a turkey is chosen at random from these 200, state the probability that its oven-ready weight is at least 7 kg.
(e)   If two are chosen at random, calculate the probability that both are at least 7 kg in weight.

(For the purposes of this question weight may be assumed to mean the same as mass.)   (AEB)

Question 8.19

When asked to plot a scatter diagram of the marks in Mathematics and Statistics of a set of ten students A, B, C, D, E, F, G, H, I, J, a candidate incorrectly produced the graph on the next page.

(i)   Copy the table below and use the graph given to complete it.

Student	A	B	C	D	E	F	G	H	I	J
Marks in Mathematics (x)										
Marks in Statistics (y)										

(ii)   Hence draw a correct scatter diagram of the marks in Statistics (y) against the marks in Mathematics (x), using 1 cm to represent 1 mark on each axis.

(iii)   Calculate $\bar{x}$ and $\bar{y}$.

(iv)   Plot the point ($\bar{x}$, $\bar{y}$) and hence draw the line of best fit by eye.

(v)   Obtain the equation of the line in the form $y = mx + c$ where m and c are given to one decimal place.

(vi)   Use your equation to find the mark in Statistics which you would expect to correspond to a mark of 20 in Mathematics, giving your answer to the nearest whole number.

(vii)   A student was chosen at random from the set. Calculate the probability that the student had a higher mark for mathematics than he had for Statistics.

(viii) Two students were chosen simultaneously and at random from the set. Calculate the probability that each student had the same mark for Mathematics as he had for Statistics. (The two students need not necessarily have the same mark as each other.)   (AEB)

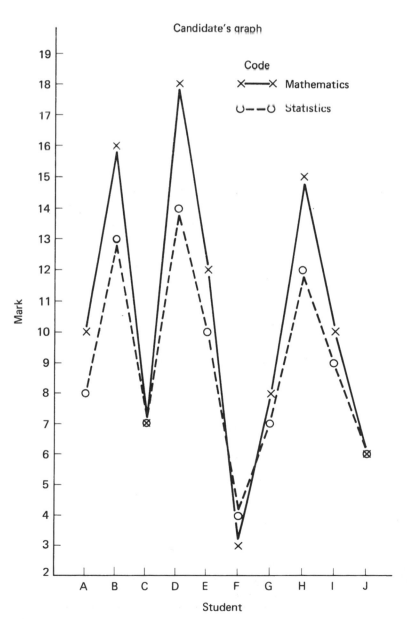

Comparing Statistics: Index Numbers

9

Objectives	By the end of this chapter the following terms and methods of calculation should be understood:

	Date attempted	Date completed	Self-assessment
Index numbers			
Calculating an index number			
Index of retail prices			

Summary	This chapter describes index numbers and their calculation. The index of retail prices is used as an example.

9.1 Introduction

An index number is a measure designed to show average changes in the quantity, value or price of a group of items, over a period of time.

Index numbers are:

(i) a device to simplify comparison over time,
(ii) calculated on a percentage basis,
(iii) usually weighted averages,
(iv) produced for prices, wages, production, sales, transport costs, share prices, imports and exports and so on.

9.2 Problems in index number construction

(a) The choice of items – a decision has to be made about the 'basket of goods'.
(b) The choice of weights – to reflect the relative importance of an item.
(c) The choice of the base year (the year with which other years are compared) – the attempt is to find a 'normal' year.
(d) Comparing indexes – if the base date changes indexes have to be 'spliced' together; changes in other factors (such as the choice of items) may make comparison impossible.

9.3 Calculating an index number

(a) Calculating a simple index number

For example: the average price of houses can be compared between two years.

Year	Average house prices (£)	Index number (price related to 1982)
1992	80 000	$\frac{80\,000}{80\,000} \times 100 = 100$
1996	90 000	$\frac{90\,000}{80\,000} \times 100 = 112.50$

In this index, 1992 is the base year (the year on which the price changes are based) and is written 1992 = 100. The index for 1996 (112.50) indicates that on average house prices have risen by 12.5% between 1992 and 1996.

The formula for a price or value index $= \frac{p_1}{p_0} \times 100$.

Where p_0 is the price in the base year and p_1 in the year to be compared:

$$\frac{90\,000}{80\,000} \times 100 = 112.50$$

(b) Calculating a weighted index number

For example: the average prices of a number of commodities can be computed over time. The commodities are given different weights according to their importance (if food is given a weight of 300 points and housing a weight of 150 points, then a change in the price of food is felt to be twice as important as a change in the price of housing).

Item	(1) Base price (£)	(2) Price 1986 (£)	(3) % increase	(4) Weight	(5) Product (3) × (4)
Food	25	30	20	300	6 000
Housing	20	22	10	150	1 500
Transport	5	10	100	100	10 000
Services	10	12	20	50	1 000
				600	18 500

$$\text{Index Number} = \frac{18\ 500}{600} = 30.83\%$$

The formula for this calculation is $\dfrac{\sum\left(\dfrac{p_1}{p_0} \times 1000 \times w\right)}{\Sigma w}$

where the calculation in the bracket is made for each item. Thus, in the example

$\sum\left(\dfrac{p_1}{p_0} \times 100 \times w\right)$ will be 18 500 (that is 6000 + 1500 + 10 000 + 1000).

If the index was assumed to be 100 in 1984 it would be 130.83 in 1986, showing a 30.83% increase in average prices for these commodities in two years.
Different types of index numbers use different systems for base years and for weights:

(i)   the Laspeyres index uses base-year quantities and weights;
(ii)   the Paasche index uses current year quantities and weights. In this system new weights are calculated every year.

(c)   Calculating a chain-based index number

This is a system in which each period in the series uses the previous period as the base. Each year, for example, can use the previous year as the base date.

For example: Conversion from a fixed to a chain base.

Year	Fixed		Chain
1993	100		100
1994	110	$\dfrac{110}{100} \times 100 \ = $	110
1995	125	$\dfrac{125}{110} \times 100 \ = $	113.6
1996	130	$\dfrac{130}{113.6} \times 100 \ = $	114.4

A chain-based index is useful where information on the immediate past is more important than information relating to the more distant past.

(d) Fisher's ideal index

The imperfections of the Laspeyres and Paasche systems of index numbers have led to attempts to find compromise solutions. These have usually involved the averaging of some component of the base and current year indices. Fisher's 'ideal index' involves the averaging of the full Laspeyres and Paasche indices, using the geometric mean. This is a complicated solution and is seldom used because it is not practicable.

**9.4
The Index
of Retail
Prices**

In the UK this is used as a 'cost-of-living' index to provide an indicator of the level of inflation. It 'measures the change from month to month in the average level of prices of the commodities and services purchased by nearly nine-tenths of the households in the United Kingdom' (Department of Employment).

As a cost of living index, the Index of Retail Prices has to be used with caution and the figures from the Index provide no more than a general and average indication of inflation: this is because:

(i)   for particular households, inflation may be greater or less than average depending on their patterns of expenditure,

(ii)   households may have very different expenditure patterns which do not coincide with the weighting system of the Index.

**9.5
Worked
examples**

Example 9.1

Discuss the problems involved in constructing an index number, with particular reference to a 'cost-of-living' index.

Solution 9.1

An index number is a measure designed to show average changes in the quantity, value and price of a group of items, over a period of time. The objective of constructing an index number is to provide a device to simplify comparison over time on a percentage basis.

The problems of constructing an index number arise from this objective and from the design necessary to achieve this. Index numbers are produced on a number of subjects including prices, wages, production, sales, costs and so on. The first problem is the choice of items to be included in any particular index. In the Index of Retail Prices, for example, there is the question of which items to include to provide a good indication of changes in retail prices. This choice of items or 'basket of goods' has to be changed every so often to reflect changes in consumer spending. The importance of 'meals eaten away from home', for example, has increased over the years so that it has eventually become a separate item in the Index.

The relative importance of items can be reflected in the choice of weights. If food, for example, is found to be twice as important in consumer expenditure as housing, then food can be given a weight of 300 and housing a weight of 150. Individual items can be weighted, such as bread or meat, and their relative weights can be used to reflect changes in their importance as consumer tastes and expenditure changes. The 'Family Expenditure Survey' provides up-to-date information in the UK on changes in the pattern of consumer spending and provides the data on which relative weights can be based. Weights can be changed either on a year by year basis or the weights can be changed at wider intervals as the base year is changed. The Laspeyres Index uses base year weights, while the Paasche Index uses current year weights.

The choice of the base year can be a problem. It is the year with which other years are compared. This means that an attempt is made to find a 'normal' year which is neither at the top of a boom or at the bottom of a slump. Any year compared with a boom year may appear to be poor, while any year compared with a slump year may appear particularly good. The Paasche Index overcomes this problem but may make comparison over a number of years more difficult.

Comparing index numbers over a number of years is a problem because the factors on which the index is based will change. These factors include weights, the basket of goods and the structure of consumer expenditure. Tastes and fashions change, the pattern of expenditure changes and the structure of society will change. It is very difficult for an index number such as the Index of Retail Prices to reflect these changes over a large number of years. If only the base date is altered, then indices can be 'spliced' together and comparisons can be made over many years, but as fundamental factors change then comparison between indices may become impossible except in a very general way.

Example 9.2

Calculate a weighted index number for the following table of figures for 1995 based on 1990.

Item	1990 price (£)	1995 price (£)	Weight
Food	30	33	50
Housing	25	25	30
Transport	5	15	10
Services	8	10	10

Solution 9.2

Item	1990 price (£)	1995 price (£)	% increase	Weight	Product
Food	30	33	10	50	500
Housing	25	30	20	30	600
Transport	5	15	200	10	2000
Services	8	10	25	10	250
				100	3350

$$\text{Weighted Index Number} = \frac{3350}{100} = 33.5\%$$

If the Index was assumed to be 100 in 1990 it would be 133.5 in 1995.

Example 9.3

Your company, based in the United Kingdom, has subsidiaries in seven countries. The table below shows the Bank of England Index of Currency Movements (that is the Trade Weighted Index) as at recent date for the eight countries in the corporate operation.

Currency	Bank of England Index
Sterling	91.7
US Dollar	122.1
Canadian Dollar	90.1
Deutsche Mark	125.2
Swiss Franc	145.3
Dutch Guilder	117.1
French Franc	72.2
Japanese Yen	130.2
Base average 1975 = 100	

Source: *Financial Times*

Required:

(a) Present the above data on a suitable bar chart and interpret it as for a layman.
(b) Explain the usefulness of a weighted index number, using the above data for illustrative purposes.
(c) Contrast the use of a base weighted index number with the use of a current weighted index number.
(d) As the company may be setting up another subsidiary in another country shortly, describe the main published sources of economic, accounting and business data to which you would turn for background information about that country (Belgium may be taken as a suitable example of that other country if you wish).

Solution 9.3

(a) Bar Chart of the Bank of England Index of Currency Movements

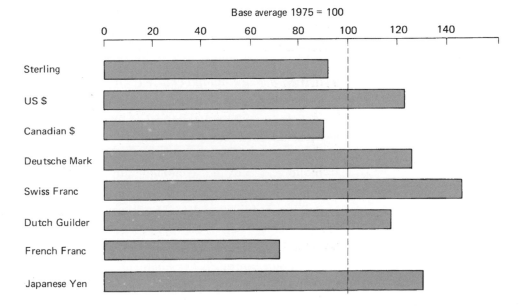

The bar chart displays the currency indices in such a way that they may be visually ranked from strongest to weakest, Swiss Franc, Japanese Yen, ... French Franc and the relative difference between the performance of any two currencies can be easily assessed visually. The chart also shows the increase and decrease in the strength of each index since the base period, that is Sterling is only 'worth' 91.7% of its value in 1975.

(b)   The data tabulated in the question reflect the change in the value of the currencies of the eight countries concerned. It would be possible to create an index for one single currency, but in this case the trade between the countries of the world influences the movements in the various currencies. However, many countries of the world do not trade equally with their partners, and consequently, the effect reflected in currency movement will not be uniform. Weights which reflect the international trading position are used to produce a weighted average effect, thus the movement in the US dollar will not have total impact on the movement of the £ Sterling, since movements in other currencies will be taken into effect in computing the index.

(c)   The distinction between these two types of index numbers arises in the selection of the weights. In the case of a base weighted index number, the weights are chosen to reflect the position at the base period of the index, whereas with the current weighted index, the weights reflect the current position, and new weights have to be established every time a new index is published. Establishing the current weights is usually more time consuming and expensive than for the prices.

In the case illustrated in the question, whilst the Index was changed in 1981 the figures were based on the trading position of 1975, simply because it was impossible to determine the up-to-date position. The contra view can be expressed about the base weighted index, in that the base period does not reflect the most up-to-date picture. In this case the base needs to be brought closer to the period under consideration.

(d)   The sources that the company could turn to for information about Belgium can be split into those from Government sources both for the United Kingdom and Belgium, and from semi-public and private sources.

The type of source that you can start with in the United Kingdom could be the *Annual Abstract of Statistics*. From this we can get some idea of the trade situation, that is Imports and Exports between the two countries and also obtain details of the movement in currency. Currency movements can be further referred to in the *Bank of England Quarterly Review*. It is possible to update the figures given in the *Annual Abstract of Statistics* by referring to the *Monthly Digest of Statistics*. No one journal published by the Government or some other body, can serve as the only source of data and so it will be necessary to turn to other sources.

In this case it would seem natural to turn to international bodies such as the European Community and the Organisation for Economic Cooperation and Development for more data. The International Monetary Fund is another possible source.

Quality newspapers and journals frequently provide information and statistics about other countries – *The Financial Times* and *The Economist* are two examples in the United Kingdom. In Belgium the relevant trade and industry associations publish business data. Specific market information could be commissioned from a market research agency.

The Banking Sector can also be another useful source of data. In the United Kingdom, the major banks publish intelligence on a regular basis. In short, a background picture of Belgium can be built up to begin an assessment of the state of that country, and whether it is worthwhile setting up a subsidiary there.

(Association of Certified Accountants, Numerical Analysis and Data Processing, 1983 – Question and Answer).

Example 9.4

Index of Industrial Production in the UK: July 1982: 1975 = 100

	Weight	Index
Mining and quarrying*	41	361
Manufacturing		
Food, drink and tobacco	77	106
Chemicals	66	109
Metal	47	72
Engineering	298	86
Textiles	67	70
Other manufacturing	142	91
Construction	182	91
Gas, electricity and water	80	115

*Including North Sea oil.
Source: *Monthly Digest of Statistics.*

(i) Calculate the index of industrial production for
    (1) all industries;
    (2) all industries except mining and quarrying;
    (3) manufacturing industries.
(ii) Comment on your results.   (ICSA)

Solution 9.4

(to calculation only)

(1) 102.5   (2) 91.5   (3) 88.9

Example 9.5

Prodco Ltd is considering constructing a weighted index of prices for the components P, Q, R and S of its stock. The weightings of the components together with the prices for the years 1976–80 are shown in the following table.

Component	Weighting of component	Prices (£) 1976	1977	1978	1979	1980
P	10	6.00	7.50	9.25	11.00	13.50
Q	12	3.00	4.50	6.00	8.00	10.50
R	17	2.50	4.00	5.80	7.00	9.20
S	9	4.75	6.00	7.25	8.75	10.00

Required:

(a) Calculate a series of weighted price index numbers (correct to one place of decimals) for 1977 to 1980 based on the 1976 figures.
(b) Compare and contrast the calculation of a set of index numbers if the Laspeyres and Paasche Price Index Numbers are calculated.
(c) Explain what practical problems are likely to be encountered in establishing an index number to measure changes in consumer prices. (ACA)

Solution 9.5

(to calculation only)

(a) 1977 143.9, 1978 192.9, 1979 238.5, 1980 324.9

Example 9.6

Given that the index of retail prices for the following data is 105, calculate the value of x (AEB)

Item	Price relative	Weight
Food	102	1
Rent	100	2
Clothing	110	x
Fuel	105	3
Others	103	1

Solution 9.7

$x = 3$

9.6 Questions and exercises

Question 9.1

Compare the latest available figures for the Index of Retail Prices and the Index 5 years ago. How good is the Index as an indication of changes in the cost of living?

Question 9.2

Wages, pensions, prices and savings can be linked to an index. Consider the advantages and problems involved in index-linking.

Question 9.3

Given that the combined index for the commodities shown in the table is 109 calculate the value of b. (AEB)

Commodity	X	Y	Z
Index	112	b	97
Weight	4	2	3

Question 9.4

The index number of a commodity in 1980 was 135, taking 1978 as base year. Given that the 1980 price was £297 calculate the price in 1978.   (AEB)

Question 9.5

Commodity	A	B	C	D
Index	107	118	94	105
Weight	2	x	1	$2x$

Given that the combined index for all four commodities is 108, calculate the value of x.   (AEB)

Question 9.6

(a) Discuss the relative advantages and disadvantages of Laspeyres and Paasche price index numbers.

(b) An investor's holding in the shares of three companies in 1977 and 1982 is shown in the table below. The average prices of these shares in each year is also given.

	1977 Price	Number of shares	1982 Price	Number of shares
Share A	145	300	420	600
B	280	500	130	200
C	205	400	240	400

(i)   Calculate Laspeyres and Paasche price index numbers for the investor's holding of shares with 1977 as base year.

(ii) Explain briefly why your results in part (i) differ.   (ICSA)

Question 9.7

(a) A firm uses three raw materials, A, B and C. The prices in pounds per kg are given below. In the past the firm has spent approximately the same amount of money on each material and regards them as of equal importance.

Material	Price £/kg June 1979	June 1980	June 1081
A	12	6	8
B	15	20	25
C	30	55	50

(i)   Calculate an index of materials prices for June 1981, using June 1979, as base.

(ii) What would be the index for June 1981, if a chain base were used?

(iii) In 1982 weights were introduced into the index. The index for June 1982, using June 1979 as base, was 146. Use the following information to calculate the prices of material C in June, 1982.

Material	Weight	Price £/kg June 1982
A	3	10
B	2	22
C	5	

(b) What is the General Index of retail prices in the United Kingdom and how is it calculated?   (SUJB)

Question 9.8

The table below shows the average production figures and prices for three models of radio in a certain country for the years 1975, 1978 and 1981.

	Quantities produced (thousands)			Price (£)		
	1975	1978	1981	1975	1978	1981
Model A	47.8	42.1	41.9	15.7	23.4	29.3
Model B	78.5	79.7	85.6	17.3	26.6	33.8
Model C	51.3	81.4	86.2	21.8	32.1	36.3

(a) Distinguish between the Paasche and Laspeyres index numbers.
(b) Calculate the Paasche price index number for 1981 with 1975 as base year.
(c) Calculate the Laspeyres price index number for 1978 with 1975 as base year.

(AEB Additional Statistics)

Question 9.9

(a) For some index numbers the base value is chosen on a particular day, for others it is the average of several months' values and again in other cases it is obtained from the value for the whole year.
    Explain why these differences arise and explain also what other considerations are to be taken into account in choosing a base period for an index number.
(b) Calculate the price relative index for the overall change for the commodities listed in the following table, using base quantities as weighting factors.

Commodity	Base year		Current year	
	Price (£)	Quantity	Price (£)	Quantity
A	2.84	53	2.93	62
B	9.61	87	8.25	95
C	3.56	49	4.51	52
D	1.87	62	3.36	68
E	14.62	35	12.48	32

(Chartered Institute of Marketing)

Question 9.10

UK Index of Retail Prices for 1977

Group	Weight	Group Index
Food	247	191.1
Alcoholic drink	83	183.0
Tobacco	46	209.7
Housing	112	165.0
Fuel and light	58	209.3
Durable household goods	63	165.0
Clothing and footwear	82	154.7
Transport and vehicles	139	191.5
Miscellaneous goods	71	187.0
Services	54	171.7
Meals outside home	45	181.6

(a) Using the above information calculate an all items index for the UK Retail Prices for 1977 and also an index for the first five groups alone. A weighted arithmetic mean of group indices should be used

(b) Explain what is meant by 'weight' in the heading in the table and comment on the difficulties that will have arisen in determining these values. (Institute of Marketing)

Question 9.11

(a) Define what is meant by a 'fixed base index number' and a 'chain base index number' and explain the different ways in which these alternatives have to be interpreted.

(b) For the following data calculate
    (i) a Laspeyres *price* index for 1980
    (ii) a Paasche *quantity* index for 1980
    in each case using 1978 as the base year. (Chartered Institute of Marketing)

Commodity	1978		1980	
	Average price (£)	Quantity	Average price (£)	Quantity
A	3.65	156	3.75	194
B	7.82	274	9.20	305
C	1.40	115	1.80	187
D	2.95	432	4.54	378
E	14.84	89	20.36	126

Question 9.12

(a) Discuss the problems of identifying suitable weights for an index number, giving appropriate examples from published indices.

(b) From the following information of the Transport and Vehicles sub-group of the Retail Price Index calculate a weighted price-relative index for 1980 based on 1974 prices.   (Chartered Institute of Marketing)

	Weight	1974 price £	1980 price £
Purchase of motor vehicles	56	1731	4623
Maintenance of motor vehicles	15	50	158
Petrol and oil	43	114	372
Motor licences	7	36	85
Motor insurance	10	68	184
Retail transport fares	8	20	69
Road transport fares	12	8	26

Source: Department of Employment

Question 9.13

What do you understand by the term 'Index Numbers'?

Give an account of the usual methods of compiling a price index, illustrating your answer where possible by reference to official published indices.

(Chartered Institute of Marketing)

Question 9.14

Your company has two factories, the buildings of which are insured through an index-linked scheme. Under this scheme the sum insured of a policyholder's buildings is automatically changed each month in line with the Cost of Construction Materials Index which is shown below.

Cost of Construction Materials Index (1975 = 100)

	1980	1981	1982
January	200.3	225.0	244.5
February	205.1	226.8	249.3
March	210.2	229.9	251.4
April	212.9	232.2	253.4
May	217.3	234.3	254.9
June	218.1	235.4	255.6
July	220.2	236.3	
August	221.3	236.6	
September	222.3	237.1	
October	223.1	239.6	
November	223.6	240.4	
December	224.0	241.0	

Source: *Monthly Digest of Statistics*, July 1982

(a) Explain briefly why weights would be used in the construction of this index. (No specific technical details of the Construction Materials Index are required.)

(b) What is the importance of the phrase '1975 = 100'?

(c) What was the percentage increase in the cost of construction materials over the two-year period ended in June 1982?

(d) Factory A was insured for £1.5 million in January 1981. What was the sum insured for June 1982? Assuming the percentage increase to be the same in the second half of 1982 as in the first half of 1982, estimate the sum insured on Factory A for December 1982.

(e) Factory B was insured for £1.1 million in June 1982. Find an estimate for the sum insured for November 1983, assuming that the same average monthly increase in the cost of construction materials between January 1980 and June 1982 also applies to the period from June 1982 to November 1983.

(ICMA)

Question 9.15

(a) A Laspeyres (base-weighted) price index may be regarded *either* as a weighted mean of price relatives *or* as an indicator of the price of a fixed 'basket of goods'.
     Explain *precisely* the meaning of these two concepts.

(b)

Component type	Price in January 1983 (pence)	Price in May 1983 (pence)	Weekly quantity of components used in January 1983
Clips	10	15	3000
Seals	16	24	6000
Tubes	12	12	2000
Widgetts	10	11	5000

Using *either* of the methods referred to in (a) calculate an all-items price index for components for May 1983, using January 1983 = 100.

(c) Is it possible to regard a Paasche (current-weighted) price index in either of the ways referred to in (a) above?
     Explain your answers.

(d) What is involved in the *splicing* of index numbers?   (ICMA)

Question 9.16

The wages paid to manual workers of a company in 1976 and 1981 are given below.

	1976 Average wage (£)	Numbers employed	1981 Average wage (£)	Numbers employed
Skilled	70	70	160	60
Semi-skilled	55	150	120	190
Unskilled	40	80	100	50

(i)   Calculate an index for wages for 1981 with 1976 = 100 as base year.
      (1) Base year weighted (a Laspeyres index)
      (2) Current year weighted (a Paasche index)

(ii) Briefly explain why your results differ.   (RSA)

Question 9.17

Discuss the Department of Employment's Index of Retail Prices, indicating its purpose, the items included and the method of collection of data.

Why is the index important to members of the general public?   (RSA)

Question 9.18

(a) Explain the terms:
(i) base year
(ii) weights
used in index number construction.

(b) The table below gives the UK Retail Prices Index and average charge for cinema admissions over the period 1975–80.

	UK Retail Prices Index (1974 = 100)	Average charge for cinema admissions (new pence)
1975	134.8	61.2
1976	157.1	73.0
1977	182.0	82.6
1978	197.1	93.7
1979	223.5	113.4
1980	263.7	141.3

Source: *British Business*

(i)   Change the base year of the Retail Prices Index to (1975 = 100).
(ii) Construct a simple index (1975 = 100) for the admissions charge to cinemas.
(iii) Compare the two sets of index numbers and comment on the results obtained. (RSA)

Question 9.19

Describe the construction and use of:
either   The General Index of Retail Prices;
or   The Index of Industrial Production. (RSA)

Question 9.20

In 1981 the production index for a certain commodity was 154. In 1982 production rose by 50%. If the same year is used as base for both the 1981 index and the 1982 index, calculate the 1982 production index. (AEB)

10

Comparing Statistics: Correlation

Objectives

By the end of this chapter the following terms and methods of calculations should be understood:

	Date attempted	Date completed	Self-assessment
Correlation			
Scatter diagrams			
Correlation tables			
Product moment coefficient of correlation			
Coefficient of rank correlation			
Regression			

Summary

This chapter describes methods of comparing statistics through correlation and the calculation of coefficients of correlation and regression.

10.1 Introduction

Correlation is concerned with whether or not there is any association between two variables.

It is useful to know:

(i)   whether any association *exists*,
(ii) the *strength* of the association:
      from −1 (strong negative association) to −0.1 and +0.1 (weak association) to +1 (strong positive association),
(iii) the *direction* of the relationship: whether it is positive (in the same direction) or negative (in the opposite direction),
(iv) the *proportion* of the *variability* in one variable that can be accounted for by its relationship with the other variable: if r (correlation) = +0.8 then r^2 = +0.64. It can be said that 64% of the variability in one variable can be accounted for by its linear relationship with the other variable.

For example: an increase in the sales of a company may show a strong association with increases in the money spent on the advertising of its products. There might appear to be a strong positive association between sales and advertising.
However:

(a) causal relationships: correlation does not prove causation;
(b) indirect connections: high correlation does not prove a direct connection;
(c) coincidence: may produce spurious correlation;
(d) reliability: little reliance can be put on the value of r when there are few observations;
(e) lag: there may be a time lag before one variable influences the other, giving an impression of negative correlation.

Relationships between two variables may be linear or non-linear. Many variables do have a linear relationship (based on a straight line) but few are perfect. As one variable increases the other variable may increase or decrease, but the changes are not necessarily in proportion.

10.2 Methods of indicating correlation

(a)   Scatter diagrams

Each pair of figures from two variables is plotted as a single point on a graph to see whether there is a pattern among the points.

If there is one, a 'line of best fit' can be drawn with the same number of points or co-ordinates on each side of the line (Fig. 10.1).

For example:

(i)

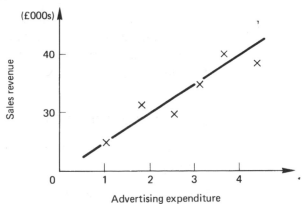

Figure 10.1 Line of best fit

(ii)

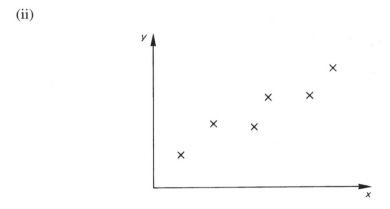

Figure 10.2 Positive correlation

(iii)

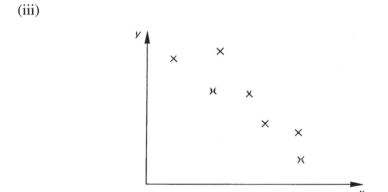

Figure 10.3 Negative correlation

(iv)

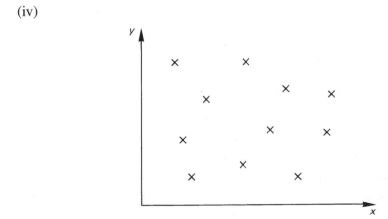

Figure 10.4 No correlation

Figure 10.2 indicates positive correlation so that as the variable *x* increases so *y* will increase, while Fig. 10.3 indicates negative correlation so that as *x* increases *y* will decrease and Fig. 10.4 indicates that there is no correlation between the two variables, so that there are a number of lines of best fit which could be drawn with equal validity.

(b) Correlation tables

These can provide an approximate indication of correlation by tabulating one variable against the other.

For example: see Table 10.1.

Table 10.1   Correlation table

Age of employee (to the nearest year)	Length of service (to the nearest year)						
	Under 5	5–9	10–14	15–19	20–24	25–29	30+
16–25	35	15					
26–35	1	22					
36–45		3	42	5			
46–55			16	28	5		
56–65		2		8	10	6	2

(c)   The product moment coefficient of correlation

Sometimes referred to as Pearson's coefficient, *this is a measure of linear correlation which attempts to show the closeness of the relationship between two variables.*

$$r = \frac{\Sigma(xy)}{n\sigma_x\sigma_y}$$

where r is the product moment coefficient,

      x is one variable (sometimes referred to as the subject),

      y is the other variable (sometimes referred to as the relative),

      n is the number of items (subject or relative, not both),

      σ_x is the standard deviation of variable x,

      σ_y is the standard deviation of variable y.

This formula can be rewritten based on the basic formula for the standard deviation:

$$r = \frac{\Sigma(xy)}{\sqrt{\Sigma x^2 \Sigma y^2}}$$

(Note: x and y are used here as the deviation from the mean of a variable)

where $\Sigma(xy)$ represents the sum of the products of the deviations from the mean,

      x is the deviation from the mean of one variable,

      y is the deviation from the mean of the other variable.

For example: see Table 10.2.

Table 10.2   Product moment correlation

Year	Investment (£000s)	Profit (£000s)	x (deviation from $\bar{x}$ of investment) ($\bar{x}=6$)	y (deviation from y of profit) ($y=8$)	x^2	y^2	xy
1989	3	6	−3	−2	9	4	6
1990	5	4	−1	−4	1	16	4
1991	6	8	0	0	0	0	0
1992	6	10	0	+2	0	4	0
1993	10	12	+4	+4	16	16	16
	30	40			26	40	26

$$\bar{x} \text{ (Investment)} = \frac{30}{5} = 6 \qquad\qquad \Sigma(xy) = 26$$
$$\Sigma x^2 = 26$$
$$\Sigma y^2 = 40$$

$$\bar{x} \text{ (Profit)} = \frac{40}{5} = 8$$

$$r = \frac{26}{\sqrt{26 \times 40}}$$

$$= \frac{26}{32.2}$$

$$+0.84$$

This result (+0.84) shows a strong positive correlation between the two variables.

(d)   Coefficient of rank correlation

This is a measure of correlation for information provided on an ordinal scale or for information on an interval scale that has been ordered or ranked.

For example: see Table 10.3.

Five brands of a commodity are tested and ranked and are then ranked by consumers to give the following results:

Table 10.3   Rank correlation

Commodity	(1) Test rankings	(2) Consumer rankings	(3) d (2) − (1)	(4) d^2 $(3)^2$
A	1	5	4	16
B	2	3	1	1
C	3	4	1	1
D	4	2	2	4
E	5	1	4	16
				38

Coefficient of Rank Correlation (sometimes referred to as 'Spearman's Coefficient'):

$$r' = 1 - \frac{6\Sigma d^2}{n(n^2 - 1)}$$

where r' is the coefficient of rank correlation (interpretation is for r),
   d^2 is the square of the differences or deviations in the ranking,
   n is the number of units.

$$r' = 1 - \frac{6 \times 38}{5(25 - 1)}$$

$$= 1 - \frac{228}{5 \times 24}$$

$$= 1 - \frac{228}{120}$$

$$= 1 - 1.9$$

$$= -0.9$$

This indicates a high level of negative correlation between the test rankings and the consumer rankings.

(e) Regression

This attempts to show the relationship between two variables by providing a mean line which best indicates the trend of the co-ordinates on a graph. (See Chapter 11 for the method of calculating the least squares method and linear estimation.)

Values can be fixed for x (the variable on the horizontal scale) and a line found which minimises the vertical distance between the co-ordinates and this line. This is the regression line of y on x; it gives an estimate of y for a known value of x. Or, values can be fixed for y (the variable on the vertical scale) which minimises the horizontal distances between the co-ordinates and this line. This is the regression line of x on y; it gives an estimate of x for a known value of y.

The method used is to minimise the squared deviations, the least-squares method (see Chapter 11).

For example: if the regression coefficient of y on x is found to be $+2$, then for each value of x, y will change by $+2$.

x	1	2	3	4	5
y	14	16	18	20	22

If the figures for x are: 0   1   2   3   4   5   6
and for y are: 0 -1.5 -3 -4.5 -6 -7.5 -9
then the regression coefficient of y on x will be -1.5;
when x is 10, y will be -15.

Regression coefficient: this is the value of b (see page 242), that is the slope or gradient of the regression line.

10.3 Worked examples

Example 10.1

Draw scatter diagrams which show:

(i)   strong positive correlation,
(ii)   weak negative correlation,
(iii)   zero correlation.

Solution 10.1

(i)

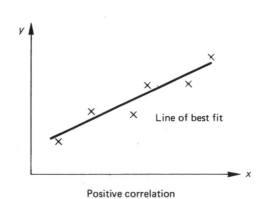

Positive correlation

(ii)

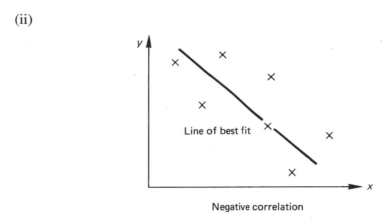

Negative correlation

(iii)

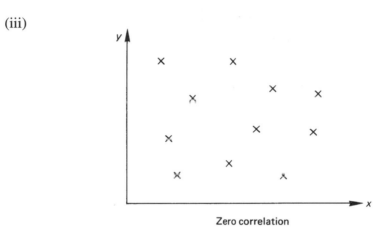

Zero correlation

Example 10.2

Explain the terms (a) 'regression' and (b) 'correlation'.

Solution 10.2

(a) 'Regression': this attempts to show the relationship between two variables by providing a mean line which best indicates the trend of the co-ordinates on a graph. The aim is to produce a line which minimises all positive and negative deviations of the data for a straight line drawn through the data. This straight line is based on an equation $y = a + bx$, where y and x are the two variables, a represents the intercept and b represents the slope of the line.

The slope of the line shows changes in one variable against the other. This is illustrated in the following graph:

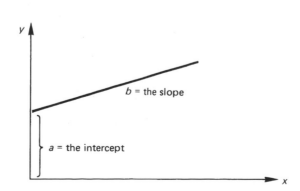

(b)   'Correlation': this is concerned with whether or not there is any association between two variables. If two variables are related to any extent then changes in the value of one are associated with changes in the value of the other.

Correlation can show the strength of any association, the direction of the relationship and the proportion of the variability in one variable that can be accounted for by its relationship with the other variable.

Many relationships between two variables are linear, but few are perfectly linear. There are many non-linear relationships as well. A high correlation coefficient does not prove that there is a causal relationship between two variables. There may be indirect connections between two variables so that, for example, the rise in the sales of two commodities may be due to improvements in the economy and not due to one commodity causing increased sales of the other commodity. Some apparent connections may be coincidental.

Correlation and regression analysis are no more than indicators of possible association between variables. They provide evidence which can lead to further investigation and analysis. They can help in planning, decision making and forecasting although they are not substitutes for looking carefully at the original data.

Example 10.3

Calculate the product moment coefficient of correlation for the following data, which compares percentage price changes (A%) and changes in sales (B%) in a particular sector of distribution:

A%:	5,	8,	10,	15,	17
B%:	17,	24,	13,	15,	11

Solution 10.3

A%	B%	x	y	x^2	y^2	xy
5	17	−6	1	36	1	−6
8	24	−3	8	9	64	−24
10	13	−1	−3	1	9	3
15	15	4	−1	16	1	−4
17	11	6	−5	36	25	−30
55	80			98	100	−64 + 3 = −61

$$\bar{x}(A) = \frac{55}{5} = 11$$

$$\bar{y}(B) = \frac{80}{5} = 16$$

$$r = \frac{\Sigma(xy)}{\sqrt{\Sigma x^2 \Sigma y^2}} = \frac{-61}{\sqrt{98 \times 100}} = \frac{-61}{\sqrt{9800}}$$

$$= \frac{-61}{98.9} = -0.62$$

This answer indicates some negative correlation between percentage price changes and percentage changes in sales. The correlation is not particularly strong but shows that it is possible that to some extent as prices rise, sales fall.

Example 10.4

Paintings completed by a group of ten students are assessed by two independent judges. The marks awarded are shown below. Calculate Spearman's coefficient of rank correlation for the marks awarded by the two judges.

Completed paintings	A	B	C	D	E	F	G	H	I	J
Judge 1	30	35	35	40	50	55	60	65	70	80
Judge 2	50	45	45	45	60	55	75	70	65	80

Solution 10.4

(1) Judge 1	(2) Rank	(3) Judge 2	(4) Rank	(5) d (4) − (2)	(6) d^2
30	10	50	7	3	9
35	8.5	45	9	0.5	0.25
35	8.5	45	9	0.5	0.25
40	7	45	9	2	4
50	6	60	5	1	1
55	5	55	6	1	1
60	4	75	2	2	4
65	3	70	3	0	0
70	2	65	4	2	4
80	1	80	1	0	0
					23.5

$$r' = 1 - \frac{6 \times 23.5}{10(10^2 - 1)}$$

$$= 1 - \frac{141}{10(100 - 1)} = 1 - \frac{141}{990} = 1 - 0.14$$

$$= 0.86$$

Example 10.5

If a regression line was drawn for the data below and its equation obtained in the form $y = a + bx$, which one of the following conditions would be true?

x	1	2	3	4	5
y	1.5	2.2	2.9	3.6	4.3

A *a* and *b* are both negative
B *a* and *b* are both positive
C *a* positive and *b* negative
D *a* negative and *b* positive

Solution 10.5

B (*a* and *b* are both positive). *a* is the value of the intercept and is positive. *b* is the value of the slope of the line which shows changes in one variable against the other. The relationship between the two variables is one of positive correlation, as is shown in the graph below:

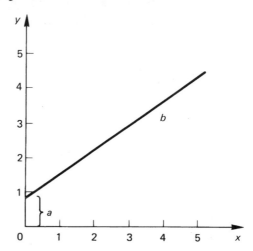

Example 10.6

Corresponding values of variables *x* and *y* are given in the following table:

x	3	6	9	12
y	−1	−2	−3	−4

The regression coefficient of *y* on *x* is:
A −1   **B** +3   **C** $-\frac{1}{3}$ **D** −3

Solution 10.6

$$\mathbf{C}\left(-\frac{1}{3}\right)$$

When *x* is 4, *y* will be $-1\frac{1}{3}$; *x* = 5, *y* = $1\frac{2}{3}$; *x* = 6, *y* = −2.

Example 10.7

The scatter diagram for which the correlation coefficient is a negative fraction is

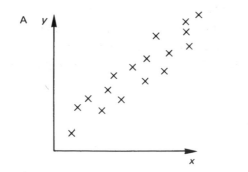

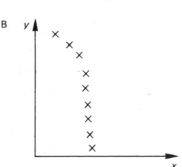

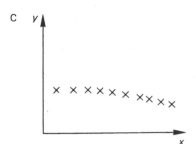
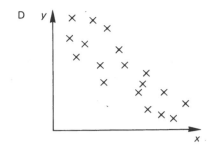

Solution 10.7

D

Example 10.8

The three scatter diagrams below show five points corresponding to five pairs of observations of the variables x and y. Given that in each case the coefficient of correlation takes one of the values $-0.8, 0$ or $+0.8$, state the particular value corresponding to each diagram. (AEB)

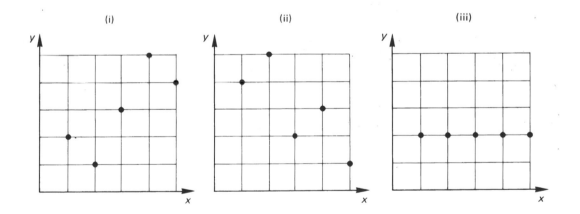

Solution 10.8

(i) $+0.8$, (ii) -0.8, (iii) 0

Example 10.9

Observations are taken of three variables x, y and z. The correlation coefficient between x and y is found to be 1 and the correlation coefficient between y and z is found to be -1. The correlation coefficient between x and z is:

A -1 **B** 0   **C** 1   **D** cannot be calculated from this information (AEB)

Solution 10.9

D

Example 10.10

A skater is given a rank for technical skill and a rank for artistic merit by each of eight judges. The marks are to be ranked so that Spearman's rank correlation coefficient may be calculated. In the table below insert the ranks corresponding to the marks obtained for technical skill. (AEB)

Judge	A	B	C	D	E	F	G	H
Technical skill	5.8	5.5	5.4	5.7	5.5	5.6	5.5	5.7
Rank								

Solution 10.10

1, 6, 8, 2.5, 6, 4, 6, 2.5

Example 10.11

x	1	2	3	4	5
y	3.7	2.5	1.9	1.4	0.2

If a regression line were drawn for the above data and its equation obtained in the form $y = ax + b$ which one of the following conditions would be true?

A a and b both positive   **C** a negative and b positive

B a positive and b negative   **D** a and b both negative   (AEB)

Solution 10.11

C

10.4 Questions and exercises

Question 10.1

The figures below show the mean daily profit and the mean daily sales revenue for a sample of 6 shops in a town in 1980.

Shop	1	2	3	4	5	6
Mean daily profit (£)	30	60	45	90	120	70
Mean daily sales revenue (£)	400	500	500	800	900	600

(i)   Draw a scatter diagram to represent this data.

(ii)   Calculate the product moment correlation coefficient.

(iii)   Comment on your results.   (RSA)

Question 10.2

Permanent House Building – Completions (England and Wales)

	For local housing authorities	For private owners
1976	70	54
1977	68	53
1978	53	44
1979	42	35
1980	42	37
1981	31	28

Unit: thousands
Source: *Monthly Digest of Statistics*

(a) Draw a scatter diagram to represent these data.

(b) Calculate the product moment correlation coefficient.

(c) Interpret your results. (RSA)

Question 10.3

Explain fully the meaning of the two terms 'Regression' and 'Correlation'.

Calculate the product moment coefficient of correlation for the following data which compares market penetration ($y\%$) and retail price mark up ($x\%$) for a particular sector of manufactured products.

x:	15	18	20	25	28	32	36	40
y:	62	69	53	55	37	36	24	22

(Chartered Institute of Marketing)

Question 10.4

(a) Describe the differences in form between the product-moment coefficient and the rank coefficient of correlation (merely quoting the formulae which are given will not earn marks). How should one choose between these two coefficients?

(b) Using the data shown below calculate the rank coefficient of correlation for the Import penetration and Export sales ratios for the products of the stated manufacturing industries and comment on the significance of your result.

(Chartered Institute of Marketing)

	Ratio: imports/ home demand %	Ratio: exports/ total sales %
Food and drink	21	5
Chemical and allied industries	27	34
Metal manufacture	24	17
Mechanical engineering	28	40
Electrical engineering	29	20
Vehicles	23	39
Textiles	24	25
Clothing and footwear	20	11
Timber, furniture, etc.	32	5
Paper, printing and publishing	23	9

Source: Department of Industry

Question 10.5

(a) 'Correlation does not prove causation'. Discuss this statement.

(b) Figures for cinema admissions and colour television licences are given below.

Year	Cinema admissions (millions)	Colour television licences (millions)
1973	134	5.0
1974	138	6.8
1975	116	8.3
1976	104	9.6
1977	103	10.7
1978	126	12.0
1979	112	12.7
1980	96	12.9

Source: *Annual Abstract*

Calculate the product-moment correlation coefficient between the number of cinema admissions and the number of colour television licences issued. Briefly comment on your results. (ICSA)

Question 10.6

The table below shows the marks awarded to 10 candidates, A, B, . . . J, in History and Economics.

	Economics				
		40	50	60	70
	40	I	B		
History	50	C	F	J	
	60		H	D	E
	70			G	A

Calculate the product-moment coefficient of correlation between marks in the two subjects. Draw up a table to show the rank obtained by each candidate in each subject and hence calculate Spearman's coefficient of rank correlation. Comment on the values of the correlation coefficients. (AEB Additional Statistics)

Question 10.7

Correlation may be measured by either a product-moment coefficient or a rank coefficient. Explain the difference between these two coefficients making it clear when it is wise or convenient to use one or the other of these alternatives.

Calculate the rank coefficient of correlation from the following data which compare product recall in a test market with the price range of the product tested (one in each of nine ranges). Comment upon the significance of the result.

Price range (£)	1–3	4–6	7–9	10–12	13–15	16–19	20–24	25–29	30–39
Recall (%)	18	26	14	22	18	19	23	17	15

(Chartered Institute of Marketing)

Question 10.8

(a) Draw scatter diagrams which show:
  (i) Very strong positive correlation;
  (ii) Weak negative correlation;
  (iii) Zero correlation.

(b)

Year	Coal Production (millions tons)	Rail Freight (millions tons)
1970	159	209
1971	150	199
1972	126	178
1973	134	198
1974	119	178
1975	129	177
1976	127	176
1977	125	172

Source: *Annual Abstract*

Calculate a correlation coefficient and comment on your results. (RSA)

Question 10.9

(a) Explain, with the use of a diagram, the term 'positively correlated'.

(b)

Date	Minimum Lending Rate	Yield on $2\frac{1}{2}$% consuls
December 1972	9	10
December 1973	13	12
December 1974	12	17
December 1975	11	15
December 1976	15	15
December 1977	8	11
December 1978	13	12

Source: *Monthly Digest of Statistics*

(i) Calculate a correlation coefficient between Minimum Lending Rate and Yield on $2\frac{1}{2}$% consuls.

(ii) Comment on your results. (RSA)

Question 10.10

(a) Make use of scatter diagrams to distinguish variables which display:

    i) perfect positive correlation,

    (ii) weak negative correlation,

    (iii) zero correlation.

(b)

	Crude Steel Production (million tonnes)	
	British Steel Corporation	Private Sector
1972	22.9	2.4
1973	23.9	2.7
1974	19.2	3.1
1975	17.2	2.9
1976	19.1	3.2
1977	17.2	3.2
1978	16.7	3.6
1979	17.8	3.7

Source: *British Business*

    Calculate Spearman's Coefficient of Rank Correlation for the above data.

(c) Explain the meaning of your result in (b). (RSA)

Question 10.11

The table below shows the amount, in milligrams, of a certain drug absorbed by five patients on two successive days. Calculate Spearman's coefficient of rank correlation. (AEB)

Patient	A	B	C	D	E
Day 1	35.5	16.7	29.4	19.8	30.1
Day 2	28.4	14.9	14.6	16.8	32.4

Question 10.12

Six petrol stations A–F were ranked three times, firstly according to quality of service (rank 1 indicating best service), secondly according to price (rank 1 indicating lowest price) and thirdly according to sales (rank 1 indicating largest sales). The results are given below.

Station	Quality of service	Petrol price	Sales
A	5	1	2
B	3	2	1
C	2	6	4
D	6	4	5
E	1	3	3
F	4	5	6

(i) Using *rank* correlation coefficients examine whether price of petrol or quality of service is likely to be the more important factor in determining volume of petrol sales.

(ii) The *rank* correlation coefficient between quality of service and petrol price is -0.2. What does this result indicate? (RSA)

Question 10.13

Five pupils obtain marks of 11, 9, 13, 14, 10 out of 20 in a French test and in a Chemistry test the same five pupils obtain 13, 16, 8, 8, 10 out of 20 respectively. Calculate the product-moment coefficient of correlation between the marks in the two subjects.

Calculate the Spearman coefficient of rank correlation. Comment on your result. (AEB Additional Statistics)

Question 10.14

United Kingdom Footwear Manufacturers' Sales

Year	1972	1973	1974	1975	1976	1977	1978	1979
All footwear (million pairs)	184.4	189.3	173.1	163.5	156.5	159.6	161.0	156.7
Sports shoes (million pairs)	3.3	3.2	3.1	3.7	4.4	5.3	5.5	4.6

Source: *Annual Abstract of Statistics*, 1981

(a) Illustrate the data above graphically.

(b) Calculate a rank correlation coefficient between the two series.

(c) Comment briefly on the trends revealed by the data. (SUJB)

Question 10.15

From a set of observations of a pair of variables, x and y, it is found that the mean of the x values is 2 and the mean of the y values is 4. Given that the coefficient of regression of y on x is -1, draw the line of regression of y on x. (AEB)

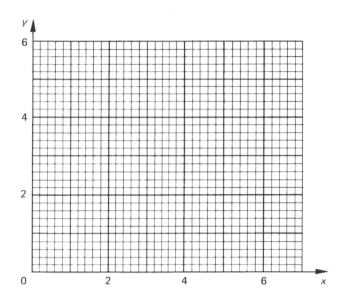

Question 10.16

A sample of eight employees is taken from the production department of a light engineering factory. The data below relate to the number of weeks experience in the wiring of components, and the number of components which were rejected as unsatisfactory last week.

Employee	A	B	C	D	E	F	G	H
Weeks of experience (x)	4	5	7	9	10	11	12	14
Number of rejects (y)	21	22	15	18	14	14	11	13

$\Sigma x = 72$, $\Sigma y = 128$, $\Sigma xy = 1069$, $\Sigma x^2 = 732$, $\Sigma y^2 = 2156$

(a) Draw a scatter diagram of this data.
(b) Calculate a coefficient of correlation for these data and interpret its value.
(c) Find the least squares regression equation of rejects on experience. Predict the number of rejects you would expect from an employee with one week of experience.   (ICMA)

Question 10.17

Ten pupils took a Statistics examination in which they had to answer 4 questions out of 6, each question carrying a maximum of 20 marks.
   An analysis of the marks of the ten pupils gave the following data:

Question number	Topic	Pupil A	B	C	D	E	F	G	H	I	J
1	Mean and mean deviation	12	8	6	19	1	2	5	9	11	7
2	Pictorial presentation	14	13	12	11	9	10	13	14	11	13
3	Scatter diagrams	2	—	—	15	—	—	—	0	7	—
4	Cumulative frequency	—	0	—	—	4	13	—	—	—	8
5	Moving average	—	—	5	—	—	—	14	—	—	—
6	Rank correlation	8	9	11	11	4	6	3	12	16	20

(i)   Calculate the mean and the mean deviation of the marks for (a) question 1
         (b) question 2.
         Comment on your answers.
(ii)   Which topic gave the greatest range of marks? State the greatest range.
(iii)   Which topic gave the smallest range of marks? State the smallest range.
(iv)   Calculate, for question 3 in the table, the mean score per attempt. Give two
         factors, each of which would account for a low mean score per attempt for
         a question.
(v)   Calculate Spearman's coefficient of rank correlation between the marks for
         question 1 and those for question 6.   (AEB)

Question 10.18

x	2	4	6	8
y	6	9	14	21

For the set of pairs of observations above, the regression line of y on x passes
through the origin. Find the equation of the regression line.   (AEB)

Question 10.19

The following data gives the actual sales of a company in each of 8 regions of a
country together with the forecast of sales by two different methods.

Region	Actual sales	Forecast 1	Forecast 2
A	15	13	16
B	19	25	19
C	30	23	26
D	12	26	14
E	58	48	65
F	10	15	19
G	23	28	27
H	17	10	22

(i)   Calculate the *rank* correlation coefficient between
         (1) Actual sales and forecast 1;
         (2) Actual sales and forecast 2.
(ii)   Which forecast method would you recommend next year?   (ICSA)

Question 10.20

(a)   Construct the scatter diagram for the following data which shows figures
         which are related to a company's quarterly expenditure on advertising (X)
         and its turnover for the following quarter (Y).

X:	38	49	61	48	53	36	56	45
Y:	139	152	175	144	153	141	168	160

(b) Calculate the equation of the regression line Y on X.
(c) Estimate the likely value of Y for $X = 60$ and indicate the advice you would give someone using this estimate. (Institute of Marketing)

Question 10.21

From a set of observations of a pair of variables, x and y, it is found that the coefficient of regression of y on x is 1.2 and that the line of regression of y on x passes through the point (5, 7). Find the value of y corresponding to $x = 2$.

(AEB)

Question 10.22

On the diagram below plot five points such that the regression line of y on x is $y = 3 - 1.5x$ and the correlation coefficient is -1. (AEB)

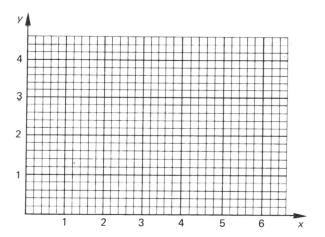

Question 10.23

Abinda is investigating the pocket money received by pupils in her school. She draws a scatter diagram of the pupils' ages and the pocket money they each receive.

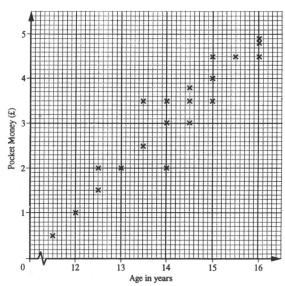

(a)   How much pocket money does the youngest pupil receive?

(b)   How many pupils receive more than £3 a week?

(c)   Describe accurately the type of correlation shown by the diagram.

(d)   Abinda has forgotten to plot the information for herself. She is 15 and is given £2.50 per week pocket money. Make this information on the diagram for her.

(e)   Abinda decides to group her data.

(i)   Complete the table, to include Abinda's own result.

Amount of pocket money (p)	Number of pupils
0–	
100–	
200–	
300–	
400–	

(ii) Draw the histogram for Abinda.

(iii) Label the modal group.   (SEG)

11

Forecasting and Trends

Objectives   By the end of this chapter the following terms and methods of calculation should be understood:

	Date attempted	Date completed	Self-assessment
Forecasting and trends			
Moving averages			
Seasonal variations			
Linear trends			
Three point linear estimation			
Least squares linear estimation			

Summary   This chapter describes methods of forecasting and calculating trends through moving averages and linear estimation.

11.1 Introduction

Forecasts are based on information about the way in which variables have been behaving in the past.

The charting of trends can provide the means for:

(i)   control,
(ii)   interpolation,
(iii)   extrapolation.

A *time series* consists of numerical data recorded at intervals of time. *Trends* include:

(i)   long-term or secular;
(ii)   cyclical fluctuations;
(iii)   seasonal variations;
(iv)   irregular fluctuations.

11.2 Techniques used to analyse trends

(a)   Moving averages

This is a method of repeatedly calculating a series of different average values along a time series to produce a trend line. Some figures will be above the average, others below it; by using an average, fluctuations are offset one against another to produce the trend.

This method can be referred to as the 'additive model', to distinguish it from other methods, and the moving average is 'centred'.

For example: annual sales of a company over a fifteen year period (see Table 11.1).

The moving average is calculated by:

(i)   adding up the sales figures for the first five years and dividing by five to produce an average ($32 \div 5 = 6.4$);
(ii)   subtracting the first year and adding the sixth year to obtain the next moving average ($(32 - 5 + 17) = 32 + 12 = 44, 44 \div 5 = 8.8$). This is continued through the series;

Table 11.1   Moving average

Year	Sales (£m)		5-year moving average
1982	5		
1983	2		
1984	4	$32 \div 5 = 6.4$	6.4
1985	9	$44 \div 5 = 8.8$	8.8
1986	12		10.4
1987	17		10.8
1988	10		11.6
1989	6		13.2
1990	13		13.4
1991	20		13.2
1992	18		15.2
1993	9		17.0
1994	16		17.0
1995	22		
1996	20		

(iii) plotting the moving average trend line against the sales figures, as shown in Fig. 11.1.

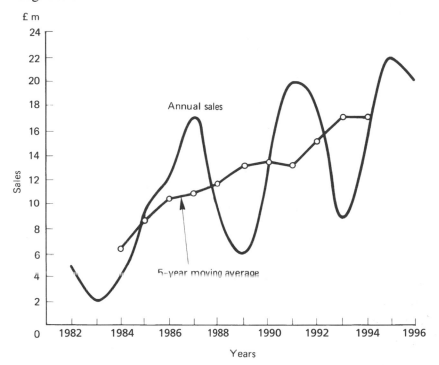

Figure 11.1 Moving average

(b) Seasonal variations

The effects of seasonal variations are often eliminated from data in order to clarify the underlying trend, data is 'seasonally adjusted'.

A commonly used method (there are others), is as shown in Table 11.2.

Table 11.2 Seasonal adjustments

Years + quarters		(1) Sales £m	(2) 4-quarterly totals	(3) Centred totals	(4) Trends	(5) Variations from the trend
1992	1	11				
	2	8				
	3	13	50	104	13	0
	4	18	54	109	13.6	+4.4
1993	1	15	55	115	14.3	+0.7
	2	9	60	126	15.8	−6.8
	3	18	66	133	16.6	+1.4
	4	24	67	136	17	+7
1994	1	16	69	145	18.1	−2.1
	2	11	76	156	19.5	−8.5
	3	25	80	162	20.3	+4.7
	4	28	82	165	20.6	+7.4
1995	1	18	83	165	20.6	−2.6
	2	12	82	166	20.8	−8.8
	3	24	84			
	4	30				

(i) Column (1) shows the sales in £m;

(ii) column (2) shows the 4-quarterly totals (11 + 8 + 13 + 18 = 50, 8 + 13 + 18 + 15 = 54 etc.);

(iii)   column (3) shows the total of each pair of 4-quarterly totals (50 + 54 = 104, 54 + 55 = 109 etc.);

(iv)   column (4) shows the trend, arrived at by dividing the centred totals in column (3) by 8 (104 ÷ 8 = 13, 109 ÷ 8 = 13.6 etc.);

(v)   column (5) shows the variation between sales in column (1) and the trend in column (4) (13 − 13 = 0, 18 − 13.6 = +4.4, 15 − 14.3 = +0.7 etc.).

It is from column (5) of Table 11.2 that the seasonal variations are calculated:

Table 11.3   Seasonal variations

Year	Quarters			
	1	2	3	4
1992	—	—	0	+4.4
1993	+0.7	−6.8	+1.4	+7
1994	−2.1	−8.5	+4.7	+7.4
1995	−2.6	−8.8	—	—
Totals	−4	−24.1	+6.1	+18.8

(1) Average:	−1.3	−8.03	+2.03	+6.27
(2) Adjustment:	+0.26	+0.26	+0.26	+0.26
(3) Seasonal variations:	−1	−7.8	+2.3	+6.5

(i)   The average (1) is the total for each of the quarters divided by the appropriate number of quarters (+0.7 − 2.1 − 2.6 = −4 and −4 ÷ 3 = −1.3 etc.);

(ii)   the adjustment (2) is based on the 'unexplained' deviations that have not been entirely eliminated – if they had, the sum of the averages would have been zero;

(iii)   this excess negative figure is taken from each quarter equally by dividing by 4 (1.03 ÷ 4 = 0.2575) and adding this figure (0.26) to each quarterly average – it is *added* because it is not clear where the difference arises;

(iv)   the final row (3) is the estimate of seasonal variations for each quarter (−1.3 + 0.26 = −1.04, −8.03 + 0.26 = −7.77, +2.03 + 0.26 = +2.29, +6.27 + 0.26 = +6.53). These figures are rounded to one decimal place, because to extend the figures further would indicate a higher degree of accuracy than is likely (−1, −7.8, +2.3, +6.5).

These figures can be used to produce a seasonally adjusted series and they can be applied to future years:

Table 11.4   Seasonally adjusted sales figures: 1996 sales figures

Quarters	Sales (£m)	Seasonal adjustment	Seasonally adjusted sales (£m)
1	20	+1	21
2	15	+7.8	22.8
3	25	−2.3	22.7
4	35	−6.5	28.5

N.B. The minus figures for seasonal variation have been added and the plus figures subtracted. This is being done to eliminate seasonal variations and therefore additions are made to the generally low seasons, and subtractions made to the seasons in which the variable has a high value.

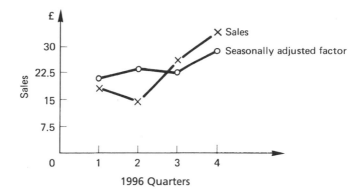

Figure 11.2 Seasonally adjusted sales

(c)   Residual factors

Irregular and residual fluctuations give an indication of the extent to which the series has been affected by irregular external factors. The curve of the graph in a time series reflects the trend, seasonal variations and irregular factors. The value of the irregular and residual fluctuations can be calculated once the trend and seasonal variations have been calculated.

For example: see Table 11.5.

Table 11.5   Residual factors

Years + quarters		Original series (see Table 11.2)	= Trend	+ Seasonal variation	+ Residual
1992	1	11			
	2	8			
	3	13	13	+2.3	−2.3
	4	18	13.6	+6.5	−2.1
1993	1	15	14.3	−1	+1.7
	2	9	15.8	−7.8	+1
	3	18	16.6	−2.3	−0.9
	4	24	17	+6.5	+0.5
1994	1	16	18.1	−1	−1.1
	2	11	19.5	−7.8	−0.7
	3	25	20.3	+2.3	+2.4
	4	28	20.6	+6.5	+0.9
1995	1	18	20.6	−1	−1.6
	2	12	20.8	−7.8	−1
	3	24			
	4	30			

The residual = the original series − (trend + seasonal variations)
13 − (13 + 2.3) = −2.3

(d)   Linear trends

Trends can be shown by a straight line if there is a linear relationship between the variables. The straight line can be based on a mathematical equation, such as with *the least-squares method*; or the straight line can be drawn by eye to provide a *line of best fit* (as for scatter diagrams, see Chapter 10); where there is a strong linear correlation between two variables it is possible to use the method of *three-point* (or two-point) *linear estimation* (also known as three-point linear regression and the method of partial averages), to produce a straight line or an approximation to it.

(i)   Line of best fit

For example: see Fig. 11.3.

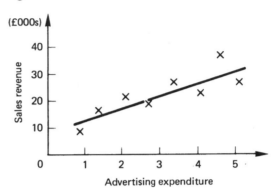

Figure 11.3 Line of best fit

(ii)   Three-point linear estimation

This is a method of finding a trend line which will approximate to a straight line, by finding three averages for a series:

(i)   calculate the arithmetic mean of each variable: this co-ordinate provides point (1);

(ii)   calculate the arithmetic mean of the figures which are positioned above point (1) for each variable: this provides the co-ordinate for point (2);

(iii) calculate the arithmetic mean of the figures which are positioned below point (1) for each variable: this provides the co-ordinate for point (3);

(iv)   these points are plotted on a graph to provide a trend line; the line is drawn through the overall mean co-ordinate and as nearly as possible through the other two points.

For example: see Table 11.6 and Fig. 11.4.

Table 11.6   Three-point linear estimation

Year	Sales (£m)		
1982	5		
1983	2	Average sales $= \dfrac{59}{7} = 8.4$	(3)
1984	4	below mean	
1985	9	Central year = 1985	
1986	12		
1987	17		
1988	10	Arithmetic mean $= \dfrac{183}{15} = 12.2$	(1)
1989	6	of sales	
1990	13	Central year = 1989	
1991	20		
1992	18		
1993	9	Average sales $= \dfrac{118}{7} = 16.9$	(2)
1994	16	above mean	
1995	22	Central year = 1993	
1996	20		

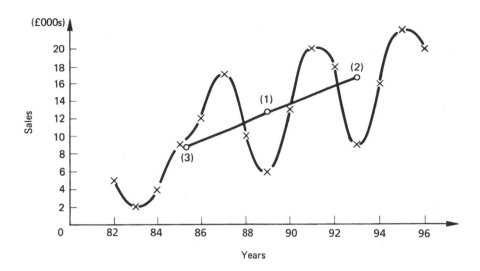

Figure 11.4 Three-point linear estimation

(iii) Two-point linear estimation

This is a method of finding a straight trend line, by finding two averages for a series:

(i)   divide the series into two equal halves, each containing a complete number of years (if the series contains an odd number of years, omit the middle year);

(ii) calculate the mean of each half;

(iii) plot the two mean values on a graph and then join them to produce a trend line.

For example: in the example in Table 11.6, the two means would be £8.4 m and £16.9 m. These two points are plotted and joined to form the trend line.

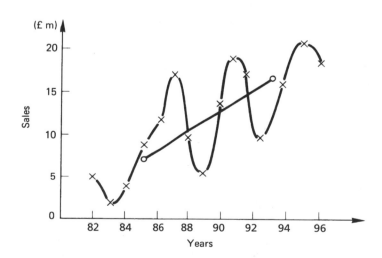

Figure 11.5 Two-point linear estimation

N.B. This method is not very accurate if there are any extreme values in the series. Both this method and three-point linear estimation are approximations to a mathematically produced linear trend, but they are likely to be more accurate than a line of best fit drawn by eye.

(iv)   Least-squares method

The aim of this method is to produce a line which minimises all positive and negative deviations of the data from a straight line drawn through the data. This is carried out by squaring the deviations (to remove minus items), and therefore, the least squares is the 'best' line, the line which minimises the error in the direction of the variable being predicted.

The straight line equation can be used where:

$$y = a + bx$$

where y and x are two variables, a represents the intercept, and b represents the slope or gradient of the line (see Fig. 11.6).

$$\text{The slope, } b = \frac{\Sigma xy - \dfrac{\Sigma x \times \Sigma y}{n}}{\Sigma x^2 - \dfrac{(\Sigma x)^2}{n}} \quad \text{or} \quad \frac{n\Sigma xy - \Sigma x \Sigma y}{n\Sigma x^2 - (\Sigma x)^2}$$

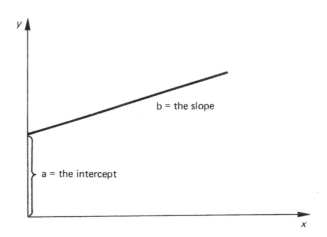

Figure 11.6 The slope and the intercept

The intercept, $a = \bar{y} - b\bar{x}$

The straight line equation: $y = a + bx$ can be re-written as $y = \bar{y} - b\bar{x} + bx$

where $\bar{y}$ and $\bar{x}$ are the arithmetic means of the two variables.

In a time series one of the two variables is time and this usually increases by equal amounts. The time factor does not have a 'value', but it is possible to number the years (months, weeks or days) in order as an increase of one on the last. When the variable x is not time, then the straight line produced by the least-squares method is a regression line (see Chapter 10).

For example: see Table 11.7.

Table 11.7 The least-squares method

Year x		Sales (£m) y	x^2	y^2	xy
1982	(0)	5	0	25	0
1983	(1)	2	1	4	2
1984	(2)	4	4	16	8
1985	(3)	9	9	81	27
1986	(4)	12	16	144	48
1987	(5)	17	25	289	85
1988	(6)	10	36	100	60
1989	(7)	6	49	36	42
1990	(8)	13	64	169	104
1991	(9)	20	81	400	180
1992	(10)	18	100	324	180
1993	(11)	9	121	81	99
1994	(12)	16	144	256	192
1995	(13)	22	169	484	286
1996	(14)	20	196	400	280
	105	183	1015	2809	1593

$$\bar{x} = \frac{105}{15} = 7 \qquad \bar{y} = \frac{183}{15} = 12.2$$

$$b = \frac{1593 - \dfrac{105 \times 183}{15}}{1015 - \dfrac{(105)^2}{15}} = \frac{1593 - 1281}{1015 - 735}$$

$$= \frac{312}{280} = 1.11$$

$$y = 12.2 - (1.11 \times 7) + (1.11 \times x)$$
$$= 12.2 - 7.77 + 1.11x$$
$$= 4.43 + 1.11x$$

Each year (x) there will be an average increase of £1.11 (million) in sales. When $x = 5$, y will equal $4.43 + 1.11 \times 5 = 9.98$. This can be applied to the data to produce a linear trend (Table 11.8 and Fig. 11.7).

Table 11.8 Linear trend

Year		Sales (£m)	Linear trend
1982	(0)	5	$y = 4.43 + 1.11 \times 0 = 4.43$
1983	(1)	2	$y = 4.43 + 1.11 \times 1 = 5.54$
1984	(2)	4	$2 = 6.65$
1985	(3)	9	$3 = 7.76$
1986	(4)	12	$4 = 8.87$
1987	(5)	17	$5 = 9.98$
1988	(6)	10	$6 = 11.09$
1989	(7)	6	$7 = 12.2$
1990	(8)	13	$8 = 13.31$
1991	(9)	20	$9 = 14.42$
1992	(10)	18	$10 = 15.53$
1993	(11)	9	$11 = 16.64$
1994	(12)	16	$12 = 17.75$
1995	(13)	22	$13 = 18.86$
1996	(14)	20	$14 = 19.97$

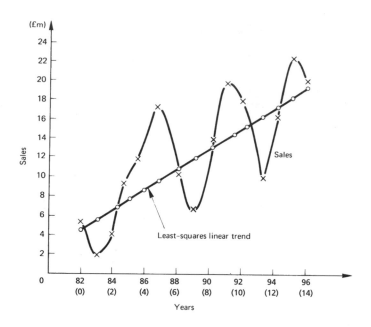

Figure 11.7 The least-squares trend line

Example 11.1

Briefly describe the components that make up a typical time series. Explain the purpose of moving averages.

Solution 11.1

A time series consists of numerical data recorded at intervals of time, such as days, weeks, months, quarters, years. Typically the variable recorded against time consists of such items as sales, costs and output, but can include many other types of data. Usually the information is shown in a table and plotted on a graph.

Trends can be observed by looking at the table and the graph, however to clarify these trends a line can be calculated. One method of doing this is by a moving average. A moving average is a method of repeatedly calculating a series of different average values along a time series to produce a trend line. Some figures will be above the average, others below it; by using an average, fluctuations are offset one against another to produce the trend.

Moving averages show the long-term trend. It is useful to see what the trend is so as to be able to have some control over future policy. For example, if sales appear to be rising this may encourage plans to expand output. A trend for sales to fall may lead to policies to alter this situation. It is possible also to interpolate information from within the trend line and to extrapolate information into the future. However, extrapolation needs to be used cautiously because internal and external factors can cause unforeseen changes in the trend. Allowing for seasonal variations may help to indicate the underlying trend. A typical time series may include a long-term or secular trend if the data covers some years. Cyclical fluctuations may be clear, linked, for example, to the business cycle. Seasonal variations may be an important component of some series and there may be irregular fluctuations. By distinguishing a trend on a graph it may be possible to forecast future development based on past experience. This can be useful in many areas, such as in market research and business forecasting and in areas such as the demand for health and education services which may be indicated by trends in the birth rate.

Example 11.2

The table below shows the sales of sportswear for a particular company over a period of three years.

Sales of sportswear (£ millions)				
Quarter	1	2	3	4
1992	10	15	14	12
1993	14	20	15	15
1994	12	18	15	12

(a) By means of a moving average find the trend of sales;

(b) plot both the original figures and the trend on a graph;

(c) by calculating the variation from the trend establish the seasonal components;

(d) forecast the sales for the first two quarters of 1995;

(e) comment briefly on your results.

Solution 11.2

(a)

Quarter		Sales (£m)	4-Quarterly Totals	Central Totals	Trends (moving average)	Variation from trend
1992	1	10				
	2	15				
	3	14	51	106	13.3	+0.7
	4	12	55	115	14.4	−2.4
1993	1	14	60	121	15.1	−1.1
	2	20	61	125	15.6	+4.4
	3	15	64	126	15.8	−0.8
	4	15	62			
1994	1	12	60	122	15.3	−0.3
	2	18	60	120	15	−3
	3	15	57	117	14.6	+3.4
	4	12				

(b)

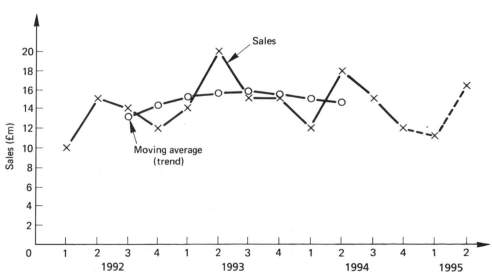

(c)

Year	Quarters			
	1	2	3	4
1992			+0.7	−2.4
1993	−1.1	+4.4	−0.8	−0.3
1994	−3	+3.4		
	−4.1	+7.8	−0.1	−2.7
Average	−2.05	+3.9	−0.05	−1.35
Adjustments	−0.11	−0.11	−0.11	−0.11
Seasonal variation	−2.2	+3.8	−0.2	−1.5

Total + 0.45 ÷ 4 = +0.11

(d) Sales for 1995:   1st Quarter   £11 million
                        2nd Quarter   £16 million

(e) The moving average indicates that the trend of sales rose in 1993 but has then started to fall. It could be expected therefore that the sales for 1995 could be lower than for the equivalent periods of 1994. The first quarter of 1995 could show sales of £11 m as compared with £12 m for 1993; the second quarter would normally show an upturn on the first quarter, but again a smaller change than in 1994, perhaps to £16 m.

These forecasts can be only estimates because the evidence available is limited and there could be unknown factors which could alter the pattern.

Example 11.3

For the data below, plot the points on a graph and draw a line of best fit through the points. Calculate a three-point linear estimation and plot this line on the graph. Discuss the results briefly.

Year	Sales (£)	Answer
1988	8	
1989	12	$\frac{45}{4} = £11.25$
1990	10	
1991	15	$\frac{120}{8} = £15$
1992	14	
1993	16	
1994	20	$\frac{75}{4} = £18.75$
1995	25	

Solution 11.3

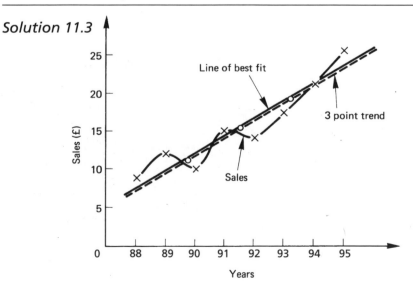

In this case the three points calculated by averages approximate to a straight line. This will coincide with a 'line of best fit' because there are approximately the same number of co-ordinates on either side of the line. The lines indicate that the sales are rising over the years. Any extrapolation of this line would depend for its accuracy on the trends continuing without any major changes in the market for this commodity.

Example 11.4

The mid-day temperature on a number of days is compared with the sales from iced drinks dispensers on the same day, to give the following results:

Mid-day temperatures (°C)x	Sales of iced-drinks (£000s)y
10	2
12	3
16	3
20	5
22	6
32	10
33	9
35	12
38	15
42	15

Calculate the two-point linear estimation and plot these points on a graph.

Solution 11.4

(i) x: $10 + 12 + 16 + 20 + 22 = 80$ and $80 \div 5 = 16(°C)$

(i) y: $2 + 3 + 3 + 5 + 6 = 19$ and $19 \div 5 = 3.8$ (£000s)

(ii) x: $32 + 33 + 35 + 38 + 42 = 180$ and $180 \div 5 = 36(°C)$

(ii) y: $10 + 9 + 12 + 15 + 15 = 61$ and $61 \div 5 = 12.2$ (£000s)

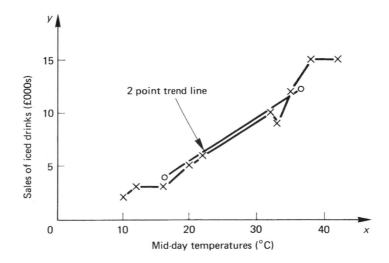

Example 11.5

Calculate the least-squares regression line of cost on output from the following table and plot the line on a graph. Comment briefly on the result.

Week	Units of output	Cost (£)
1	3	5
2	6	9
3	8	10
4	10	12
5	13	14
6	17	16

Solution 11.5

Week	Units of output x	Cost (£) y	x^2	y^2	xy
1	3	5	9	25	15
2	6	9	36	81	54
3	8	10	64	100	80
4	10	12	100	144	120
5	13	14	169	196	182
6	17	16	289	256	272
	57	66	667	802	723

$$\bar{x} = \frac{57}{6} = 9.5 \qquad \bar{y} = \frac{66}{6} = 11$$

$$b = \frac{723 - \dfrac{57 \times 66}{6}}{667 - \dfrac{(57)^2}{6}} = \frac{723 - 627}{667 - 541.5} = \frac{96}{125.3}$$

$$= 0.8$$

$$y = 11 - (0.8 \times 9.5) + (0.8 \times x) = 11 - 7.6 + 0.8x$$
$$= 3.4 + 0.8x$$

Week	Units of output (x)	Cost (£) (y)	Regression of y on x
1	3	5	$y = 3.4 + 0.8 \times 3 = 5.8$
2	6	9	$= 3.4 + 0.8 \times 6 = 8.2$
3	8	10	$= 9.8$
4	10	12	$= 11.4$
5	13	14	$= 13.8$
6	17	16	$= 17$

The graph shows the regression line for total cost (y) on output (x). This indicates that for an increase in output of x units the total cost will increase by

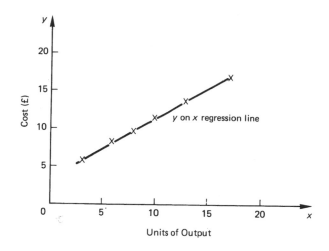

2.45 + 0.8. Therefore, for an output of 12 units, the total cost will be 3.4 + 0.8 × 12 = £13.00. It is possible to extrapolate and to forecast, for instance, that for an output of 20 units the total cost will be 3.4 + 0.8 × 20 = £19.40. Any such forecast will depend upon the trend continuing in the same direction it has in the past.

Example 11.6

The time series given below shows the cost of production of Marco plc for a four year period spanning 1977–81.

Cost of production (£000s) of Marco plc

Year	Quarter			
	I	II	III	IV
1987			55.8	53.6
1988	55.5	57.5	57.2	54.6
1989	56.3	56.0	55.4	50.4
1990	56.1	57.5	53.9	53.4
1991	60.1	63.0		

Required:
(a) By using the method of moving averages calculate the trend of the production costs. Plot both sets of figures on a graph and comment on the trend.
(b) By calculating the variation from the trend establish the seasonal variations.
(c) Deseasonalise the original data using the figures from (b) and interpret the results.

Solution 11.6

(to calculation only)

(a) Trend −, −, 55.8, 56.1, 56.3, 56.2, 55.8, 55.1, 54.5, 54.7, 54.7, 54.9, 55.7, 56.9, −, −.
(b) Seasonal variations: 0.78, 1.85, 0.25, −2.88

(c)   Seasonally adjusted trend: $-$, $-$, 55.6, 56.5, 54.7, 55.6, 57.0, 57.5, 55.5, 55.1, 55.2, 53.3, 55.3, 55.6, 53.7, 56.7, 56.3, 59.3, 61.1.

Example 11.7

United Kingdom passenger movement abroad by sea and air (100 000s):

Quarter	1	2	3	4
1979	46	86	120	61
1980	53	89	125	61
1981	51	91	132	66

Source: *Monthly Digest of Statistics*

(i)   By means of a moving average find the trend and the seasonal adjustment.

(ii)   Forecast passenger movements for the first two quarters of 1982.   (ICSA)

Solution 11.7

(i)   Trend values: 79.175, 80.375, 81.375, 82.0, 81.75, 81.75, 82.875, 84.375, 84.375

Seasonal factors:

Quarter	1	-29.80
	2	7.14
	3	42.39
	4	-19.73

(ii)   56, 93 (depending on forecasting method).

Example 11.8

What is the value of the third average in a set of three point moving averages calculated from the following numbers?   (AEB)

4	5	7	6	8	3	4	9	7	8	6

A 5   **B** 6   **C** 7   **D** 8

Solution 11.8

C

Example 11.9

Observations of a variable are made on the 15th day of each month of 1981. How many values of a five-point moving average could be calculated?   (AEB)

Solution 11.9

8

Example 11.10

The figures given below are observations of a variable taken at consecutive equally spaced times.

12	14	13	16	18	17	21	23	22	27	29	28

Determine:

(i)   the most appropriate number of observations to use as a basis for moving averages;

(ii) the value of the ninth moving average. (AEB)

Solution 11.10

(i) 3,   (ii) 26

Example 11.11

Find the value of the fifth average in a series of six-point moving averages for the following sequence:

25	27	32	31	30	35	40	46	41	42	42	45

Solution 11.11

39

11.4 Questions and exercises

Question 11.1

For what sort of data is it useful to plot a moving average? (SUJB)

Question 11.2

A milkman collects money on Thursdays, Fridays and Saturdays. The amount collected on each day over a three-week period was as follows:

	T	F	S	T	F	S	T	F	S
Amount collected (£)	196	340	413	212	354	$2x$	x	312	382

If an appropriate moving average were calculated, what would be the value of the third point? (SUJB)

Question 11.3

If in question 11.2 the fourth moving average has a value of £328, what is the value of the sixth moving average? (SUJB)

Question 11.4

Meteorological records of a certain station showed that the number of days in the years from 1970 to 1979 on which snow fell were as follows:

Year	1970	1971	1972	1973	1974	1975	1976	1977	1978	1979
Days	4	5	7	5	8	11	7	12	16	10

(i)   Calculate the 3-point moving averages and their mean value.
(ii) Plot the data on graph paper and indicate on your diagram the moving averages you calculated in (i). Does there appear to be any change in the data over time?
(iii) Draw, by eye, a suitable straight line through the moving averages. Calculate the gradient of your line and explain what this tells us about snowfall over the period 1970–79.   (WJEC)

Question 11.5

Explain the purpose of moving averages. Define the terms secular trend, seasonal variation and random variation as used in the analysis of time series.

The table below shows the number of houses sold by an estate agent per quarter from 1977.

	Houses sold 1st quarter	2nd quarter	3rd quarter	4th quarter
1977	160	300	275	180
1978	200	325	310	215
1979	225	350	320	240
1980	245	370	—	—

(a) Using 2 cm to represent 50 houses and 1 cm to represent one quarter, draw a graph of the given data.
(b) Calculate, to the nearest whole number, a set of appropriate moving averages and plot these on your graph.
(c) Estimate the number of houses the estate agent may expect to sell during the third quarter of 1980.   (AEB)

Question 11.6

An amateur geologist collected 12 specimens of minerals, which she believed to be either quartz or barite. The mass and the volume of each specimen were determined and the results are tabulated below.

Specimen	A	B	C	D	E	F	G	H	I	J	K	L
Volume (cm³)	3.3	5.3	3.2	1.7	4.3	4.1	1.9	6.0	2.3	3.7	1.8	5.0
Mass (g)	8.7	14.0	14.4	7.7	19.3	10.9	8.5	16.0	6.1	16.7	18.6	22.5

(i)   Using 1 cm to represent 1 g on the vertical axis and 2 cm to represent 1 cm³ on the horizontal axis, plot a scatter diagram of mass against volume, lettering each point.

(ii) The mass of 1 cm^3 of quartz is 2.65 g. By drawing an appropriate straight line on your diagram, list, in alphabetical order, the five specimens which appear to be quartz.

(iii) List, in alphabetical order, the six specimens which appear to be barite.

(iv) Calculate the mean volume and the mean mass of the six specimens which appear to be barite.

(v) Draw the line of best fit by eye through the points which represent these barite specimens.

(vi) Use the line of best fit to estimate
(a) the mass of a specimen of barite of volume 3.0 cm^3,
(b) the volume of a specimen of barite of mass 18.0 g.

(vii) One of the twelve plotted points does not lie on either of these two lines. Suggest three possible reasons, each of which might account for this.

(AEB)

Question 11.7

The table shows the average household quarterly expenditure on all fuels for the years 1975–79. Identify the trend by the method of moving averages, and by examining the fluctuations of the series about the trend, estimate the quarterly seasonal variations. (Chartered Institute of Marketing)

	1975	1976	1977	1978	1979
1st quarter	75	89	104	116	138
2nd quarter	42	51	59	66	79
3rd quarter	35	42	49	55	67
4th quarter	63	75	88	98	117

Question 11.8

From the data supplied obtain a forecast of sales for each of the quarters of 1983 by a simple extrapolation of trend and seasonal variation, using the method of moving averages. (Chartered Institute of Marketing)

	Sales of linoleum (in thousands of square metres)		
	1980	1981	1982
1st quarter	39	26	14
2nd quarter	47	30	21
3rd quarter	48	35	28
4th quarter	37	24	18

Question 11.9

Calculate a five month moving average for the following series and plot the moving averages and the original time series on one graph.

Hence, by graphical means or otherwise, obtain a forecast of production for each of the last four months of 1981. (Chartered Institute of Marketing)

					Monthly production of bricks in millions							
Month	J	F	M	A	M	J	J	A	S	O	N	D
1980	38	45	46	32	36	41	46	51	34	38	43	49
1981	54	39	44	46	52	59	40	45	—	—	—	—

Question 11.10

The data below give the monthly sales of wine (thousands of one-litre bottles) of an importer, together with a 5-point moving total.

	Jan.	Feb.	Mar.	Apr.	May	June	July	Aug.	Sep.	Oct.	Nov.	Dec.
1981 Sales							1.4	1.0	1.3	1.4	1.4	2.9
Moving total									6.5	8.0	8.0	7.5
1982 Sales	1.0	0.8	0.9	0.9	1.4	1.5	1.8	1.9	1.9	0.9	1.0	3.3
Moving total	7.0	6.5	5.0	5.5	6.5	7.5	8.5	8.0	7.5	9.0	8.0	7.0
1983 Sales	0.9	0.9	0.9	1.0	1.8	1.9	1.9	1.9	2.0	1.3		
Moving total	7.0	7.0	5.5	6.5	7.5	8.5	9.5	9.0				

(a) Assuming an *additive* model, calculate a 5-point moving average and determine the trend and hence obtain a seasonally adjusted series.

(b) Plot the original series, trend and seasonally adjusted series on one graph.

(c) Comment on your results.   (ICMA)

Question 11.11

Marriages in the United Kingdom (thousands)				
Quarter	1	2	3	4
1978	80	101	147	88
1979	78	109	142	89
1980	76	112	140	86

Source: *Monthly Digest of Statistics*

(i) By means of a moving average find the trend and the seasonal factors.

(ii) Give the figures for 1980 seasonally adjusted.   (RSA)

Question 11.12

Sale of men's socks (million pairs)				
Quarter	1	2	3	4
1979	8.2	9.4	9.7	11.9
1980	7.1	8.2	9.4	11.4
1981	7.0	7.9	8.4	11.0

Source: Department of Industry

(a) Smooth this time series by means of a centred four quarterly moving average.

(b) Plot the original and moving average figures on the same graph.

(c) Discuss the essential feature of this time series as shown by the graph, suggesting why this product has this sales pattern. (RSA)

Question 11.13

Total sales of gas by the public supply system (units: therms $\times 10^9$)				
Quarter	1	2	3	4
1979	5.9	3.6	2.4	4.6
1980	6.1	3.3	2.3	4.9
1981	5.9	3.6	2.2	5.2

Source: Department of Energy

(a) Calculate, using the method of centred moving averages, the average seasonal variation for this data.
(b) Give the seasonally adjusted figures for 1981.
(c) Would you expect a similar sales pattern for electricity? Give a reason for your answer. (RSA)

Question 11.14

Sales of women's jumpers, cardigans, etc. (millions)				
Quarter	1	2	3	4
1977	22	17	19	22
1978	16	17	19	21
1979	15	14	14	17

Source: *Monthly Digest of Statistics*

(i) By means of a moving average find the trend and the seasonal components.
(ii) Forecast sales for the first two quarters of 1980.
(iii) Comment on the likely accuracy of your results. (RSA)

Question 11.15

(a) Briefly describe the components which make up a typical series.
(b) Sales by Mail Order Business (£100m)

Sales by Mail Order Business (£100m)				
Quarter	1	2	3	4
1977	14	13	13	20
1978	17	16	16	20
1979	19	20	19	26

Source: *Monthly Digest of Statistics*

By means of a moving average find the trend and the seasonal component. (RSA)

Question 11.16

The number of sales assistants employed by a store chain each quarter was recorded over a four year period as follows:

Year	Quarter			
	1	*2*	*3*	*4*
1988	250	238	220	342
1989	234	166	156	265
1990	168	150	132	250
1991	152	133	115	234
1992	134	117	98	219
1993	120	100	83	202

(a) Draw a graph of the time series.

(b) Determine the trend and plot it on your graph.

(c) Discuss the nature of the time series and that of the most appropriate model to be used for forecasting purposes. Plot on your graph, by eye, the trend line to be used in this model.

(d) Detrend the time series and determine the seasonal components of the model chosen in (c).

(e) Use your model to forecast the number of sales assistants that will be employed during 1994.

(f) The sales assistants' trade union writes requesting you to forecast numbers to be employed in 1996. Draft a brief memorandum replying to its request.   (ICSA)

Answers to Questions and Exercises

Chapter 1

1.7 B **1.8** D **1.10** (i) E (ii) A, D (iii) B, C **1.12** (a) colour (b) size

Chapter 2

2.16 (d)(i) £84 **2.23** (i) A (ii) E (iii) D (iv) C

Chapter 3

3.1 (a)(i) 700 ± 98 (ii) 700 ± 0.14 or $700 \pm 14\%$ (b) 76.73 **3.2** 5 **3.3** C
3.4 B **3.5** 62 **3.6** 466 **3.7** (a)(i) $25.4 \text{ cm} \pm 0.05 \text{ cm}$
(ii) $406.402\,5 \text{ cm}^2 \pm 2.07 \text{ cm}^2$ (iii) $3\,739.006\,5 \text{ cm}^3 \pm 39.364\,1 \text{ cm}^3$, 3680 cm^3,
1.57% (b)(i) 0.35 kg, 4.0 kg (ii) 0.3 kg, 4.0 kg (iii) 3.7 kg (iv) 3.604 kg, 3.6 kg
(v) 3.6 kg **3.9** 124.5 g **3.10** 0.17

Chapter 4

4.1 (a) £39 338 (b) 45.6% (c) $2\frac{1}{2}$ years **4.2** (a) £14 641 (b) £6204 (c) £4164
(d) £13 743 **4.3** (a) 9% (b)(i) B (ii) A **4.4** (a)(i) £71 869 (ii) 57%
(b) £48 686 **4.5** D **4.6** B **4.7** C **4.8** (i) 5, 3, 7, 60 (ii) 16 (iii) 17.5
(iv) 10.34 (v) 29 **4.9** (i) 21 hotels (ii) £7.20 (iii) 1.62 (iv) 1.45 (v) D
4.10 A **4.11** 0.66 **4.12** 50% **4.13** (a) A: crude death rate = 7.1,
standardised death rate = 4.93; B: crude death rate = 4.9, standardised death
rate = 7.55 (b) 12.6 km, 7587.75 m^2, 417.3 m^3 **4.14** (b) 10.77, 14.01 (e) 1250,
140, 200, 265, 365, 280

Chapter 5

5.11 3 h 20 min **5.12 B** **5.13 D** **5.14** (a) Dogs (b) Cats **5.15** (i) 10
(ii) 23 **5.16 C** **5.17 D** **5.18** (i) 110 (ii) 200 **5.21 B**
5.22 (b) Conservative 110.25°, Labour 126°, Alliance 58.5°, Nationalist 45°,
Don't know 20.25° (c) radius = 3 cm **5.27** (a) Spain (b) America (c) France,
Italy, Spain (d) France (e) 100° **5.28** (a) 800 (b)(i) 120° **5.29** (a) 65–70
(b)(i) 10–15 (ii) 45% (c) 6.5% **5.31** (a) 371 000 (million) (b) 15 days
5.32 (a) 1200 (b) 900 (c) Andrée

Chapter 6

6.4 36.13 **6.5** 7.4 **6.6** (a) 10.2 (b) 9.1 **6.7** 2 **6.8 D**, 12 **6.9** Median
6.10 C **6.11** 31 calls **6.12** Median **6.13 B** **6.14** 70 kg **6.15** 6.085 mm
6.16 1 **6.17** 30 calls **6.18** (i) £4000–£6000 **6.19** (i) £3200 (ii) £5500
(iii) 9%, mean wage = £3917, 38% **6.21** 6.2 g **6.22** 12 **6.23** 8
6.24 60 000 **6.25** (a)(i) $5000 (ii) $9000 (iii) 70% (b) $1000
6.26 (a) 33 min (b) 64 min (c) 60 min

Chapter 7

7.1 A **7.3 B** **7.4** 5.9, 3.1 **7.5** 1.83 **7.6** 55 **7.7** Semi-interquartile range
7.9 0.1 **7.10** $x = 11$ **7.11 A** **7.12** 9.2 (a) 230 (b) 230 **7.13** 13.6 **7.14** 7.4
7.15 25.9 **7.17**

No. of letters (x)	1	2	3	4	5	6	7	8	9	10
No. of words (f)	0	6	6	10	3	1	0	1	0	3

(i) 4.3 (ii) 2.30 (iii) 4 (iv) 5, 3 (v) 1.5 **7.18 C** **7.19** Mean, coefficient of
skewness, mode **7.20** (i)(a) 4.66 cm (b) 4.54 cm (c) 4.74 cm (d) 0.1 cm
(ii) 720 (iii) 4.66 cm **7.21** (a)(i) 16 (ii) 15.5 (c) 14, 17, 1.5 (d) 108, 97
(e) Mathematics **7.22** (a) 19.75 min, 6.42 min (c) 20.24 min
7.23 Mode = 23 (a) 22.5 (b) 21.94, 2.18 **7.24** (i) 7.5 h, 2.5 h (ii) £72,
£2.40/h (iii) £90, £7 (vii) 8.5 h, 0.61 h **7.25** (b) 55 min, 37 min, 83 min,
23 min (d) 0.78

Chapter 8

8.1 (a) 45.5 min, 38 min, 51 min, 6.5 min (b) 47 min, 42nd percentile, 0.52,
0.12 **8.2** 13/15 **8.3** 4/15 **8.4** (a) 1/216 (b) 3/216 **8.5** (i) 5/14 (ii) 11/28
(iii) 17/26 (iv) 1/4 **8.6** (iv)(a) 3.195 cm (b) 3.191 cm (c) 3.20 cm
(d) 0.0045 cm (v) 90% (vi) 0.22 (vii) 0.0085 **8.7** (a) 1/114 (b) 91/228
(c) 137/228 (d) 9/38 **8.8** (a) 0.000 335 (b) 1.0 (c) 0.0107 **8.9** (a) 0.737
(b) 0.398 (c) 0.0228 **8.10** 0.92, 0.08. We can accept hypothesis that mean is 77
units. **8.11** We can accept hypothesis that means are equal. **8.12** (a)(i) 0.3024
(ii) 0.0024 (iii) 0.0948 (b) 0.096 **8.13** (a) 781 210 (b) 0.047 (c) 0.185
(d) 0.993 **8.14** (i) **D** (ii) **A** (iii) **B** **8.15** 0.012 **8.16** (a) 1/55 (b) 8/11

8.17 (i) 75p (ii) 0.78 (iii) 22% (iv) 51% **8.18** (b) 6.1 kg, 5.6 kg, 6.6 kg, 0.05 kg, (c) small: up to 5.6 kg, medium: 5.7 kg to 7.1 kg, large: over 7.2 kg (d) 0.17 (e) 0.028

Student		A	B	C	D	E	F	G	H	I	J
x		10	16	7	18	12	3	8	15	10	6
y		8	13	7	14	10	4	7	12	9	6

(iii) $\bar{x} = 10.5, \bar{y} = 9.0$ (v) $y = 0.7x + 2.0$ (vi) 16 (vii) 0.7 (viii) 0.02

Chapter 9

9.3 $b = 121$ **9.4** £220 **9.5** $x = 4$ **9.6** (i) 130.7, 191.7 **9.7** (i) 133 (ii) 116 (iii) £55 **9.8** (b) 182.1 (c) 150.6 **9.9** (b) 116.4 **9.10** (a) 111.04, 188.02 **9.11** (b)(i) 133.2 (ii) 124.7 **9.12** 296.3 **9.14** (c) 17.2% (d) £1.7m, £1.8m (e) £1.3m **9.15** (b) 131.3 **9.16** (i)(1) 229.1 (2) 225.5 **9.18** (b)(i) 1975 = 100, 1976 = 116.5, 1977 = 135.0, 1978 = 146.2, 1979 = 165.8, 1980 = 195.6 (ii) 1975 = 100, 1976 = 119.3, 1977 = 135.0, 1978 = 153.1, 1979 = 185.3, 1980 = 230.9 **9.20** 231

Chapter 10

10.1 (ii) 0.98 **10.2** (b) 0.997 **10.3** −0.95 **10.4** (b) 0.22 **10.5** (b) −0.69 **10.6** 0.71, 0.79 **10.7** −0.25 **10.8** (b) Product-moment correlation coefficient = 0.90 **10.9** (b)(i) Product-moment correlation coefficient = 0.53 **10.10** (b) −0.64 **10.11** 0.6 **10.13** −0.84, −0.83 **10.14** (b) −0.69 **10.16** (b) Product-moment correlation coefficient = −0.87 (c) $y = 24.9 − 0.99x$, 24 **10.17** (i)(a) 8, 3.8 (b) 12, 1.4 (ii) Question 1, 18 (iii) Question 2, 5 (iv) 6 (v) 0.53 **10.18** $y = 2.5x$ **10.19** (i)(1) 0.52 (2) 0.84 **10.20** (b) $y = 91.3 + 1.3x$ (c) 169 **10.21** $y = 3.4$ **10.23** (a) 50p (b) 11 (c) positive

Chapter 11

11.2 3rd 3-point average = 326.3 **11.3** 313 **11.4** (i) 5.3, 5.6, 6.6, 8, 8.6, 10, 11.6, 12.6, mean = 8.5 (iii) gradient = 1 **11.5** (b) 229, 239, 245, 254, 263, 269, 275, 278, 284, 289, 294 (c) 345 **11.6** (ii) A, B, F, H, I (iii) C, D, E, G, J, L (iv) 3.3 cm³, 14.85 g (vi)(a) 13.5 g (b) 4 cm³ (vii) K **11.7** 35.1, −15.6, −26.1, 6.5 **11.9** 39.4, 40.0, 40.2, 41.2, 41.6, 42.0, 42.4, 43.0, 43.6, 44.6, 45.8, 46.4, 47.0, 48.0, 48.2, 48.4. **11.10** 5-point averages: 1.3, 1.6, 1.6, 1.5, 1.4, 1.3, 1.0, 1.1, 1.3, 1.5, 1.7, 1.6, 1.5, 1.8, 1.6, 1.4, 1.4, 1.4, 1.1, 1.3, 1.5, 1.7, 1.9, 1.8; seasonally adjusted series: 1.4, 0.9, 1.2, 2.1, 1.9, 1.3, 0.6, 1.4, 1.2, 1.3, 1.3, 1.5, 1.8, 1.8, 1.8, 1.6, 1.5, 1.7, 0.5, 1.5, 1.2, 1.4, 1.7, 1.9, 1.9, 1.8, 1.9, 2.0 **11.11** (i) Trend: −, −, 103.8, 104.5, 104.9, 104.4, 104.3, 104.4, 104.5, 103.9, −, −; seasonal factors: −28.5, 5.6, 39.7, −15.1 (ii) 104.5, 106.4, 100.3, 101.1 **11.12** (a) 9.7, 9.4, 9.2, 9.1, 9.0, 9.0, 8.8, 8.6 **11.13** (a) 1.9, −0.7, −1.8, 0.7 (b) 4.0, 4.3, 4.0, 4.5 **11.14** Trend: −, −, 19.3, 18.5, 18.5, 18.4, 18.1, 17.6, 16.6, 15.5; seasonal components: 2.1, 1.5, −0.2, −3.4 **11.15** (b) Trend: −, −, 15.4, 16.1, 16.9, 17.3, 17.5, 18.3, 19.1, 20.3; seasonal components: 0, 1.6, 3.9, −5.6

Glossary

1 Statistics

Descriptive statistics: the presentation of data and the calculation of descriptive measures which help to summarise data.

Inductive statistics: the inferring of characteristics of a population on the basis of known sample results.

Macro-statistical information: data produced by the public sector and which relates to the country as a whole.

Micro-statistical information: data produced by private firms and private organisations.

Primary data: collected by or on behalf of the person or people who are going to make use of the data.

Qualitative data: where differences between variables cannot be measured, although they can be described.

Quantitative data: where differences between variables can be measured.

Secondary data: used by a person or people other than the people by whom or for whom the data was collected.

Secondary statistics: statistics compiled from secondary data.

Standard Industrial Classification: a system of classification of establishments according to industry.

Statistics: is concerned with scientific methods for collecting, organising, summarising, presenting and analysing data, as well as drawing valid conclusions and making reasonable decisions on the basis of this analysis.

2 Collecting information

Cluster (area) sampling: clusters are found by breaking down the area to be surveyed into smaller areas, a few of these areas are chosen at random and units, selected at random, are interviewed in these selected areas.

Interviewing: a conversation with a purpose.

Law of inertia of large numbers: large groups of data show a higher degree of stability than small ones.

Law of statistical regularity: a reasonably large sample selected at random from a large population will be, on average, representative of the characteristics of the population.

Master samples: samples covering the whole of a country to form the bases (a sampling frame) for smaller local samples.

Mechanical observation: the use of mechanical and electronic means of observation.

Multi-phase sampling: some information is collected from the whole sample and additional information is collected from sub-samples.

Multi-stage sampling: a series of samples taken at successive 'stages' such as geographical regions, towns, households.

Non-sampling errors: due to problems involved with the sample design.

Observation: collecting information by looking at it.

Panels: groups of people, selected at random from a survey population, who are surveyed at various times over a period of time.

Participant observation: the observer becomes a participant in the activity being observed.

Questionnaire: a list of questions aimed at discovering particular information.

Quota sampling: quotas (of people or items) are chosen so that the overall sample reflects the known population characteristics in a number of respects; this is non-random but representative stratified sampling.

Random route sampling: a form of random sampling involving a route.

Random sampling: each unit of the population has the same chance as any other unit of being included in the sample.

Replicated or *interpenetrating sampling:* a number of sub-samples, rather than one full sample, are selected from the population.

Sample: anything less than a full survey.

Sample frame: list of people, items or units from which the sample is taken.

Sampling error: difference between the estimate of a value obtained from a sample and the actual value.

Sampling population: group of people, items or units under investigation.

Sampling units: people or items which are to be sampled.

Sampling with replacement: units selected at each draw are replaced into the population before the next draw.

Sampling without replacement: only those units not previously selected are eligible for the next draw.

Stratified random sampling: a form of random sampling involving dividing people or items in the sampling frame into groups, categories or 'strata' which are mutually exclusive.

Survey: an investigation with the objective of collecting information on a subject.

Systematic observation: used to observe only events which can be investigated without the participant knowing.

Systematic sampling: a form of random sampling involving a system.

3 Accuracy

Absolute error: the actual difference between an estimate or approximation and the true value.

Biased, cumulative or *systematic error:* all the errors lying in one direction.

Degrees of tolerance: the level of accuracy required in the measurement and use of particular statistics.

Error: the difference between what is acceptable as a true figure and what is taken for an estimate or approximation.

Relative error: absolute error divided by the estimate.

Unbiased or *compensating error:* when approximations cancel each other out.

4 Basic mathematics

Algebra: a method of investigating the properties of numbers using general symbols.

Binary system: has a base of two digits, 0 and 1.

Compound interest: a geometric progression, where in a series of numbers the difference between the numbers is found by multiplying the preceding number by a fixed amount (the 'common ratio').

Decimal system: based on groups of ten.

Fraction: unit of measurement expressed as one whole number divided by another.

Integer: any positive whole number, any negative whole number, or zero.

Interval scale: ranks objects with respect to the degree with which they possess a certain characteristic, and also indicates the exact distance between them.

Nominal scale: a method of classification where the function of numbers is the same as names.

Ordinal scale: the ordering of categories with respect to the degree to which they possess particular characteristics, without being able to measure exactly how much of the characteristic they possess.

Percentage: per hundred.

Powers: a shorthand method of representing a series of multiplications.

Ratios: a relationship between two quantities expressed in a number of units which enables comparison to be made between them.

Simple interest: an arithmetic progression, where in a series of numbers the difference between them is the same.

Standardisation: techniques used to enable like to be compared with like.

Tally: to keep score or account by ticks, notches, or marks.

5 Frequency distributions

Bar chart: a form of pictorial presentation where bars are used to provide comparison between items.

Frequency distribution: shows the frequency with which a particular variable occurs.

Graph: a 'grid' on which curves are plotted to illustrate the relationship between two variables.

Histogram: a method of representing a frequency distribution diagrammatically.

6 Averages

Arithmetic average (mean): the sum of the items divided by the number of them.

Averages: measures of central tendency and measures of location.

Box and whisker diagram: displays the values of the smallest observation, the largest observation, the median and the quartiles of a set of data.

Deciles: divide an ordered distribution into ten equal parts.

Geometric mean: the nth root of the product of the distribution.

Harmonic mean: used to average rates rather than simple values.

Median: the value of the middle item of a distribution which is set out in order.

Mode: the most frequently occurring value in a distribution.

Percentiles: divide an ordered distribution into one hundred equal parts.

Quartiles: divide an ordered distribution in four equal parts.

7 Dispersion

Coefficient of variation: the standard deviation divided by the mean.

Dispersion: measures of deviation or spread around a central point.

Interquartile range: the difference between the upper quartile and the lower quartile.

Mean deviation: the arithmetic mean of the absolute differences of each value from the mean.

Range: the highest value in a distribution minus the lowest.

Standard deviation: the square root of the sum of the square of the deviations of the individual values from the mean of the distribution, divided by the number of items in the distribution.

Variance: the average of the square of the deviations.

8 Statistical decisions

Conditional events: two or more events are said to be conditional when the probability that event B takes place is subject to the proviso that event A has taken place, and so on.

Confidence limits: intervals that will, at specified levels of probability, include the population mean.

Event: an occurrence.

Independent events: two or more events are said to be independent if the occurrence or non-occurrence of one of them in no way affects the occurrence or non-occurrence of the others.

Mutually exclusive or *complementary events:* two events are said to be mutually exclusive if the occurrence of one of them excludes the occurrence of the other.

Normal curve: a bell-shaped symmetrical distribution whose shape depends on the values of the mean and the standard deviation.

Probability: the probability of an event is the proportion of times the event happens out of a large number of trials.

Sample space: the set of possible outcomes to an experiment.

Significance tests: how far differences between an hypothesis and a sample result can be reasonably ascribed to chance factors operating at the time the sample was selected.

Standard error: the extent to which sample means deviate from population means; the standard deviation of the sampling distribution of the mean.

Tree diagrams: used to reduce the need to produce a complete sample space for complicated combinations.

z-value: the distance any particular point lies from the mean, measured in units of standard deviation.

9 Index numbers

Chain-base index: each period in the series uses the previous period as the base.

Index numbers: a measure designed to show average changes in the price, quantity or value of a group of items, over a period of time.

Index of retail prices: 'measures the changes from month to month in the average level of prices of the commodities and services purchased by nearly nine-tenths of the households in the United Kingdom' (Department of Employment).

Laspeyres index: indicates how much the cost of buying base-year quantities at current-year prices is compared with base-year costs.

Paasche index: indicates how much current-year costs are related to the cost of buying current-year quantities at base-year prices.

10 Correlation

Correlation: whether or not there is any association between two variables.

Product moment coefficient of correlation: a measure of linear correlation which divides the mean product of the deviations from the mean, by the product of the standard deviations.

Rank correlation coefficient: measure of correlation based on an ordinal scale or an interval scale that has been ordered or ranked.

Regression: attempts to show the relationship between two variables by providing a mean line which best indicates the trend of the points or co-ordinates on a graph.

11 Trends

Least-squares method: produces a line which minimises all positive and negative deviations of the data from a straight line drawn through the data.

Linear trends: methods of arriving at a linear or straight line trend.

Moving average: a method of repeatedly calculating a series of different average values along a time series to produce a trend line.

Three-point linear estimation: a method of finding a trend line which will approximate to a straight line, by finding three averages for a series.

Time series: numerical data recorded at intervals of time.

Two-point linear estimation: a method of finding a straight trend line, by finding two averages for a series.

Formulae

Financial mathematics

Simple interest $A = P(1 + tr)$
Compound interest $A = P(1 + r)^t$

Present values $P = \dfrac{A}{(1 + r)^t}$

Averages

Arithmetic mean: $\bar{x} = \dfrac{\Sigma x}{n}$

Arithmetic mean of a frequency and grouped frequency distribution:

$\bar{x} = \dfrac{\Sigma fx}{\Sigma f}$

Arithmetic mean of a frequency and grouped frequency distribution using an assumed mean:

$\bar{x} = x \pm \dfrac{\Sigma fd_x}{\Sigma f}$

Position of the median for a discrete series:

$M = \dfrac{n + 1}{2}$

Position of median for a continuous series:

$M = \dfrac{n}{2}$ or $\dfrac{f}{2}$

Position of lower quartile:

$$Q_1 = \frac{n}{4} \text{ or } \frac{f}{4}$$

Position of upper quartile:

$$Q_3 = \frac{3n}{4} \text{ or } \frac{3f}{4}$$

Position of deciles:

$$D_1 = \frac{n}{10} \text{ or } \frac{f}{10}$$

$$D_2 = \frac{2n}{10} \text{ or } \frac{2f}{10} \text{ and so on}$$

Position of percentiles:

$$P_1 = \frac{n}{100} \text{ or } \frac{f}{100}$$

$$\mathbf{P}_2 = \frac{2n}{100} \text{ or } \frac{2f}{100} \text{ and so on}$$

Geometric mean = the nth root of the product of a distribution.

Dispersion

The range = highest value − lowest value

Interquartile range = $Q_3 - Q_1$

Semi-interquartile range = $\dfrac{Q_3 - Q_1}{2}$

Standard deviation:

$$\sigma = \sqrt{\frac{\Sigma x^2}{n}} \quad \text{or} \quad \sqrt{\frac{\Sigma(x - \bar{x})^2}{n}}$$

Standard deviation of grouped frequency distribution:

$$\sigma = \sqrt{\frac{\Sigma fd_x^{\,2}}{\Sigma f} - \left(\frac{\Sigma fd_x}{\Sigma f}\right)^2} \times \text{class interval}$$

Variance:

    Variance = average of the square of the deviation
    or the square of the standard deviation
    Variance = σ^2

Coefficient of variation:

$$V = \frac{\sigma}{\bar{x}}$$

Areas under the normal curve

68%	1σ on either side of the mean
95%	2σ on either side of the mean
99%	2.58σ on either side of the mean
99.74%	3σ on either side of the mean

$$z\text{-value} = \frac{x - \bar{x}}{\sigma}$$

Standard error

$$\text{S.E.} = \frac{\sigma}{\sqrt{n}}$$

Probability

$$\text{Probability} = \frac{\text{the number of ways an event can happen}}{\text{the total number of outcomes to an experiment}}$$

Significance tests

Ho: μ = the population mean
H₁: $\mu \neq$ the population mean

Type I error is rejecting the null hypothesis (Ho) when it is in fact true
Type II error is accepting the null hypothesis when it is in fact false

Index numbers

$$\text{Price index} = \frac{p_1}{p_0} \times 100$$

Weighted index number:

$$\text{Price index (Laspeyres)} = \frac{\Sigma p_1 q_0}{\Sigma p_0 q_0} \times 100$$

$$\text{Quantity index (Laspeyres)} = \frac{\Sigma q_1 p_0}{\Sigma q_0 p_0} \times 100$$

$$\text{Price index (Paasche)} = \frac{\Sigma q_1 p_1}{\Sigma q_1 p_0} \times 100$$

$$\text{Quantity index (Paasche)} = \frac{\Sigma q_1 p_1}{\Sigma q_0 p_1} \times 100$$

Correlation

Product moment coefficient of correlation

$$r = \frac{\Sigma(xy)}{\sqrt{\Sigma x^2 \Sigma y^2}}$$

or $r = \dfrac{\Sigma(xy)}{n\sigma_x\sigma y}$

Coefficient of rank correlation

$r' = 1 - \dfrac{6\Sigma d^2}{n(n^2 - 1)}$

Linear trends

Straight line equation $y = a + bx$

or $y = \bar{y} - b\bar{x} + bx$

The slope, $b = \dfrac{\Sigma xy - \dfrac{\Sigma x \times \Sigma y}{n}}{\Sigma x^2 - \dfrac{(\Sigma x)^2}{n}}$

The intercept, $a = \bar{y} - b\bar{x}$

Calculations which are not included in the formulae

Accuracy and approximation
Mathematics: fractions, decimals, powers, roots, ratios, proportions
Birth and death rates
Mode, median, geometric mean
Mean deviation
Moving averages, seasonal variations, two and three point linear estimation, least-squares method

Standard normal distribution

The standard normal distribution is a way of stating an actual value in terms of its standard deviation from the mean in units of its standard deviation. This new value can be called a 'z' value.

$$z = \dfrac{\text{The value} - \text{The mean}}{\text{The standard deviation}} = \dfrac{x - \bar{x}}{\sigma}$$

where z = The distance any particular point lies from the mean measured in units of standard deviation.

x = Any particular value.

$\bar{x}$ = The arithmetic mean.

σ = The standard deviation.

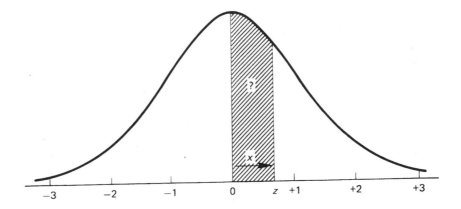

z	Area	z	Area
0.0	0.0000	1.5	0.4332
0.1	0.0398	1.6	0.4452
0.2	0.0793	1.7	0.4554
0.3	0.1179	1.8	0.4641
0.4	0.1554	1.9	0.4713
0.5	0.1915	2.0	0.4772
0.6	0.2257	2.1	0.4821
0.7	0.2580	2.2	0.4861
0.8	0.2881	2.3	0.4893
0.9	0.3159	2.4	0.4918
1.0	0.3413	2.5	0.4938
1.1	0.3643	2.6	0.4953
1.2	0.3849	2.7	0.4965
1.3	0.4032	2.8	0.4974
1.4	0.4192	2.9	0.4981
		3.0	0.4987

References for Further Reading

More explanation and discussion

Tim Hannagan, *Mastering Statistics*, 3rd edn, Macmillan, Basingstoke, 1996.
This is in the Macmillan Mastering series and is designed for GCSE, GNVQ,
business and professional qualifications and for all areas of basic statistics
and numeracy. It includes more detailed explanation and discussion of the
main areas of statistics and establishes the way forward to more advanced
statistical techniques.

More advanced statistics

C.A. Moser and K. Kalton, *Survey Methods in Social Investigation*, Heinemann,
London, 1971.
This is the classic book on survey methods.
M.R. Spiegal, *Theory and Problems of Statistics*, McGraw-Hill, New York, 1960.
This remains the most comprehensive, advanced text on statistical techniques.

Examples of the use of statistics

Social Trends, Central Statistical Office, published by HMSO, London, annually.
This provides as many tables of figures, graphs and diagrams as most people
would want, but there are many other government and international
publications full of statistical data. Company annual reports also provide
many examples of the use of statistics.

Index

Macmillan Work Out Series

For GCSE examinations
Accounting
Biology
Business Studies
Chemistry
Computer Studies
English Key Stage 4
French (cassette and pack available)
Geography
German (cassette and pack available)
Modern World History
Human Biology
Core Maths Key Stage 4
Revise Mathematics to further level
Physics
Religious Studies
Science
Social and Economic History
Spanish (cassette and pack available)
Statistics

For A Level examinations
Accounting
Biology
Business Studies
Chemistry
Economics
English
French (cassette and pack available)
Mathematics
Physics
Psychology
Sociology
Statistics